The Noise of Infinite Longing

"Muscular, passionate, and rigorously honest prose . . . compelling . . . always gorgeously written, *The Noise of Infinite Longing* is made of prose at once lush and well modulated."
—*LA Weekly*

"There have been acclaimed, bestselling memoirs about overcoming poverty or criminality, about the upheavals of immigrating to America, even about growing up with incest or insanity in the family. But there hasn't been a memoir quite like *The Noise of Infinite Longing*. . . . Remarkable."
—*Dallas Morning News*

"No habla español? When Luisita López Torregrosa uses Spanish in *The Noise of Infinite Longing*, the reader is so under her spell, language is not important. . . . Once in a while you're lucky enough to read a book that compels you to ask questions: What part does memory play in grief? Can you love a person who hurts you? And most difficult: Can you love a person who hurts someone you love? . . . Ms. Torregrosa pulls off an oxymoronic feat: she is ferocious yet lyrical. She makes you see the other Puerto Rico, her Puerto Rico—it's Fajardo, El Vedado, and Perez Galdos, places of trammeled beauty."
—*New York Times*

"*New York Times* editor Torregrosa's debut recalls with rueful affection an unsettled childhood in a tropical paradise. . . . Bittersweet and beautifully written."
—*Kirkus Reviews* (starred review)

"Told with honesty and anger . . . vivid writing."

—*New York Times Book Review*

"A family tale that is as devastating as it is inspiring. And it is beautifully told. . . . The family's saga in *The Noise of Infinite Longing* becomes a springboard for talking about Puerto Rico and what it means to be Puerto Rican—even living far from the island. . . . Torregrosa moves from confusion and desperation to understanding of her family and culture, and finally into an awakening and embracing of a past she can call her own."

—*Orlando Sentinel*

"A family can move so often and change so much that children lose their sense of belonging. This dynamic is strongly illuminated in *The Noise of Infinite Longing*, an evocative memoir by Luisita López Torregrosa."

—*Charlotte Observer*

"*The Noise of Infinite Longing* is both the moving story of a family torn between the Anglo and the Latino cultures, and the tragic yet courageous tale of a woman's struggle to assert her right to love as she chooses. This engaging memoir challenges the reader to find solutions to the problems it presents. A poignant read deserving a wide audience."

—José Raúl Bernardo, author of *The Wise Women of Havana*

"Torregrosa's deft, vivid characterizations capture a multigenerational cast, and her keen sense of sound and scene makes this a moving, believable, and fresh story of growing up Puerto Rican and being American."

—*Publishers Weekly*

"*The Noise of Infinite Longing* is groundbreaking, tender, and wondrously written."

—Jaime Manrique, author of *Twilight at the Equator* and *Latin Moon in Manhattan*

"A lush and lyrical sadness permeates *The Noise of Infinite Longing*, Luisita López Torregrosa's exquisite memoir about growing up in Puerto Rico in the 1950s. . . . Torregrosa writes with skill, candor, and grace."

—*Camden Courier-Post*

"The author and her five siblings come together for the first time in ten years at their mother's funeral in Texas. In the days that follow, the stories of their divided family unfold, providing revealing glimpses into half a century of their native Puerto Rico's *historia*."

—*Latina* magazine

Tiffany Richards Leohnis

LUISITA LÓPEZ TORREGROSA is an editor at the *New York Times*. Her articles have appeared in the *Times, Vanity Fair, Condé Nast Traveler*, and *Vogue*. She lives in New York City.

The Noise of Infinite Longing

A Memoir of a Family—and an Island

Luisita López Torregrosa

An Imprint of HarperCollinsPublishers

A hardcover edition of this book was published in 2004 by Rayo, an imprint of HarperCollins Publishers.

First Rayo paperback edition published 2005.

Designed by Fearn Cutler de Vicq

The Library of Congress has catalogued the hardcover edition as follows:

López Torregrosa, Luisita.

The noise of infinite longing: a memoir of a family—and an island / Luisita López Torregrosa—1st ed.

p. cm.

ISBN 0-06-053460-5 (hc: alk. paper)

1. López Torregrosa, Luisita—Family. 2. Family—Puerto Rico. 3. Puerto Rico—Social life and customs. 4. Puerto Ricans—Foreign countries. 5. Social values—Puerto Rico. 6. Puerto Rico—Biography. I. Title.

F1960.L68 2004

306.8'5'097295—dc22 2003056796

ISBN 0-06-053461-3 (pbk.)

05 06 07 08 09 ❖/RRD 10 9 8 7 6 5 4 3 2 1

This book is for my sisters,

Angeles, Carmen, Sara, and Olga,

and my brother, Amaury.

In memory of our mother.

"I am not certain as to how
the pain of learning what is lost
is transformed into light at last."

—W. S. Merwin, "Testimony"

Contents

The Noise of Infinite Longing

Prologue

Texas, 1994, a Reunion

The day my mother died, I was standing at the butcher-block counter of my kitchen, the sunlight harsh against the window-panes, and in my ear, on the telephone, my sister was shouting. She didn't make it. She's gone. I looked into the sun, blinded. Sara was sobbing into the phone. I heard my voice, deepening, slowing, as if my voice alone could rise against that flood and stop it. I wanted the details, the hour, the place, the last minutes. She was in the car, on the way to the post office, Sara said. Suddenly she grabbed her chest and said, It hurts, and then she was dead. None of it made sense to me. A car, a country road, mother on a stretcher, medics trying to revive her, the sirens. She was declared dead on arrival. But why did she die? I kept asking. We don't know, Sara said. She spoke in bursts, in little cries, incoherent.

I was standing inside the spread of sunlight that burned through the panes, leaning hard against the kitchen counter. My sister's words seemed muffled, as if they were coming from an immense distance, farther and farther, until I could barely hear her, her words becoming unintelligible. The room, the spot on the terra-cotta tiles where I stood holding the phone, became brighter, lighter. I could hear the birds in my garden, swooping down and out of the limbs of the old tree that leaned over the back fence.

They are all coming today, she said.

Tomorrow, I said, I'll come tomorrow.

I hadn't seen my mother in two years, the years when her hair had finally begun to gray and her voice had become thinner, tremulous. Her face, in her seventies, had become her own mother's face, the cheeks sunken, her eyes deep sockets, still dark and opaque, stonewashed black. The crook of her nose was now more pronounced, like her mother's, with her nostrils widened. But the skin of her face had almost no lines, without the indentations of her years. In the last pictures taken of her, at a candlelit dinner in New Orleans a month before her death, she was wearing her dangling emerald earrings, a short black sheath, and black sheer hose that showed off the calves she was so proud of. Her fine hair had been freshly trimmed, straight and feathery around her face. She looked ten years younger than her age.

Now she was gone, just like that. Later I would snap my fingers to remind myself, like a broken twig.

Angeles is already on her way, Sara was saying. She was coming from Tegucigalpa, flying over a thousand miles, believing that our mother was still alive. She would arrive in her snap-on sunglasses, smoking her unfiltered Honduran Camels, wearing those comfortable sandals with the heels worn down. She was careless with her appearance, like women who were beautiful when they were very young. When we were teenagers I envied her looks, her femaleness, her cheekbones, her eyes so black, large, and unknowable—the ones keeping the secrets. She was a year younger than I, but from the time we were young girls she seemed fully shaped, nearly a complete woman. Now her beauty had aged, but it had deepened, the flavor fuller, thicker. She wore the marks of a life lived with abandon. She was Ava Gardner after Sinatra, after the high life.

My brother, Amaury, was flying in from New York, and he would arrive with his eyes bloodshot, heavy from crying. He had a mustache, thick bristles that shadowed lips that were like my mother's. His voice was loud, either mocking or angry like our father's. He would arrive half drunk, his hands trembling, laughing and crying out of the same pain.

My younger sisters were coming, too. Olga, the youngest, who had in her blood the combustion of my parents' temperament, was flying up from New Orleans with her husband and their two boys; and Carmen was driving in from West Texas, where her life was tennis and card games with the other ladies and raising perfect children, and the big house with the swimming pool. My aunt, Angela Luisa, was flying in from San Juan, coming all that way to see her only sister be buried in a countryside cemetery in a rural town in East Texas.

Over the phone I could hear the commotion in Sara's house—in the background of her words, the slamming of refrigerator doors and the footfalls of people coming and going, people crying out, shouting. Her husband was calling out questions to her, making arrangements—did they have enough cars to take everyone back and forth from Dallas to my mother's house some fifty miles away; who was going to sleep where; who was arriving when at the airport—the mundane logistics that come with a sudden death.

Then the phone connection was abruptly scrambled. Sara had to take another call, and she hung up in mid-sentence. And now there was only silence. I held on to the phone, still hearing my sister's first words. She didn't make it. She's gone.

I was trembling head to foot, shaking uncontrollably, and at one in the afternoon, in the torpor of that Saturday in September, a time of year that was almost tropical in all that sunlight of late summer, I poured myself two fingers of gin, splashed the tonic, and squeezed the lime. I called the only person in the world who I thought could make sense of this for me, and she said, crying before I could, I'll be right there. She came over and found me sitting tearless on a patio chair in my garden. She picked up the hose and watered the drooping bamboo stalks and the withered azaleas, and we drank all afternoon.

That night in my empty apartment, now emptier, I lay in my bed, dead myself. The walls seemed higher and whiter and empty of shadows. I left the bed and went to my living room and sat up all night, eyes grained, stinging, dry, as if I were waiting for somebody to come and tell me that it wasn't true, that she was not dead, not at all.

At five in the morning, when the sky was beginning to break free of night, I pulled the duffel bag off the top shelf of my closet. Slowly, counting the minutes and wanting to stop them at the same time, I took one shirt, then another, off their hangers and folded them carefully into the bag. I went through the mental list of travel, a list I knew from my years flying from one magazine assignment to another, and I was done in no time at all. I called up a taxi, and it showed up too soon, before I could make my rounds, locking doors, turning off lamps.

The taxi's lights beamed on the still street. The driver opened the door for me, and I heard a click as it closed, loud in that silence of dawn. The airport terminal was already crowded. Lines formed at the ticket counters, bags pressed against me. People on holiday, people on urgent errands. I didn't notice their faces.

At the counter, the clerk punched the computer keyboard, found my name. I blurted out, before I could stop myself, my mother is dead, I'm going to her funeral. The clerk's face turned to me, eyes softening. She had heard this before, and her hand patted mine. I knew I would drink all the way to Dallas.

Sara was at the airport, waiting for me. I hadn't seen her in four, five years. She was taller than I remembered. Her light, long hair fell around a face that seemed gaunt to me, full of mourning, no, not yet, full of shock. Her eyes found me, and when I held her I could feel her bones, her long hands clasping my back. She was the next to the last of my parents' six children, and when she was a child, when she was burned by scalding water and we believed she would die, even then she had a smile the rest of us didn't have, a light about her that made her the only one of us who had what people call a good nature.

In the car, driving to my mother's house an hour away, she was valiantly trying to distract me, retelling the details, the funeral plans, the sleeping arrangements. She was the first among us to learn that mother was dead. She lived only an hour away and in those last years had become very close to mother. Telling me about mother's last moments alive, details she had heard from mother's husband, Sara's voice, always high-pitched, was hitting higher notes, like a broken chord on a violin. Her light brown eyes had darkened with loss, pitched dark like black screens.

We are going to mother's house, she said. They are waiting for us.

I looked out the window at dry, flat land, the road straight and long. She talked all the way.

She is at the mortuary, she said. They embalmed her, her coffin is open, you may see her tonight.

No. I shook my head. I'm not looking at her. I don't want to see her embalmed.

But she looks very good, Sara said.

No, I said. She's dead.

I blew smoke out the window.

Part One *In the Beginning*

"The truth which I intend to set forth here is not particularly scandalous, or is so only to the degree that any truth creates a scandal."

—Marguerite Yourcenar, *Memoirs of Hadrian*

Chapter One

An Island of Illusions

The box lay on my lap. I did not want to open it. Angeles sat across from me, in the torn leather chair in the room in Edgewood, Texas, where my mother had kept her books, her photo albums, and the trinkets she had picked up in her travels. I had arrived just a few hours before and had walked around the house as if it were a church, slowly, gazing up at the pictures my mother had chosen to hang on the walls, looking at her bed, at her bottles of Arpège and her felt-lined jewelry box, staring unbelievingly at her faded red robe still hanging on the back of the bathroom door.

My mother's room had not been touched. The bed was made, the rose-colored bedspread smoothed around it, not a wrinkle in it, the way she had left it. Beside her bed, on her night table, she had a framed picture of my grandmother, a picture I had always loved, my grandmother in a gray and white housedress with dark stripes. Her face was powerful, nothing frail about it. It was the face of Spanish doñas, those Goya faces, smileless, almost ruthless, eyes long lost in some past. Next to the picture was a paperback edition of Toni Morrison's *Beloved,* a book I had recommended to her. It lay there as if it had just been bought, no pages turned. Closest to the bed and my mother's pillow was her latest crossword puzzle, which she had clipped from a newspaper. It was unfinished. I wanted to take it but didn't dare touch it. I couldn't touch any of it.

I glanced up and down the hallway, where her diplomas were hanging in the same frames I remembered, and the picture of her I most loved, taken when she was twenty-three, just before I was born. It was in a cluster of family pictures. I stood before it the way I stood, when I was very young, before the statues of the Virgin Mary, the way I later looked at posters of movie stars.

I want a copy of that, I said.

The house where she had lived for the last five years of her life was full of people, more people, I was sure, than had ever been in it when she was alive. Townspeople, neighbors, her husband's relatives, people I had not met or had forgotten. My sisters were already there, and my brother, and my aunt, Angela Luisa, with her son, Jacobo. I was startled to see him, immaculately dressed in a dark business suit, resolute and somber, standing at her side, just a step behind her, attentive but distant, at her elbow but not quite touching it. I wouldn't have recognized him now except for the close-set eyes and foxlike face, the same look he had when he was a boy.

One by one they came to me.

But, nena, you look the same, my aunt said. It had been many years, more than two decades since I had last seen her.

You look the same, too, I lied, throwing my arms around her, relieved to see someone who had shared my mother's life, who had shared our childhood.

She said, I came because I knew that if I didn't come you and your sisters and brother would not have anyone here that was real family. I embraced her again. She was right. The sadness in her, the sorrow that had to be in her after losing her only sister, her older sister, seemed muted, cut off. She had never been one to show much emotion.

When I was a child, she had been a spire to me. She was a writer, a journalist, the center of attention in rooms crowded with powerful men whom you read about in the papers, and with women in demure cocktail dresses who kissed her on both cheeks. She had been my model, tall and light-haired, unadorned yet shining in her silk scarves, elegant like a swan. But she didn't look the same, how could she? She was seventy-four years old, two years younger than my mother, and she was less agile and a bit stooped. Her hair was a blond gray curled by beauty parlor hot rolls, combed in tight waves. She had on a silken dress with long, flowing sleeves, the sort she would wear to a theater opening. Her strand of pearls was draped loosely around her old woman's neck. But she had the brightness about her that I remembered, her glow, her playful smile, and the warmth she seemed to hold mostly for Angeles and me.

Your mother, she said, taking me aside, should have lived the life I had (she meant fame, travel, awards all over the walls), and I should have had hers.

I didn't believe her, didn't believe that she would've traded lives with my mother, but I did believe that my mother would have wanted my aunt's life. This was a comment, I thought, meant to suggest something about my mother more than about my aunt, and she said it as if revealing a secret, something she had thought about all those years. It felt like the point of a blade touching briefly, coldly, against my skin, before it fell to the ground.

When she embraced me again, she let her long, ringless fingers rest on my shoulder, and stood back to look at me. I wanted to scream, Where is she, where is she?

Angeles came out of a room, and we held each other for a very long time. She looked older than I, her hair a sea gray that was oddly almost black like the depths of the sea. She held me like a doll, tight to her, and her tears touched my face, making it impossible for me to cry. Holding her was as close as I could ever get to holding my mother again, but we still played the roles we had played since we were children. She cried, I didn't.

She looked so tired after a twelve-hour flight, arriving only to learn that she was too late, that our mother was already dead. She felt so small in my arms, even though she was bigger than I, and I brushed back her hair.

She laughed suddenly, pulling away from me, and took me to the room where she had been hiding from the crowd in the living room and in the kitchen, where my mother's second husband, Leon, a Texan with the bearing of a onetime football quarterback, was receiving the townsfolk.

We didn't want to have anything to do with those people, in-laws we didn't know, the mayor of the town, the beautician, the storekeepers, the women who set up bingo games in the annex of the church, who belonged to the ladies' auxiliary and put up notes on missing pets on the town hall's bulletin board—the people who had been my mother's everyday acquaintances, people who called my mother a Good Samaritan, so ready to help with all the town's activities.

Your mother was so kind to our community, they said with little variation as they filed in, carrying pies and casseroles, the usual in those parts. She was so good to our town, so interesting, so charming. We will miss her so.

Angeles looked around and said, Who are these people?

I found a chair, and Amaury swayed toward me, his eyebrows raised in anger.

Where have you been? You're the last one to arrive.

I couldn't come any faster, I said, brusque, lying.

He knew. I glared at him, turning away. He had that way about him, saying the wrong thing, miscalculating, and he reminded me of my father.

I've been here since yesterday, he said, an accusation. I took the first flight out of New York.

He was the good son, he was saying, and I was the selfish daughter. He was wrecked, his face darker than I remembered, the limp in his right leg more pronounced. When he was a boy, maybe four years old, he fell off a swing and broke his arm. I let him lie on the ground while he cried. It was Angeles who came running to him. She still did that, and now, when he needed to stop crying, she came to him again. They cracked a joke that I didn't get. I was separate; they separated me from them. We smoked, we had Lone Star beer. We let the ashes fall on the floor and the bottles pile on a table.

Angeles refused to go out to the kitchen and meet all the people and thank them for coming. But I went, my aunt insisted. I found room at the kitchen table, and sat quietly, thanking strangers who took my hands and looked at me with blurred eyes. Are you the journalist? I smiled, nodding.

Your mother talked about you all the time, the ladies said.

I knew that; she talked about all her children, always pulling our old pictures out of her wallet.

In front of me, on the table, was a bowl of fake fruit (mother loved fresh fruit—why would she buy waxed apples, pears, bananas? I wondered). Scoops of potato salad and slices of honey-glazed ham were put on a plate for me and I pushed it aside. How could I eat? Finally, it was time to go view the body.

I'm not going, I said. Angeles is not going. Amaury is not going.

The others—Carmen, Sara, and Olga—all went, parceling their cars, dragging their husbands and children with them.

Angeles and I stayed in the den, and Amaury stayed with us. Together, we thought ourselves a trinity—the three oldest, the ones who really knew the story. We were our parents, their reflection. Angeles more than any of us.

Now we were going through my mother's things, her boxes, plain shoe boxes, all unmarked. We were looking for anything of hers.

Angeles had already gone through the box on my lap, holding each letter, some many years old, in her own childlike handwriting. She took the letters out of envelopes, glancing over them, and putting them back in the box, in order, just as they had been placed there by my mother.

She said nothing when she handed me the box. She reached for a cigarette and lit it with the burning butt of the one she had just smoked.

Mother wanted to be cremated, Angeles said finally. It's in there, in her handwriting.

I opened the box. I found the note, on top of the pile of yellowing papers. I read it quickly. I never saw this before, I said, injured.

I did, years ago, Angeles said.

Why not me? I said, our little jealousies rising above the pain.

The letter was undated, not addressed to any of us. Mother wrote it on plain drugstore stationery and she had folded the single page in half. The ink was fading, the paper stiff. In handwriting that still retained her fluid slope, but was now a little more crooked and shaky in her old age, she had written that she wanted her ashes spread in her garden.

So why was she not cremated? I asked. Amaury looked at the floor. He didn't know. He had just read the letter for the first time.

Angeles whispered, It's too late. She's already embalmed, everything had been arranged before we got here. We didn't know.

But why is she being buried here? I said, repeating myself, helpless, furious that I had not known before, that her wishes had been ignored. Why were we not asked? What does she have to do with this town? She belongs in Puerto Rico, I kept saying, a meaningless thought since she had not lived on the island for thirty years. But it was the dream I thought she had, a dream I had for her. It was her home, I said. It was our home.

I was born in a place of no particular consequence, on an island of certain beauty, at the intersection of two cultures, where the Atlantic meets the Caribbean, a place of crosswinds and hurricanes, jumbo jets and puddle jumpers, a stopover for travelers going by sea or by air to one or another tourist resort in the American tropics. Island colonies, all of them, outcrops of sunken landmasses, dead rims of ancient volcanoes, pieces of land conquered and abandoned, hot, sensuous, primitive, ocean-lapped and wind-lashed. Places like this island have no history, their beginnings pulverized by time and indifference, their moments of heroism and cowardice passing unnoticed by the grander world.

We have known voyagers in armor, and voyagers who happen upon us, travelers who come to invent us, enamored of islands and of their moist seduction. Poets are born under the susurration of coconut palms, in the black nights of the islands, and out of the incomprehensible beauty around us, out of this brilliant palette, come these people, who over centuries of copulation have shed and grown layers of skin and color, a people indefinable, irreducible, passionate and unforgiving, penitent and superstitious, rootless, insular, without horizons.

A people confined by water, surrounded by the infinite, with nothing but dreams.

They dream they came from a land across the water, from a continent of magnificent riches and ancient races, a place they could only dimly remember so many centuries later, but that gave them a strength in the blood, a way of moving and talking, a music older than any memory. They dream they came in royal galleons, across cold purple seas, to conquer lands of fabled treasures, a red earth engorged with gold and silver, and endless shores of sands without footprints. They came, those in armor and those in tri-cornered hats, the barons and dukes, the knights and masters of empire, sailing under the silken banners of a kingdom, to plunder and Christianize, to spread their seed, to take.

Blood flowed in rivers, and in the openmouthed bays of the islands, deathless stone monuments were built to the conquest. Fortresses in Habana, in Santo Domingo, in San Juan, all proclaimed Spain's sovereignty, and cathedrals proclaimed the triumph of the Church over the primitive and uncivilized. In the cities spawned by the Spaniards, once scattered settlements of fruit-laden jungle and sheltering palm trees where the Taínos had made their bohíos and tended their yuccas and corn and cassavas, in nearly every new capital of the West Indies, the face of history became Spain. The French came later, and the English, and the Dutch, and the Africans in chains. But the bloodlines were to Spain, the passions and fatalism and poetry, the madness and the isolation, the irrational pride, the treachery and cruelty.

Those dreams, that history, became transmuted in time, embellished, living on in a few, the historians and artists, the poets, and in the families who claimed ancestors from the arid mountains of Galicia, from the vineyards of Andalusia, from the Mediterranean coast of Catalonia. And in those stories, the life of the island became ancient and romantic, filled with treasures found and lost, with nobility and bravery.

Illusions are the breath of life in a place of little importance.

The northwestern coast of the island runs jagged against the pounding surf of the Atlantic, a moody sea along that coast, heaving high, rugged waves against rocky beaches the color of bones. Ships and sailboats and adventurers cruise those waters, finding anchor and shelter in the seaside town of Aguadilla, where, they like to say, Columbus first landed in Puerto Rico, stopping for water at a spring that is now the center of the town's Parque El Parterre. The town has its Mediterranean airs, and retains some of the architectural curlicues and social snobbery of colonial times.

Out of this storied town, where family name and position determined destinies, came my mother's family. She was born there, in September 1918, when a Great War was devastating Europe and the island was a colony of the United States. She was a middle child, one of three children. The three of them, a boy and two girls, were born into a family where nothing but brilliance was expected, where certain things were assumed—manners and social graces, discipline and studiousness, and in time, good marriages.

My grandmother, a woman of the old world, had been brought up by governesses and tutors, had grown up at dinner tables frequented by men who would one day figure in history books. She was the oldest in a family of six girls, daughters of Josefa Muñoz Rivera, who in a picture my grandmother kept in a gold-leaf frame on her dresser seemed forbidding and severe, with a stern, dour look. It was a face rounded by middle age, with hardened eyes, and hair so dark it seemed dyed. Doña Josefa's ancestors had come from Spain in the eighteenth century and settled in the central mountains of the island. Her grandfather, Luis Muñoz Iglesias, a captain in the Spanish militia, had gone into politics after making the months-long journey from Castilla la Vieja, a province north of Madrid. One of his sons, another Luis Muñoz, became a mayor and had five boys and three girls, among them Josefa, my great-grandmother. His oldest boy, Luis Muñoz Rivera, became a journalist, a poet, and a nationalist (the history books call him a statesman). Josefa did what women of that time usually did, marry and have children.

Josefa's oldest daughter, my grandmother, Monserrate Guevara

Muñoz, was born in Aguadilla, and grew up with the privileges and comforts enjoyed by only a few on the island. Along with this came the emotional distance from her parents that was the custom in families whose names were passed on to the next generation like heirlooms.

I can't see my grandmother ever being an infant or a child, playing freely, getting dirty in the mud with other children. But I can see her at the piano, her back straight, shoulders high. I can see her embroidering a dress, and dancing in a white gown, the hem of which she would hold up with a long, manicured hand. She was a striking young woman, long-necked and lean, who held forth in any conversation, sprinkling bon mots and charm on the serious talk of politics and theater she grew up hearing around the dining table in that house where her father, Agustín Guevara Santini, a marshal of the courts, was a quiet force.

When she was in her early twenties, still living in Aguadilla, she married a shy and bookish lawyer and journalist, Angel Torregrosa, a slight man with wavy light brown hair and owlish eyes that were made more owlish by his wire-rimmed reading glasses. There are no letters and no family stories about a great passion between them, nothing to tell us that their marriage was the culmination of a soulful love affair. It was a proper marriage, a matter of accommodation and tradition. He was an inch shorter than she and stoutly reserved, son of a family of note, whose father, Luis Torregrosa, a pharmacist who, like many men of his class at that time, was more politician than businessman. He served in the parliament and helped establish the Republican Party.

The strain of politics ran thick in my grandfather's blood. Even before my mother was born, Angel Torregrosa was publishing a weekly newspaper of political debate, fighting for the end to American colonialism and for independence. They were the only Torregrosa family on the island, tracing back their origins to Torregrossa, a Catalán village near Barcelona.

My mother once tried to trace the family's history and she got as far back as the nineteenth century, when the Torregrosas left Spain, not to escape persecution or to find fortune, but, according to lore, to minister to the New World colony in the name of Spain, to claim land and farm it, to educate the people and improve health services. They were professors, lawyers, and pharmacists, and they spawned a family of professors, lawyers, and doctors.

In the town in the mountains of the Cordillera Central where my grandparents moved after having their three children, the town where my mother grew up, Don Angel was a considerable figure, a judge and a writer, and, oddly for a man of introspection, a theater producer, something of a dashing impresario, friend of the actors and writers who came through town to stage plays in the theater he supported for years.

When my mother grew old, in her last years, this was the town she most longed for; this was her Puerto Rico, where she grew from a child into a fierce girl of fixed ideas and grandiose dreams, where she learned to ride horses and had boys circling her on the dance floor. Her roots, she said, ran deepest there, in those mountains.

She dreamed that one day she would build a house at the top of one of those hills, and she would stand in her garden in those cool mornings of the hills, drinking her black coffee, looking out to the Caribbean Sea in the far horizon to the south.

The town, Cayey, was surrounded by hills of coffee and tobacco farms and pineapple fields hoed and planted on the skirts of the mountains. On the higher ground, near hilltops that seemed unreachable from the spinning two-lane road that cut through the island north to south, campesinos tended their banana and vegetable patches and lived in one-room houses they built of wood and scraps of tin, tiny houses that seemed like pin-sized spots of yellow or blue, so high up in those hills they could touch the clouds.

Cayey was built like all the other towns on the island, around the plaza. The plaza was the center of the world. The layout of the town reflected the rigid social structure that predated even colonial times: the farther from the plaza, from the municipal buildings and the church, the poorer the houses, the poorer the people. The best homes fronted the plaza, their trellised verandas looking out on the social and commercial life of the town, on the church and its processions, on the strollers and the soft glow of globe-shaped streetlamps, on the ferias of music and dancing.

Sitting on their balconies, as the sun went down, even in the heat of breezeless days and on rainy dusks, the flies gathering on meriendas of sugary coffee and cakes, the women chaperoned the passing of the day, watching out for their husbands to come home, and keeping an eye on the children playing hopscotch and jumping rope in the plaza in that hour when the children were allowed out, just before dinner and bedtime. For it was women who sat on those porches, mothers, grandmothers, greeting visitors, telling their tales, chattering about the things women chattered about, loves and children, weddings, and the situation with the servants.

My grandmother's three children were exactly two years apart, a perfect scale. Children to her were adornments, the inescapable obligation of women. In this house voices were not raised, and disapproval was shown not with screams but only with a raised eyebrow and a glowering stare. My mother, her sister and brother, all had nursemaids and cooks, and they took piano lessons and learned to recite verses and to perform in public.

They were model children, my grandmother claimed, setting for me an example. But then, pausing for a minute, she would turn to me and whisper, Except for your mother.

I learned to enumerate all my mother's sins: She was moody, disobedient, stubborn, bossy, opinionated, and, worst of all, she couldn't sit still. Children are meant to be looked at, not to be heard, my grandmother said repeatedly, another of the old sayings she seemed to have for nearly every occasion.

Grandmother painted my mother as half genius, half tyrant.

Your mother was too smart, too quick with that mouth of hers, didn't like to study but got the best grades, everything came too easily to her, and she had no patience for anything that wasn't perfect, for anything that wasn't the way she saw it. She believed she was always right, and she drove Angela Luisa to tears. Poor Angela Luisa, she was so meek, so quiet, she did everything your mother wanted. She made her dresses, she brushed her hair, she put on your mother's makeup, she ran errands for her. She was always there, in the background.

Your mother was such a terror—she said this with a sigh not of resignation but rather of admiration. Look, one day your mother left school and went to the stables and got on a horse and we didn't know where she was for hours. We couldn't find her anywhere. That was the time, my grandmother said, building up the story like a fairy tale, when your grandfather hit her. Grandmother raised her right arm high to show me how grandfather had done it. That was the only time he raised his hand against any of his children, she said. I couldn't see my grandfather hitting anyone, least of all my mother.

But this was not the time, she said, when your mother was thrown off her horse—that was later. Her boot was caught in the saddle and the horse ran wild and dragged her down a rough field, her head bouncing off rocks and pebbles, bleeding, unconscious—that time, we almost lost her, she almost died.

These stories about my mother were recycled, embroidered, woven from vaguely remembered episodes and stray moments shaped out of half-truths, dimmed and shaded by pride and hurt, and the layers of years, like all memories.

Sometimes, when the rain came in the afternoon and we had nothing to do but sit in the porch, grandmother would come out of her bedroom with her pack of old photos: mother and Angela Luisa in sailor dresses, their hair cut the same, in a bob with bangs, looking almost like twins; mother, Angela Luisa, and José Luis, teenagers posing for a formal picture, my uncle in suit and jacket, the girls in grown-up dresses; my mother, maybe sixteen years old, wearing a long party dress, her mouth slightly open in a smile, her eyes gazing directly at the camera.

Your mother was a beauty, my grandmother would say. She said that often.

She would pull out more pictures. Here was my mother in her riding jacket and tight, knee-high black boots, and in ball gowns, posing with her girlfriends, my mother standing at the front, everyone else radiating around her. She was already a full woman, her breasts clenched in a corset, her hair falling over part of her face, her eyes riveting with promises.

Her lips were shaped perfectly, as if they had been drawn on her. They were rich, defined. Even without the red lipstick that she usually wore, her mouth had a way of speaking its own language, pursed or tightly closed, crooked in disapproval, carelessly open in laughter.

On the theater stage, she was a star, carnations falling at her feet. She was not yet eighteen, still in high school, when she founded with her brother the Farándula Bohemia, a theater ensemble that for several years toured the island. Grandmother kept the old newspaper clippings and read them to me, and I saw my mother, in front of the crimson velvet curtain, her hands raised in triumph, welcoming the applause, her head thrown back. But eventually she left the theater company and left, too, a wreckage of smitten boys who serenaded her with moonlight songs, who brought her gardenias and azucenas, who swept her around dance floors.

She left Cayey for the University of Puerto Rico. She was going to study law.

A few years later, my grandparents moved to San Juan. My mother had already finished her undergraduate degree and had entered law school. My grandfather went to work for a government agency and published newspaper articles on politics and theater and adoring biographies of men he admired. They had an apartment near the university, just off the Avenida Muñoz Rivera, a modest flat where my parents came to live after they were married, where I first lived. This was where my grandfather, still wearing his suit and tie, would pick me up and, putting my baby feet on his buffed cordovans, would dance with me in his old man's shuffle.

He was a man of habit, spending his evenings secluded in his room, reading, writing, and, a family story has it, drinking. One day he came home from work with a terrible headache, took to his room, and was found hours later dead of a brain hemorrhage. He was not sixty years old.

Widowed suddenly, my grandmother left the apartment where he had died and with us moved to El Vedado, a neighborhood of old Spanish-colonial homes and smaller bungalows. We had a large house of constant breezes and the shade of big trees, a one-story house that was yellow like my grandmother's amapolas. It was a house, like all of my grandmother's houses, that seemed always to be full of company, aunts and cousins and distant relations. She didn't live there very long, perhaps two years, before she built a house nearby, on Calle Pérez Galdós, but I remember the coolness of floor tiles in that old house where I learned to walk.

Now and then I see flashes of rainy afternoons at Pérez Galdós. My grandmother has her long dark hair pulled up in a bun, her loose, faded dress falls down to her bony ankles, and she's sitting back in her rocking chair, reading the newspapers to me. She read the obituaries, pointing out this or that person she had known. For hours she would tell me these stories of our family, nationalists and journalists, writers and poets, names given to avenues in San Juan, to town streets, to public schools and parks and plazas. I grew up with their names and faces in my head, men with heavy mustaches and spectacles, austere men in dark regalia, whose sepia portraits appear in the histories of the island.

My grandmother's house, built near the Avenida Eleanor Roosevelt on a lot in a new section of El Vedado, was designed by my mother, who had an eye for architecture and liked to walk around in her heels in the unplowed lot, imagining floors being laid down and walls going up. This house, which would be my grandmother's last home, had two stories and it was square and flat-roofed in the tropical style, with a front porch that butted a rectangle of grass edged by flowers my grandmother planted. They were her favorite yellow and red hibiscuses, pink poinsettias, and shrubs I could not name.

Grandmother lived on the ground floor. It was a big flat with two large airy bedrooms, a small maid's room, and a sunny living room with crank-up slatted windows. She kept her old caned chairs there, the ones she had inherited from her mother, and her upright piano and her radio. To the side, she had a small dining area that looked on a small side porch, and a kitchen that caught the breezes when the door to the outside was opened, letting in light and the voices of neighbors from across the wall that separated our house from the building next door.

Every morning grandmother was up before sunup, in her slippers and apron, making coffee, pouring it through the damp cloth filter.

She and mother were reading the papers, drinking coffee from little cups, by the time Angeles and I woke up and got dressed. Mother left early for her job at the Justice Department, taking the bus to Old San Juan. Usually my father was away at the United States Army barracks, where he, a chemical engineer who knew nothing of war and was too old to go to the front, was serving his tour of duty shuffling papers at a desk job.

All day long I had grandmother to myself.

She was a tall woman, with a long narrow back slightly stooped by age, a deeply featured face with a hooked Roman nose, and the bluish freckled skin of someone who never sat in the sun. Her skin was wrinkled tight around the bones of her forearms, and her frame was fragile and flat, but her face, lean and creviced, with high cheekbones, loosened when she laughed, a birdlike fluttering around her favorite visitors.

On the days she went out, she wore her hairpiece. She kept it in a bottom drawer of her mahogany armoire, where her dresses were hung high, too high for me to reach. The closets in her house were for us, not for her. She would not put her things in a closet, a place without the wood scent that I could smell on her clothes. Her hairpiece was a thick round bun, like a crown, which she said had been made from her own hair. She let her long, fine hair fall down to the middle of her back. Then she would wrap it around the hairpiece with long hairpins and combs. She took great care. She powdered her face, she splashed on blush, and she wore a silk camisole over her bare, flattened, sagging breasts. In the flesh-colored stockings she always wore and her stacked-heeled black leather shoes (her feet were so big), with an heirloom brooch pinned to her blouse and her hair up in that soigné style, she looked head to foot like the matriarch she was, even taller and stronger, with an air of command in her face.

Almost every afternoon, around sundown, we had company, grandmother's sisters and her cousins. She brought out glasses full of chilled tamarind juice, or cups of freshly made coffee, and a platter of white cheese and membrillo. Standing on the ledge of the porch, by the bank of daffodils and azaleas grandmother watered at daybreak and at dusk, I spotted the visitors coming down the road and announced them to my grandmother.

One day I saw a strange woman rounding the street corner, walking in our direction in a hurry, appearing out of the rain like a mad ghost, dressed in black, the hem of her flapping dress touching the pavement. Her hair was a wild mass of wiry gray, her skin parchment white. She carried a leather-bound book of uncut pages, what turned out to be a collection of her poems.

Her unexpected appearance was a big occasion. My grandmother reddened with excitement, taking down from the shelves of her glass-fronted china cabinet her porcelain espresso cups and saucers, the ones with the blue birds and blue mountains, waterfalls and rivers and tiny Chinese houses with concave roofs. Seeing my grandmother so excited, I wanted to know who the woman was. Grandmother turned to me, putting her long index finger to her lips, quieting me, and said that this wild woman who would flit in an out of our house over the years was her cousin, a poet. Clara Lair she called herself, her pen name.

Grandmother held the book of Clara's poetry on her lap, fingering the leather jacket. She called Clara una lumbrera, a brilliant woman, a light in the firmament, a word that brought images of suns to my mind. Clara didn't stay long, ignored me as if I weren't there, and then flew out, gone as suddenly as she had appeared.

She's a little mad, grandmother said to me later, smiling. Insanity runs in the family.

Our other visitors were not quite so mad or quite so lumbreras. Mostly, they were my grandmother's sisters.

Nana was a spinster who so hated being touched by children that she squirmed and jerked back when I kissed her cheek. She sat stiffly, hands folded on her lap, in the wooden recliner by the porch table, sipping black coffee, her lips pursed, barely touching the cup. She had a government job, in the Treasury Department, in an office where she kept the books. Every day she wore her work uniform, the same round-collared, buttoned-up-to-the-neck pink cotton blouse and dark blue skirt that covered her knees. Her face was heavily caked, a chalky pink blush that she put on like a mask, stopping just below the hairline, leaving an odd thin line of white skin showing between her forehead and her hair. I was fascinated by that line, that bare space, I wanted to touch it.

Seven days a week she rose at dawn and went to Mass, walking the mile to the nearest church in a black mantilla. She rarely missed a day. The Church and baseball were her passions, the only ones I ever knew about.

Every now and then, grandmother let me go see Nana in her one-room flat in the building next door that was owned by another of my grandmother's sisters, Isabel, the rich sister, who had married sugar money. Nana had a half refrigerator with a bottle of milk and almost nothing else in it, and she had a bedside table where she kept her prayer book and a rosary of worn black beads. There was little else in that narrow room with the shuttered window, a single bed, a radio. On those evenings that she and I spent together, we didn't talk very much. We listened to the ball game, shouting and jumping with every strike and every score, her ear pressed to the radio, her fingers squeezing a handkerchief.

For a time, Tití Angela Luisa lived in the spare room in grandmother's house, where she made our party dresses, just as she had made mother's gowns. She worked on my grandmother's old Singer sewing machine, her long foot hard on the pedal, her hands guiding the cloth—silk, crinoline, satin—under the machine's needle, tat-tat-tat, a whirr filling the house.

But first, Tití, the name we always called her, lay down the crinkling dress patterns that she had bought at a store. She placed them on the floor and laid the fabric she had ironed over each paper pattern. Leaning on her knees, she trimmed and folded the cloth, her lips clamped around straight pins. Later, when the gown was sewn, by her hand and her machine, she selected from plastic bags she kept in her sewing box the sequins and the beads, glassy, slippery pieces. She squinted as she threaded the needle through holes that were invisible to me. She sewed each bead by hand.

When I was three, she dressed me like a ballerina, complete with dancing slippers and a glittery crown on my light brown curls. All through our childhood, she made pinafores and piano recital gowns for Angeles and me, and on our birthdays, she made the dresses and baked the cakes and mixed the icing, squeezing the icing through a cloth funnel, writing our names in pinks and yellows.

Sometimes, like magic, a long white dress would appear, a grown-up dress with a scooped neck and a big flowing floor-length skirt. That was the dress she made for me for my first debut, when I was seven, at a children's ball at the Caribe Hilton. She pulled my long, wavy hair away from my face and took the sides of my head into her hands. She creamed blush on my cheeks and outlined the rim of my lips with her black makeup pencil, eventually painting my small lips bright red. Just above my upper lip, she painted on a tiny black beauty mark. There I was, in the great lobby of the Caribe Hilton, with a flower in my hair, and a long lavender lily in one hand, leaning over a water fountain, looking ten years older.

Every morning she left for her newspaper job, driving off in her secondhand Volkswagen, pushing the gas pedal as hard as she pushed the pedal on the sewing machine. She was too tall for the car. She was bony, thin and angular, and, to me, quite glamorous with her loose blondish hair and her head scarves. In her late twenties, she was old for a single woman of that time, but she was different in other ways. She was a woman who traveled abroad alone, who was the hostess or the guest at the interminable lunches, interminably photographed, at the Club Cívico de Damas (she was the one without a hat), a woman whose name was the byline of a weekly column in the newspaper.

It seemed to us that she would never marry, and in her striking solitariness, she was someone who belonged alone.

But she did marry. She married late but quite romantically, to a journalist, a man almost thirty years older than she, who was quite debonair and bohemian. All her friends said he was a charming storyteller and he had written books against the death penalty and against American control of the island. These were books people called important, and he seemed to know everything and everyone.

Jacobo and Tití first lived in an apartment house in another neighborhood. The apartment was tiny—the refrigerator was in the stairwell, the bathroom had no tub, only a shower stall. But it was like a dollhouse to me. When Angeles and I visited, she made us hot chocolate and let us play canasta with them until bedtime. For a long time, for many of the years of my childhood, Tití took Angeles and me everywhere, to the movies, to restaurants, to the drive-in. She took me to my first European movie, *La Strada,* and tried to explain a plot that made little sense to me but seemed very sad. I still see Giulietta Masina in her clown face. The first time I had Chinese food, at a large, bright restaurant on Franklin Delano Roosevelt Avenue, the sort of restaurant where the waiters bowed when she came in and stood at attention near her table (she feigned modesty but clearly expected the beer to be poured just so and the cook to make whatever changes she wished), she taught me to use chopsticks. The first time I saw a newspaper coming off the presses, I was with her. That was at the old building of *El Imparcial,* a blood-and-guts tabloid where she began her career as a society columnist, chronicling births and debuts and weddings.

We were standing in a corridor, at a wall of glass through which we could see the presses churning below. Huge, noisy machines occupied the entire basement. She had to shout so I could hear her.

Mira, mira, she shouted—look, look.

My face was touching the glass. The machines roared and newspapers rolled off cylinders, piling one on top of another. She took me by the hand, and we ran down the stairs to the press room. She shouted to a pressman, and he handed her a newspaper, and she gave it to me. It was warm, like freshly pressed clothes, and it smelled like nothing I had ever known.

Some years later she was on a television quiz show modeled after *What's My Line?* With that and her Sunday column, which she had moved to another newspaper, *El Mundo,* then the island's largest, she became something of a celebrity. She took me to the television studios of Telemundo, where I was seated in a guest room behind the cameras and watched the show.

The studio was air-conditioned, freezing, and the cameras blocked my view of her face. But I could hear her voice, higher pitched when she was on the air. She was funny, I could tell. When she made a comment, the audience laughed all around me. After the show, people crowded around her, asking for her autograph. I stood beside her, watching her, and watching the people who treated her as if they knew her personally: Angela Luisa, Angela Luisa. I wanted to be her. Craning my neck, I studied how she made her signature, the rounded *A* and the curly *L,* the sharp *T,* and the flourish in the *g*'s. But after years of giving autographs and signing her name to her column, she no longer had to use her last name. Angela Luisa was enough.

The ballet, the theater, the newspaper, her world was mine, and I thought that if I grew up to be like her, I, too, would have front-row seats at the theater and fine dinners at elegant restaurants with movie stars, and newspapers hot off the presses every night.

Every day grandmother fixed our breakfast, whatever we wanted—soft-boiled eggs, cream of corn, oatmeal—and forced us to drink glasses of warm milk. She didn't eat, but she stayed in the kitchen, keeping up a commentary with no one in particular, her voice rising above the clatter of pans and running water, her hands deep in soapy water.

She had a maid to clean the house and do the daily wash out back, but she liked to do the cooking herself. Sometimes she went out, making her visits to her sisters. But she never went to church, and she seldom went shopping, having been brought up with servants to do the housekeeping and the groceries, having been brought up to make her own clothes or to have a seamstress make them for her.

When she had no maid, she managed somehow by herself. She bought vegetables and fruit off the carts that came down the street, and she made daily lists of groceries she needed and paid the street boys to get them from the supermarket at the corner. Occasionally she had lunch delivered. In those days there were places—bodegas, storefront kitchens—that made entire meals to order and delivered them in fiambreras, aluminum containers that were stacked one on top of another. All over the neighborhood, you saw delivery boys carrying fiambreras, the food steaming, the smells of rice and beans, mofongo, alcapúrrias, lingering in the air.

Each day around noon she sat beside her radio and listened to my uncle's comedy show—Now, she would say to me, sit still and listen, José Luis is on the radio. He came to my grandmother's house occasionally, making his entrances with much fanfare (which was mostly my grandmother's, who preened around him, giving up to him her rocking chair, bringing him a cup of coffee, though she knew he would've preferred a shot of rum). His voice carried from the street, full of theater. I recognized it instantly. He sounded just as he did on the radio. He was not a big man, but he had girth, blocky shoulders and a large face, a large nose, a big mustache, and thinning hair. Bluster, he had bluster, and a raucous, hoarse stage voice, and exploded with laughter at his own jokes, which he invented on the spot. Once he went to Spain and he carried on as if he had discovered it—After Spain, there's only heaven, he said over and over, looking up at the sky. Pictures of bloody bulls ran through my head.

When a crowd gathered at his house, as it often did, he entertained in his pajamas and slippers, a handkerchief soaked in bay rum on his forehead. Standing in the middle of the room, he played magic tricks, bringing on laughter each time, and dashed off verses, which he recited with expansive gestures, his arms taking in the whole room, flowery lines that he later wrote down and dedicated to any of us in even more flowery language and signed in a heavy bold hand.

My grandmother rarely went to his house, and months would pass between his visits. She seldom told me stories about him, but she didn't miss his show—those slapstick skits and street jokes she hardly understood but that people loved. The crazy but lovable down-and-out characters he created made him a familiar figure, famous, a picture in the papers, a man known just by his last name.

Late in the afternoon in those days, el panadero came by the house, always at the same time, crying out, Pan, pan, pushing his wheeled cart, which he stacked high with fresh loaves of bread wrapped in plain white paper. My grandmother would go out in her slippers, pick from the cart the warmest loaf she could find, and give the man his five cents. Then she would sit in the dining room and break off a crusty piece and spread it with soft butter. I would climb on a chair and bend over her big steaming cup of coffee, soaking my piece in it, crumbs of soggy bread and melting butter running down my chin.

Just as the sun was setting, after the rainbow that came with the afternoon showers had faded, my mother would arrive from work, walking from the bus stop, a newspaper in her hand, her heels clicking on the pavement. Angeles and I would run to her and hold her around her waist. With a cup of coffee and the newspaper folded beside her, she would sit on the porch with us, holding us to her lap, humming to us, her voice a breeze in my ear, Ese lunar que tienes, cielito lindo, junto a la boca, no se lo des a nadie, cielito lindo, que a mí me toca.

Chapter Two

Amor de Loca Juventud

On the eve of my mother's funeral I thought I would sleep, but sleep didn't come. My sisters and I had booked rooms in the town's only motel—it was too far to go back to Sara's in Dallas for the night, and my mother's house was crowded, with Angeles and Amaury staying there. It was an ordinary roadside motel, a truck stop where coffee came gritty and lukewarm out of a machine and long-haul drivers gassed up their trucks and stayed on for a couple of beers. I had a room alone, as I wanted it. No conversation, no crying, only silence. Well, not entirely. The old air-conditioning unit rattled, the occasional souped-up car roared out of the driveway, and murmurs came through the walls. I read the local papers. I leafed through a magazine. I turned on the TV and clicked it off, startled that the world was still going on, Jay Leno laughing, his cackle breaking through the impermeable quiet I was trying to build around myself. I turned off the lights.

In the dark, I saw my mother in her short, red velvety robe, the one still hanging on the back of the door of her bathroom; I saw her going to the kitchen and drinking a glass of milk before bedtime, and I saw that house of hers, with the tall trees and the garden she tried to plant, where her piano stood like a prized trophy against a living room wall. I saw her china espresso cups shining among the old dishes in her cupboards. They were a gift from Angeles, and mother had wrapped them in newspapers and carried them from one country to another. She kept the cups for a long-anticipated moment, an evening of great conversation and poetry and piano-playing, where she would serve espresso to convivial company, but that had not happened to her in those last years. So little had.

The funeral was the next day, on a Monday, at noon.

It was the first time that the six of us had been together in one place in more than fifteen years. We all sat together in the second pew, dressed up as she would have liked. We were all in black—a row of black, a row of lost faces.

The church was draped in red. Red carnations, big crimson-and-white wreaths placed around and on her coffin. The stained-glass windows seemed red, which caused the sunlight to stream through in red, like a spotlight. She liked red, and she liked black. I can hardly remember her in blue or green, but she was a tropical woman, she liked her plumage.

We held hands, Angeles on one side of me, Amaury on the other. We stood to pray, and we sat quietly, heads bowed, to listen to someone play "Für Elise," the music she had played on her piano. We listened to the eulogies, soft words about a woman, a good woman, but someone I didn't recognize as my mother, and when we filed out, when they played the "Ave Maria" on the pipe organ, I thought I might cry.

I turned to Angeles and said, She would've liked it.

Yes, all the people who came, Angeles said.

A green awning with wide white stripes shaded the chairs that lined up in front of the hole where her coffin would lie. A gravestone had been made, her name—no, not her name, but the name she took when she remarried—had been chiseled into gray marble. The years, 1918–1994. In quotes, Flor de Borínquen. A poem had been written for her in her youth called "Flor de Borínquen," and she had kept it. Borínquen, the tribal name for Puerto Rico. Meaningless and sad in this clay that wasn't hers.

We stood behind the rows of chairs. Leon, my mother's husband (I had to remind myself), was already seated in the center of the front row; their son, Leon Jr., and Leon's family around him. He was a handsome old man, had to have broken hearts when he was at Texas A&M, just like his son, my half brother, Leon Jr., had during the year he spent in College Station, playing football, skipping classes, and finally dropping out. Leon Jr. looked just like him, a tall, light-eyed Texan, brushing back his short hair. The boy had gone into the army, and I hadn't seen him since he was very young. Little Leon, we called him. He had our mother's eyelashes, but little else we could find. Old Leon saw us standing back, waved, calling us to his side. The minister, bespectacled, middle-aged, his face deeply lined beyond his years, approached us, clasping a Bible in his right hand. He spoke softly, his eyes clouded behind his glasses. He said, Come to the front row, it's for family. We nodded but said nothing. He took me by the elbow, gently. I shook my head. Then, knowing that mother would have ordered us to the front row, I smiled, thinking she would understand, and said, Thank you, but we prefer to stand back here.

Prayers were said, and the sun beat hard on my back and the soil lost its morning dampness and was now dry red, the fields around us barren.

Tití Angela Luisa stood bravely in the heat, in black, her eyes behind sunglasses. My aunt had seen her father buried, her mother buried, her husband buried. Now, her only sister. They began to lower the coffin. We turned our backs at that moment.

Amaury reached for my hand. He looked younger and taller in a suit, a handkerchief folded in the pocket of his jacket, his face shaven, his mustache clipped, his dark hair combed back. His sunglasses concealed his swollen eyes. He had cried all through the service in church, his shoulders shaking. The girls had cried; everyone had cried but Angeles and me.

I thought, If I cry, if Angeles cries, who would be there for the others?

The burial service seemed very fast. We walked away before the coffin had completely gone into the ground, and we separated to get into our cars. We rode, as in a caravan, to the church hall, where the ladies had prepared a lunch for the entire crowd.

Angeles and I didn't go in for a long time. We stood outside, smoking under the threshold, reviewing the service as if it had been a theater play, trying to see it as my mother would have. She would have liked it, I repeated.

Relatives of my mother's husband came by, cousins, nephews, aunts, everyone. We smiled, we thanked them, but we could hardly remember any of them.

What are we doing here? Angeles asked me, asking herself. What is this, a lunch after a burial? We laughed. Sara came to get us, someone came to get us, and we went inside.

Tables had been set up, as if this were a dinner party. The six of us didn't sit at the table the ladies had for us. This had been my mother's church group, and she and her husband ate lunch there every Sunday after services. My mother, incredibly, had become a churchgoer in her old age, she whom I had rarely seen in a Catholic church when I was growing up. She had become a Methodist like Leon when she remarried, and lately had been reading that booklet of prayers I saw on her bedside table.

We didn't stand and wait to serve ourselves from the buffet. We sat in a corner by a window and took pictures of one another with Olga's camera and acted exactly like my mother would have prohibited, like outsiders, like the private club we had suddenly become. Orphans against the world.

Olga was beside herself, one moment sobbing uncontrollably, the next laughing just as hard, and crying out, Mother, mother is gone. She held on to Angeles, bending as if the pain were centered in her stomach, as if the life inside her were leaving. What am I going to do without her? And suddenly shifting moods, she started taking pictures. Amaury had his arm around me. He grew up years that day, I could see it. He seemed stronger, his arm firmer, and he had lost his barrio shuffle. Angeles was the center, where she always was, even when she said nothing. She had become mother.

She was dressed like the rest of us, in black, and wore her sunglasses even inside the church hall. You look like a movie star, I said to her, half kidding, something exotic and bruised and beautiful (she had a knack for the camera). Well, in this place, she said, taking off her sunglasses, twirling them in her hand, we *are* movie stars.

We huddled side by side, running outside to smoke, and when the lunch was finally over and people dispersed, we took our places on foldout chairs that had been placed on the lawn, to take a big picture. Angeles and I, hair in place, sunglasses on, legs crossed, sat center stage, in the front. Amaury, Olga, Sara, and Carmen stood behind us. People came by, saying their good-byes, saying those sweet things to which no one expects an answer—remembering a gift my mother gave them, the way she spoke, her charming accent, they said. She was such a good person, they said, not knowing what else to say. She was so elegant. Yes, she was, thank you, I said over and over.

But they didn't know her. At least, they didn't know the woman in the picture she had given my father when she was young, a year before I was born—"Amaury, te quiero mucho, María Luisa."

They didn't know, the two of them.

In the beginning, when they met, she was a swimsuit beauty, a cheerleader and sorority queen who rode horses and played the piano. He was already out in the world, the first of eight children, the first in his family to have gone to university, the oldest son of a small-town drugstore owner. He had reached the middle age of his youth. Slender, pale-skinned, narrow-faced, jagged already, a twenty-five-year-old man of many women even then. He was a man with a past and the willful temper and ambition of the hard-born.

She was twenty-two, a face imperfectly sculpted, smooth as rain-worn stone, the nose not quite aquiline, the eyelids perhaps too sorrowful, but cheeks perfectly boned, sharp slants toward her mouth. It was the mouth, always, which betrayed the consuming ardor, the consuming longing that had been born in her. Dark-haired, with the sighful movements of a Dolores Del Río (in *María Candelaria,* flowers cascading from her goddess head) and lips just a moment before pouting, just a shade softer than rose, she played the leading roles in all the worlds she lived in, and in all those worlds, she was imperious and yet submissive, and men fell on their knees, or broke her heart.

She was a party girl. A brilliant girl, studying law like her father, but capriciously, absorbing books like air, because the stuff of books, and words in all forms, came easily to her. She liked to say that when she and my father came together, it was destiny. They met in passing, and he ignored her. She was his sister's college roommate, too young for him, virginal. But he must have noticed something because months later, after that one fleeting meeting, he still remembered her face. He called her and invited her to dance.

What a dancer he was.

The palm of his blunt broad hand on her waist, he swept her, literally, across waxed floors, heat rising on her cheek, on her bare neck, on her breasts, their hands clasped, bodies infinitesimally apart, then as one, swirling, circling, a storm rotating, dipping, brushing everyone else aside. She was his already, her legs entwined, her feet following without thinking, clouds under her. Boleros never seemed to end for them, and tangos that exhausted passion until they closed out the night. In the dawn, pearl gray like her eyes, his white dinner jacket was soaked with her, her chiffon gown limp, her mouth half open on his lips.

Era el amor de loca juventud. . . .

He wrote her letters. His unintelligible scrawl became so familiar, she knew the words by the slant. The slashes he made. They were pictures to her, and she imagined him in the port town where he lived, on the eastern end of the island, a mountain-edged region of sugarcane fields and flat sea heat. She thought she knew the details of his days, his routine. But she knew only what he wanted her to know.

His letters in those first months when they knew each other had the force of a life totally outside her own, outside the familiar circles of the life she knew in San Juan. The story of his days rushed at her, along with his desire and his raw ardor.

She found his tenacity, his strength, irresistible, and she fell in love madly—madly being the only way she could have ever loved—and in that madness she did not see the smallness in him, the earthiness, the brooding anger.

When they first met, my father was a chemical engineer. He was the first professional in a family whose ancestors came from the province of Galicia, driven out of the red-rock fallowness of Spain a century before, a poor, sullen, hardy, stocky people, their skin blanched white. His father, Ernesto López Orengo, owned a drugstore at a time when such a thing on an island town, owning any store, gave a family a certain stature in the town's society. Guayama, where my father was born, and where his father had his first drugstore, was a placid city of Spanish-colonial homes, sugarcane fields, and pasofino horses on the southeastern coast. It was out of the way of the major east-west and north-south commercial traffic of the island, but for a time it was rich in sugar, coffee, and cattle.

My father was a grown boy when Don Ernesto moved his business and his family to the northeast coast, to Fajardo, a shabby, congested port town of busy commerce and big refineries, fishing villages, sugar landowners, and the droves of mountain people who came down to the coast for work.

The drugstore was a small shop, surviving on foot traffic, doing well enough during the Depression to support my grandparents and their large family, but my grandfather was not a moneymaker. He was a man behind a desk, a courteous storekeeper rising affably to attend a customer, moving carefully around the store shelves, peering through his thick glasses, studying the labels on the potions and powders. He was not an imposing figure. He had a square, robust frame, same as his sons in their middle age, and a dour face, with somber, dark eyes behind black-frame glasses.

He died before I was born, and there are few stories about him, but everyone said he was a man of few words, reclusive and quiet around his wife, Josefina Candal Feliciano. She was a round-hipped little woman who bore eight children, four boys and four girls, and dominated the family even in her old age, when her hair had turned thin white, and her eyes had gone to a filmy light brown.

Even with her children grown and married, she commanded them with her piercing shrill voice and her pinprick, puckered, disapproving mouth. She terrified the women her sons had married; strong women themselves, they became sheepish in her presence, fearing the enraged temper her sons had inherited. Defenseless as she appeared with that sweet, little girl's face of hers (she had the face of nuns I had known), she could explode in anger over some unintended slight—an impolite grandchild, a birthday forgotten, a gift not brought.

She would rise up from her chair, wrap herself in the shawl that she almost always had around her shoulders, and taking her walking cane, demand to be taken home. One of her sons would invariably follow, apologizing, and we her grandchildren would obediently call after her, Abuela, abuela!

My father was her glory, the first of her boys to make money, enough money to send his younger brothers and sisters to college. He was twenty-one when he started working at the centrales around Fajardo and Humacao, on the eastern coast, at the old nineteenth-century sugar refineries that were left over from Spain's colonial era, when sugar was the island's gold, when acres of coastal sun-scorched fields were worked by African slaves (the native Indians, the Taínos and Arawaks, had long ago been decimated) and the grand landed families, Spaniards and criollos, lived in fabled estates in the cool mountains.

There were no longer slaves in the early 1900s—slavery was banished in Puerto Rico in the mid-1800s, before the American Civil War—but the descendants of slaves and Taínos, the mestizos, the negritos and jíbaros, the illiterate and landless, did the menial work. They were indentured servants, tenants, small-plot farmers, and seasonal sugarcane cutters in straw hats and rolled-up threadbare pants. They came down from the hills and the coastal villages season after season, brown-skinned, with hollow chests, their thin-muscled arms bearing the scars of machete cuts.

In those thick fields where the cane grew taller than they, the men endured bug bites, infections, and their bare feet sloshing in mud. At the end of the day, their backs broiled, they carried their bundles of sugarcane, long stringy poles roped around their torsos, the bundles weighing them down. On the edge of the sugar fields, they loaded the oxcarts that would take the sugarcane to the centrales, the sugar mills and refineries, a collection of sheds and brick buildings with smoke towers that filled the air with plumes of vapor that was sweet with the smell of crushed cane, boiling sugar, and molasses.

My father rarely spoke of his time at the centrales, perhaps because he had hated the heat of the sheds, the monotony of the rounds he made, looking at test tubes, gauging by color and thickness the quality of the molasses that would be distilled into a thick, cloying liquid to be poured into wooden barrels to ferment and age until it turned into prime dark rum, cinnamon-colored Puerto Rican rum, the best in the world.

Nuestra clase de gente, grandmother liked to say. I can't remember the first time I heard her say that, but it was something I understood very early, hearing her wonder aloud, while sitting in the porch with her newspaper, if such-and-such a person in the news, or someone she heard about or just met, was related to such-and-such family in Aguadilla or Lares or Aibonito. She and mother could spend hours doing this, tracing family histories, remembering the connections between a family and a town, and what came of them.

Our world was simple then, and the layers of society seemed clearly marked: good families at the top, and the gentuza at the bottom; and the gentuza were definitely not nuestra clase de gente. They were out there, my grandmother said, pointing in no particular direction. They were the masses, the unschooled, the families of the barrios, the men in the bodegas, the people who didn't know where they came from.

There was nothing new in the system. From the reign of the caciques, who kept lesser tribes away from their plaza, through the reign of Spain, which built a fortress around its garrison in San Juan to keep invaders at bay and the natives out, Puerto Rico had been ruled by class—no less than the rest of Latin America, no less than the European empires. It was a society built on manners and traditional customs and mores, on riches and exploitation, on the fiction that class was a birthright.

My father came from a good family, my grandmother declared after making her calculations. Perhaps it was not a prominent family, but they were solid, refined, and made up of serious men. My father had manners, he knew to stand up when my grandmother entered a room; he was deferential to my grandfather. He had been a good student and a devoted son, and on the occasions when he escorted my mother to a dinner or to a dance, he had the bearing of successful men. Era tan guapo, my grandmother remembered. He cut a fine figure, self-assured, a man who could join any conversation. He also had the personality my grandmother fell for; he could charm with words and had the easy confidence of a man of means, of ambition, and in those days, when he was courting my mother, in a society where appearances were everything, he was a proper suitor, nuestra clase de gente.

But his had been the life of a small-town patrón, nightlong games of dominoes, Sunday fiestas at the farms of his friends, roasting pigs and having their drinks, their beer, their tumblers of rum. Nights spent with street women, fathering unclaimed children. Putting money on the table, taking care of wives and mothers, and the campesinas, the servants, the women they took at will.

His heart had calluses, and his dreams the confines of that narrow island life, an insular life bounded by mountains and sea. He longed for possession—to have, to own, to control and command—and once he met my mother he wanted nothing more than to possess her. It took him no time.

What a distance she crossed for him. She who adored attention, who demanded and got center stage in the theaters where she played Camellia, radiant in the footlights. She could hold a room in a spell reciting the nostalgic, tormented verses of Rubén Darío and García Lorca, and she dazzled in any field she chose to enter (she even won in basketball and was photographed in swimsuits, her hair up in a turban, for society magazines). She who had everything had fallen for a man who had never set foot in a theater, who never read books, who had never thought of Madrid, Paris, Rome, the places she had longed for all her life.

He was a man who didn't send her flowers.

He was no poet, she knew, but she said she had had the poets and their fragile words, and the nervous young men who came with guitars and violins to serenade her from the street below her bedroom window. They brought orchids for her hair and sentimental sonnets she put away in scrapbooks. She had had boyfriends, men her parents liked, men from the right families, but none had made her shudder the way my father had, none could bend her to their will as he had, as he did.

Era un hombre fuerte, un hombre de ambiciones, un romántico—he was strong, ambitious, a romantic—she told me many years later, trying to explain, as she had for most of her life, his possession of her, trying to forgive not him but herself.

They married one July, on a day blazing and humid with the pent-up rains of the hurricane season. It was not a big party, not the society wedding one would have imagined considering the circles she lived in. It was a quick civil ceremony in front of a judge at city hall. All their months of romance and letters and impassioned courtship had culminated that day in July, in a plain room, in a plain ceremony with plain words.

In the island, at that time, at any time, a Catholic girl, a society girl, had no bigger dream than her wedding day, the beautiful white gown, the church dressed in flowers, music from a choir, the blessing of friends and family. Only elopement was more disgraceful than a civil ceremony.

But my mother, the incurable romantic, a woman who never lost sight of her place in society, defied convention, and denied herself her own dream.

As a child I had imagined her in white, the trail of her dress sweeping down the church aisle, my father in coattails anxiously waiting to take her hand, and I believed that picture until many years later, when I heard the stories—that my mother was pregnant and wanted to hurry the wedding, that my father had been married before and the Catholic Church wouldn't marry him again, that fearing society gossip, she had wanted to let the date of her wedding go unnoticed.

I didn't ask her, not ever. I didn't want to hear a lie, and I didn't want to hear the truth.

On that day, no pictures were taken, or none were kept. There was no announcement in the society pages, no engraved invitations, no ballroom reception. In my mother's scrapbooks, which record almost every year of her life then, there is not one remembrance of her wedding.

Those were the war years, after Pearl Harbor, when Puerto Ricans, colonials with American citizenship, were drafted to fight in lands they barely knew, whose names they could barely pronounce, heroic places they heard about in the dark of movie houses, on the grainy Movietone newsreels narrated by baritone voices with end-of-the-world urgency. The names of those places would soon become familiar, postmarks on letters home from the front. From the hills of the campesinos, from the mud slums of swampy San Juan, the men were recruited, outfitted in the drab olives of the United States Army, and sent off to fight under a flag that was not ours, a flag that bore no star or stripe of our own, to which we pledged allegiance every day in the schoolhouses of the island.

And over the airwaves that crackled and faded, beamed from Washington to the Caribbean, the voice of Franklin Delano Roosevelt was heard nightly on the radios in the living rooms of San Juan. In the distant towns of the Cordillera Central, FDR's picture was nailed to tar-board walls along with the portraits of the Virgin and Christ on the Cross you see in the homes of the humble in Catholic countries.

My father was not sent off to fight. He did not see Normandy or Naples or Corregidor. He saw nothing of the war. He was too old and flat-footed. But he joined the Army Corps of Engineers and was assigned to a desk job in the barracks in San Juan and wore his army uniform every day, creased and shiny. He wore it with that male pride that comes with stripes and snappy salutes. He was fatless and slight but looked stronger than he was, with an air of authority. By now twenty-seven years old, he was settled in, fully grown-up, mature in the way that men in their twenties were at that time, men with families and large responsibilities.

All her life my mother bragged about my father's unselfish support of her career during their first years of marriage, when she, who had never had the slightest affinity for the kitchen, who couldn't mend a sock and had absolutely no interest in keeping house, spent most of her days debating tort law, attending lectures on civil and criminal law (she favored civil law), and disputing fine legal points. Telling the story of those early years, she described my father's pride in her, his wife the lawyer, and his exuberance when he introduced her to his friends as his wife—Una mujer brillante!

How she liked to embellish her image of him.

But my mother was lying. He had not wanted her to finish law school. When I was old enough to understand, my grandmother told me that he had wanted to take her away from the city to his town on the east coast. He wanted her to give him children and cook his meals, like the wives of his friends. But he had had no choice. My grandfather insisted that she had to finish law school.

She was the only one of my grandparents' three children to follow in grandfather's steps. They took pride in that, in a family where a good name and accomplishment were the only inheritance. They had no wealth, no land, no sugar fields, no coffee farms. They had cared little for the making of money but placed immense store in lineage, in ancestors, in books written and honors gained, in their name appearing in the chronicles of the island's history.

My mother was in her last year of law school, pregnant with me, small-bellied and thin, but she did not leave the university or take to rocking chairs to wait nervously for the birth of her first child. She was close to completing her last semester in law school when I was born, in late March, in a clinic in the San Juan district of Río Piedras, in a building that no longer exists, not far from her parents' apartment, near the university.

She had an easy birth. She liked to say I was a perfect baby, perfectly shaped and perfectly behaved. I didn't cry all night. Many years later, on one of my birthdays, she sent me a few verses on bond paper, written in her slanted longhand. It was a celebration of my birth. She wrote it in tears, I was sure reading her words, feeling her intimacy, embarrassed at the lyrics overflowing with sentiment, the joy she described in the very act of having me come out of her, her flesh and blood, inseparable from her.

But I had also brought her enormous physical pain. Within weeks of my birth she had cysts removed from her left breast, caused by excess milk she produced while breast-feeding me. She went through surgery without anesthesia, with only a local painkiller, and fell unconscious from the pain when the surgeon punctured her skin and cut into her breast. She was left with six scars. She was never again able to breast-feed her children.

She romanticized even that gruesome pain, making a drama of it, telling the story when we were grown, always ending it with a flourish.

Your father says it was butchery, she said each time, almost triumphantly.

Those stitched wounds on her breast, which turned into grayish spots with time, were marks of courage, like the jagged indentations on her scalp, on the crown of her head, barely visible scars from the day when she was sixteen—or was it eighteen?—and a horse threw her off with a sudden jerk and her boot was caught in the saddle, and the horse, its reins loosened, raced off, dragging her along, her body bouncing over pebbles and hard dirt, the back and top of her head skinned, torn, soaked in blood.

At the end of the spring when I was born, she put on her black graduation robe and mortarboard and received her law degree. In a picture, my mother looks intriguing, distant, with a finely drawn face and enormous pupils of liquid black, almost translucent. She now had the title that lawyers carry with all the weight given to titles in Latin America, la licenciada, la doctora. My father's surname did not appear on her diploma, nor on the brass plaque she later hung outside her office. She would not change her name.

She was María Luisa Torregrosa, a name she said like a melody, like a declaration.

At that time, when most women were little more than the property of their fathers or husbands, women in Puerto Rico, and in much of Latin America, usually professional women and society women, didn't surrender their maiden names, their family names, when they married. They simply appended their husband's surname to their own. But on the diplomas and awards framed in my mother's office, and in the books where she was cited among other female lawyers in America, her name stood alone, without my father's surname, and when she signed her name to the thousands of papers and documents that she would sign as a lawyer, she never used his name. Maybe in doing this, I thought years later, she tried to withhold something of herself from him.

On the day of my baptism, my family—grandmothers, aunts, cousins, uncles, and my grandfather Angel, just before his death—posed for a picture in their suits and summery dresses at the bottom of the steps of the church. My parents were placed apart, like bookends. He was hatless, looking gaunt and distracted in his starched army khakis, holding me in his arms, and she was in a black lace mantilla, her eyes brooding into the camera.

In the first years of their marriage my parents had no home of their own. He was in the army; she had a law clerk's job. We lived with my mother's parents. After my grandfather Angel died, we moved with my grandmother from the flat near the university to an old house in El Vedado, a neighborhood of leafy streets and Mediterranean-style houses with red-tiled roofs and casement windows, big banyan and flamboyán trees. The streets abutted the busy avenues of Hato Rey, a crowded district of middle-class homes, stores and markets, gas stations, food stands, and wood-and-tin houses with open sewers.

In the late forties, the movement of people from the sugarcane fields and the coffee hills had already started, and San Juan, always a densely populated capital, was expanding. Slums sprouted on the edges of middle-class and upper-middle-class residential districts, and new low-cost subdivisions of modest, square-shaped cement houses were being built by the government wherever there was open land.

The island's transformation began in those years. Sugar, coffee, and tobacco farms began to fold, leaving the field hands with nothing. Factories began to take the place of farms—small textile factories where the luckiest earned their wages in stifling rooms, sewing cloth and leather on rustic machines and by hand. When the island gained a measure of independence, when it became a commonwealth of the United States in 1952, the changes accelerated. Bigger factories went up, more skilled labor was needed, and the poor flooded the cities, without jobs, without a trade. With that flow of people came a profound social and cultural change.

Tens of thousands of half-literate jíbaros, people from the slums and fields and towns, left the island for New York and cities farther west to find work, traveling more than fifteen hundred miles north with the dream—a steady daily stream of people who, like all immigrants before them, congregated naturally with their own in a strange land, creating new barrios, living in the tenements once filled with Italian and Jewish and Irish immigrants. The island was now spreading, spilling outward, eventually giving New York the flavor of the mountains of Puerto Rico, the rhythms of the plena, the Spanglish of a people with a broken language, and a broken home.

No one in my family left the island seeking their fortune. They left to study abroad, to get degrees from Harvard and Columbia, to live the bohemian life, and to tour the great cities of Europe, to visit the Louvre and the Prado Museums, to put on the layer of culture that came with traveling, with seeing the world.

Before I was three, my mother was showing me pictures in the *National Geographic,* places she wanted me to know as well as she knew them, even though she had never seen them. She and my grandmother also talked about the opera and theater in Madrid and Paris, and Sarah Bernhardt became a name as familiar to me as the name of the governor of Puerto Rico, my grandmother's cousin, who had spent years writing poetry in Greenwich Village before becoming a politician.

But it didn't occur to us that life would be better somewhere else (maybe in Madrid or Barcelona, mother used to say), and we pitied the poor families carrying their paper bags stuffed with their meager belongings—and their chickens and plátanos—that crowded the airport terminal for the flights to New York.

My family lived in a society so small that we knew no one who left, except for the maids who believed the Bronx was paved with gold. A few of my mother's friends and my father's sisters married Americans they had met during the war, men posted to the island's military bases, who went on to live in places like Pasadena and Coral Gables. But we didn't need to escape. We were not rich, yet we seemed to be on an island where more than seventy percent of the people were poor. We could move from house to house, hire servants, and attend private schools. And in that atmosphere of comfort, the island seemed idyllic to me, the island being in reality my parents, my family, what we know as children.

Chapter Three

A City of Pyramids

After the funeral, after the lunch at the church, we drove an hour away from Edgewood, to Sara's house in Dallas. Her kitchen, a large all-white room dimly lighted in the sunset glow, a kitchen she kept immaculate, had the look of a war room, the wreckage of too many people, cold leftovers, empty beer bottles, overflowing ash-trays. The dishes piled up in the sink.

Sara moved about, quiet as if in slippers, picking up after the rest of us, pushing her hair back off her tired face, with its bluish circles under her eyes. Angeles, Amaury, and I seemed glued to the kitchen chairs around the table, as if we would never get up. Olga was some-where in the house, tending to her boys. Carmen to the side of the table, not quite in the circle, her hands clasped in her lap, her eyes lowered, but she was listening.

She had on her makeup but looked drained, although she cer-tainly seemed more composed than the rest of us. She had on her earrings, her rings, her watch, gifts from her husband. She had on a short skirt that showed off her lean legs.

You look just like mother, I said to her, noticing her almond-shaped eyes, her fine cheekbones, her prim mouth. She smiled her tight faint smile, shaking her head. I don't see it, she said. Well, mother when she was very young, I said, putting my arm around her. She pressed her lips, flattered but embarrassed. She had thin lips, not at all like mother's, but I was seeing mother in all of them, in all but me.

She was happiest in Mexico, I said suddenly, just to say something. This was ground we had covered over the years. We had endlessly discussed every minute detail of our mother's life, especially mother's life with father, and the years when the first three of us were born.

The war had ended, Angeles was born, and my father left the army and his job in the sugar refineries. He had decided to become a doctor. With my mother's help, he got a government scholarship to study medicine in Mexico. For the first time in his life, he had to imagine a place outside the island, a place where he knew no one. But because he lacked imagination, he lacked fear.

My mother, whose ambitions for him were even larger than his own, left the work she loved at the Justice Department, the life of family and friends, and the four of us—I was three years old, Angeles was two—traveled two thousand miles, over the Atlantic, over the Gulf of Mexico, in bouncing, slow propeller planes, stopping in Habana, in Miami, sick to our stomachs, light-headed, to Mexico City.

Mexico? Carmen asked softly, with a look of surprise. She never talked to us much about Mexico. I turned to her. Yes, Mexico, years before you were born.

Angeles shook her head.

I don't remember anything about Mexico, Amaury interrupted.

You were a baby then, I said.

Angeles was very quiet. She was staring into some vision only she could see. Dragged on her cigarette, mashed the butt into a saucer. I watched her. She didn't look at me. She had changed into an old T-shirt and jeans. She had not slept well for days, had stayed up most of the night before the funeral with Amaury, had stayed in mother's den, had helped him fold out the sofa bed and put on the sheets and covered him with a blanket.

Those were their best years, I repeated, she told me so herself once. She said, life was simple then.

Life was simple then, I thought, pushing away the image of her body in the ground, alone in a cemetery whose name I had already forgotten. Who could think of that? But it was all I kept thinking about, her body in a dark box. Sitting in Sara's kitchen, at that moment, I wanted to think of Mexico, the smell of roasting corn and the thick smoke of coal fires, as if I were five years old again.

~

Along the Paseo de la Reforma and the Avenida Chapultepec, sweeping boulevards bordered by trees and parks, great hotels and shops, the city opens up to the clouds, the streets broaden, and flower-strewn fountains spray the tepid tropical air. Immense paintings appear on the facades of buildings, murals telling the story of Mexico: doomed faces, a blood-soaked earth, peasants in loose spun-cotton shirts, barefoot or in huaráches, carrying sticks and shovels, raising the banner of the Virgen de Guadalupe.

In the small Ford that my father drove, I stood on tiptoe on the floorboard in the back, clinging to the headrest of the front seat, with my face out the window, looking up at the murals and the giant billboards with magical pictures and words, words that had colors, shades, movement, music. I was teaching myself to read, and I began to invent stories that I kept to myself about gold treasures buried under the yellow parking strips painted on sidewalk curbs, heroic adventures in which I, much bigger in my imagination than I actually was, would dig up coins, jewels, gems, and leaping into the car, grab the wheel and somehow save my family from certain death.

All along, I was listening to my mother recount from memory the history of Chapultepec, the fortress where the Emperors Maximilian and Carlota saw their end in the time of the conquest, the same fort where, centuries later, six young cadets jumped to their death defending the castle against the invading American army. Mother pointed at the monument, six very tall columns, honoring Los Niños Héroes, at the entrance to the park, where on Sundays we paddled boats among gray swans.

At the museums mother took us to, stories and paintings of the Mexican Revolution celebrated the tattered armies of Zapata and Pancho Villa, peasants in wide-brimmed charro hats and bandoliers, carrying the Mexican flag—white, red, and green, a flaying serpent in the beak of an eagle standing on a wreath of cactus—the flag limp, torn by bullets.

I memorized the names of the men in the murals—Hidalgo, Juárez, Montezuma, Cuauhtémoc—names that I saw etched on marble and stone on the glorietas along the avenues that crisscrossed the city, monuments towering over the rumble of people and traffic that made Mexico a chaotic, mysterious puzzle to me.

It's sinking, my mother told me when we stepped down at the entrance to the cathedral in the Zócalo. The cathedral, dark and musty like a tomb, rose beyond my eyes into the sky, its floor stones worn down by centuries of damp. Mexico was sinking inches every year (I tried to imagine it, to feel it falling) into the thin-air swamp on which it had been built, the Tenochtitlán of the Aztecs, the Ciudad de Mexico of Cortés and the Spanish conquistadors.

All that blood in that place.

We lived on Calle Génova, in la Zona Rosa, in a third-floor walk-up, a flat of three small rooms in an ornate stone-fronted colonial building where the laundry was hung up to dry on clotheslines on the rooftop. The building had an open atrium, and the flats in the upper floors were arrayed along a corridor that circled it. There was nothing special about the building, but it had a tiled courtyard, splashed with light in the dry winter months and flooded in the rainy summer season.

But we liked our apartment, with the plain wooden door marked No. 23. We could see the sky from our windows, could see on fogless days the crown of the volcano Popocatepetl, almost always in mist, and we could run down the steps and the city was right there, at our doorstep.

Buses and cars constantly blew their horns, police sirens screeched, and vendors grilled ears of corn on smoky, burning coal, steamed handmade tortillas, and filled them with stringy shards of barbecued pork and chicken.

The mercados, the farmers' markets, opened early in the day. Tents were raised on poles, and straw mats thrown on the ground. Broad-faced, brown-skinned women squatted on their haunches with their wares, unglazed clay pots for cooking and serving, handmade sarapes, shawls, ponchos. There were tables with carved wooden figurines of the Virgen de Guadalupe and the baby Jesus, and straw baskets sagging with loads of dusty fruit and vegetables.

Flies hung over everything, sucking the coagulated blood off plucked chickens that were strung on hooks upside down, their necks broken with a hard twist of the hand.

My mother didn't work. She didn't have an office or a job. She didn't have her diplomas on a wall. The neighbors didn't know, or care, that she was María Luisa Torregrosa, la licenciada.

Nadie me conoce aquí, she would say, a lament. No one knows me here. She was a housewife, a young woman with children. She bathed us and dressed us, swept and mopped every day, and cooked dinner—we could hear her screams every time she burned herself at the stove. But she didn't complain that her hands had burns, that her nails kept breaking. She studied cookbooks, standing over the tiny kitchen counter, like she had once studied law books, and she did the shopping and dusted the furniture.

On Calle Génova, a two-lane road several blocks long between the Paseo de la Reforma and the Avenida Chapultepec, the farmers' market sprawled from one side of the street to the other, and mother shopped there every morning, remarking to no one in particular about the crimson color of the carnations she loved or the smell of coffee beans or the tenderness of tomatoes.

We wandered away from our block, and in these walks with her, we crossed Londres and Liverpool and Hamburgo, a grid of streets whose names she said aloud, ah, Niza, Florencia, every name transporting her, and us with her, my first lesson in European geography. She liked to make conversation with the women in the mercado, heavy women hunched down with invisible burdens, with their impenetrable dark eyes and wide, slanted Indian faces, who would stare back at her silently, smile shyly, and giggle among themselves.

I could tell they didn't know what to say to this thin, pale young woman with the ribbon in her hair. In the mornings in the mercado, in her espadrilles and headband, with her children immaculately groomed, my mother seemed a foreigner, like the wives of diplomats, like the ladies who sent out their servants and came around in chauffeur-driven cars. But my mother walked and had no servants and checked off her grocery list and counted her coins, carrying home a bag full of the tomatoes that I would later eat whole, like apples.

Soon she had three children. A year after our arrival in Mexico, she was in her eighth month of pregnancy. She didn't complain about that either. But she wanted her baby to be born on the island;

she wanted her mother with her. My father couldn't go, but she took Angeles and me with her, and we made the long, sickening trip back to San Juan.

My brother was born, a boy just as my father had wished, and a couple of weeks later, we were boarding a plane again, leaving my grandmother and Tití Angela Luisa behind, leaving San Juan, flying into the now-familiar airports in Habana and Miami, waiting in hotels and terminals on the interminable trip just to get to Miami, which in early September was hot and wet like an equatorial island.

We traveled by Greyhound to New Orleans and all the way to Mexico City. My mother, still frail, still swollen in her stomach and her breasts, carried my brother in one arm and held on to my sister and me, standing at the bus stop in her low-heeled flats, while the men loaded the luggage. Hollow-eyed and sleepless, she managed to find a hotel for the overnight stop in New Orleans, and then endured the exhausting damp heat of that late summer in a stifling, crowded bus on the twenty-hour journey from New Orleans to Mexico City.

The bus moved slowly, overloaded with villagers and their bundles, just like we seemed to be ourselves. It whimpered up and down the narrow, broken-down roads of northern Mexico, rock and desert Mexico, as arid a land as I had ever seen.

But she was happy. She was bringing my father a boy, what he had wanted, what he had waited for impatiently when first one daughter, and then another, had been born, not the sons who would carry on his name. Now she had that boy, a boy named after him, Amaury.

The apartment in Mexico was not big enough for all five of us, but my father was on a scholarship, and was making no money. We could not think of moving anywhere else. On our weekend drives around the city, my mother pointed longingly at the Spanish-style houses with their grilled balconies and the haciendas in the stone-street colonias of San Angel and Coyoacán. She would exclaim, Imagine living there, living behind the thick walls, in houses with elaborate arches, with gardens of bougainvillea and cool palm-shaded verandas.

My father was an old student, already in his early thirties, cramming to keep up with a class of much younger men at the Universidad Nacional Autónoma de México. At home in the evenings, and on weekends, he paced up and down our living room, from sofa to dining table, from armchair to front door, carrying two-pound textbooks, their spines cracked, pages dog-eared. His fingers, which were blunt and lean, flipped through the pages, stopping to scrawl notes in the margins. He kept a human skeleton hanging off a hat-rack in their bedroom, and a skull on a desk near my brother's crib. He carried them around the living room, the yellowish skull and the dangling skeleton, pointing at this bone, at that vertebra, speaking to himself. I learned to study from him, watching his furrowed forehead, his taut mouth, veined hands flaying the air.

Every weekday morning, he put on his fedora and light woolen jacket and was gone before we were up. My mother was in the kitchen making the thick black coffee she liked, reading the newspaper. She had no maid, only the lavandera who came once a week to do the laundry up on the rooftop. Now my mother had three children to look after, and the toll began to show. She was so thin, her wrists like a child's. But every day she cooked our meals and, like clockwork, bottle-fed my brother, mixing the powdery formula in the morning, keeping the bottles sterilized, warming them in boiling water, testing the temperature of the milk, pouring drops on the back of her wrist. While he slept, she cleaned the house, did the dishes, and did her nails.

Day after day, late in the afternoon, she changed into a dress, freshened up her makeup, put on red lipstick and perfume, and waited for my father to arrive from school. Oh, your father's here, she exclaimed, smoothing down her dress, when she heard his footsteps approaching the apartment.

She made occasions of his arrivals, rushing to the door to greet him, kissing him lightly on the mouth, preening as if they were courting. His entrance changed the air, a sudden loudness ripping the afternoon quiet. He had a voice that carried even when he whispered. He hugged me, he hugged Angeles, lifted Amaury up in the air, and demanded his beer. For him, she dropped everything.

Couples like them, classmates of my father's and their wives, came by on weekends. On our old RCA turntable they played Artie Shaw and Cole Porter and the boleros of the islands. I sneaked out of my bedroom, in my pajamas, and my father would let me have sips of his beer, a bitter foam I licked off his glass. Then he would send me off to bed, but I crouched behind a chair, in a corner, and watched them dance to "Bésame Mucho" and "Night and Day," my mother fragile but undulant, her breasts pressed against my father's chest, and his body curved into hers.

There were times, when the night was long and the bottles of beer and rum had been emptied, when the sound of his voice silenced everyone. She knew his rages, knew that the slightest frown on her face, a crisp tone in her voice, or an opinion he didn't like could make him explode. He would turn on her, demanding another drink, making fun of some remark she had made, mocking her, ridiculing her knowledge. It could be anything—her cooking, her poetry, her piano-playing.

I heard his words and blamed his drinking, but when I became older I realized that those words, that anger, were there inside him all the time and were simply loosened by the rum. Easy to know

now, he was a man tormented by jealousy of my mother, by envy of her class, her family, things he lashed out at when he drank.

But then, when I was four years old, five, six, I didn't understand his anger, didn't understand how he could be the same man who held me lightly, comforting me when I had nightmares, who took me to the circus and bought me popcorn, who taught me to ride a bicycle and ruffled my hair when he came home every night.

The first time he struck one of us was at dinner, a day like any other. Angeles was so small, so shy then. She longed for his attention. Tugged at his pants wanting a kiss, and when he spoke down to her, she looked up at him smiling, adoringly. That day, she and I were seated at the dining table as usual, my parents on either end. Angeles was not eating.

She is so thin, my mother complained, looking at him. Like hundreds of time before, she tried to force Angeles to eat, pushing a spoonful of rice into her mouth, but Angeles spit it out, sprayed it all over herself and the tablecloth. My mother tried again, her fingers pinching Angeles's skinny arm, forcing another spoonful into her mouth. Shaking her head, Angeles started crying. My mother barely touched her own food, she ate so little herself, spearing the peas, pushing aside the rice, glancing at my father, those glances they had.

He screamed at my sister. Eat, eat! My sister cried louder.

He unbuckled his belt, a narrow black leather belt, and yanked it through the loops of his pants and laid it, doubled up, by his plate. The belt lay there like a twisted ribbon. My sister cried harder. I stopped eating. He clutched the buckle and wrapped the belt in his right fist and with his other hand he reached out to my sister and grabbed her by her wrist, his hand a clasp around a tiny bone. He lifted her off her chair in one quick movement and dragged her to our bedroom. I heard her cries, at first loud and then like muffled whimpers, and the snapping sound of leather on flesh, a sound that became the single most frightening image in my nightmares. I held to the hem of the tablecloth, clutched it, trying not to cry, but crying all the same.

Please stop him, I begged my mother.

His voice was a growl, louder with each stroke of the belt.

In this house you do as I say, in this house you do as I say, he repeated with each blow.

My mother did not stop him. She did not leave her chair, but a faraway, clouded look came over her as if she were not there at all.

I had expected her to stop him, to march into the bedroom and take his belt away from him, but she didn't, not that time, not ever. This woman who had no fear, who spoke so fiercely to us, to her family, to her friends, who won arguments by sheer force of will, sat helpless, weak, afraid, and I saw that fear in her eyes, and I was terrified.

Many years later, on the day that would turn out to be the last time I saw her before her death, I reminded her of this. Why didn't you stop him? I demanded an answer, I wanted an apology. Why had she not stopped him from hitting us, why had she not left him and taken us with her?

She was an old woman now, and she began to cry, defending herself, and swore that she had no memory of any of it, none.

Every morning my mother walked with me the two or three blocks to the Van Dyke Academy, a colonial-era Catholic convent of gray stone spires and black iron gates. I was five, in first grade, a wisp with spindly legs and straight long hair tied back with a ribbon, a squint in my eyes, and already a furrowed brow. She left me at the gates, in the hands of nuns who wore those black habits and rimless thick spectacles that scare children. In my dark blue uniform with a starched white collar, I carried my books in a canvas bag and sat in the back row, too timid to raise my hand even though I almost always knew the answers. I had a knack for absorbing everything I heard, and soon I was getting straight tens in all my subjects—geography, sociology, reading, arithmetic, languages—and my world became filled with books and far places.

School was the life outside my parents' house. It was my world entirely. The first time I saw blood was there, when a boy in my class fell off a ledge in the courtyard and slashed his head, and I thought he was dead. The first time I had a crush was there, too, on a fair-haired boy my age and on his older sister, angelically blond and tall, who would come running to me, taking me in her arms, calling me her princess.

After school, after I did my homework, my mother let me go out to the apartment building's courtyard. I put on my roller skates and swept around the patio. I was fearless on skates, could slide down the cement embankments at Chapultepec and jump over steps. On the smooth courtyard tiles, I rushed and twirled, forward and backward, and a girl who lived next door to our flat, a girl named Rebecca, who was the first real friend of my childhood, a dark-haired girl in a ponytail, held me tightly by the shoulders and danced with me like that.

On Sundays, almost every Sunday, my father took us to Chapultepec. The park was like a jungle and a country fair, and Angeles and I rode the donkeys and I roller-skated and climbed rope while my mother put my brother in the children's swings, his fat little body convulsing with laughter. By the end of the afternoon, our faces were smeared with cotton candy, and my father, who didn't leave our side, took us for one last ride on the carousel.

One Sunday, my father rented an old girl's bicycle and lifted me to the seat. I was laughing, scared, but I wouldn't let him see that. He braced me with his arms, standing behind me, and suddenly he let me go free. The bike wove madly, and I screamed, laughing at the same time, and fell right on my side. He ran to me and lifted me again, straightened up the bike, and put me back on the seat. He didn't give up. He let me go again, and I fell again, and again he picked me up. You've done fine, he said when I started crying. Try again. He got on the bike himself to show me how to control the handles, and he let me go, giving the bike a push. I didn't fall again.

In our last year in Mexico, when he had a holiday from the university, we drove all the way to Acapulco, a two-day drive.

It was January, and the hotel was empty but for the five of us.

Angeles and I ran wild up and down the empty terrace restaurant, dancing to the band that played just for us. We had five days there, my mother keeping out of the sun under an umbrella, my father swimming against the current, his body flowing with the water. One day the three of us, my mother, my father, and I, were playing in the surf at Caleta, the roughest beach, jumping up and down with the waves, holding hands, when a big wave knocked us apart. My hand slipped from my father's. Underwater, I saw my mother's head scarf floating by, and I felt myself sinking. It seemed an eternity and the water felt heavy on me, pushing me down, but it had to have been only a matter of seconds before my father's hand grabbed my leg and lifted my body above the water, and I could breathe again.

Sometimes on those weekends, we spent a day in the canals of Xochimilco, in the pretty boats they had then, when the waters were clear and covered in petals and mariachis in their big hats and black garb, carrying violins and guitars, came by to sing, and peasant women in loose dresses of peacock colors made tortillas by hand, pounding and kneading the corn flour, twisting and stretching the dough, clapping it hard between their palms until the dough was round and wafer-thin. Afternoons passed by in the water, with music and the light splashing of paddleboats.

On the other side of Mexico City, we had the ruins of Tenochtitlán, what was left of Aztec Mexico, and to Teotihuacán and the Pyramid of the Moon. Holding my mother's hand, I climbed up the slippery steps of the pyramid, nothing but clouds above me. At the top of the pyramid, at the highest level, the world seemed like a painting, and the air was tinged with sunlight but no breeze. Climbing down was an ordeal, a steep decline that I climbed down backward, not on my feet but on my hands.

We had afternoons when we drove around a city that seemed to have nothing but great monuments, statues, pyramids, and volcanoes. We stopped at road stands at dusk, in the chill of Mexico City's gray, wet air for ears of corn charred over coal fires, and since that time the smell of those Sundays, the thick smoke from the coal fires, the roasting of corn was Mexico for me.

Life was simple then.

Part Two *A Childhood in Pieces*

"Juventud, divino tesoro,
ya te vas para no volver!
Cuando quiero llorar, no lloro
y a veces lloro sin querer."

—Rubén Darío, "Canción de Otoño en Primavera"

Chapter Four

Playing in the Fields

His picture had been crumpled, the corners torn as if it had been pulled in anger from a frame or a photo album. It lay under a stack of family pictures my mother had tossed in her boxes when she ran out of room in the scrapbooks. He was wearing the white coat with a round collar that doctors wear, and a stethoscope hung around his neck. He was in his early thirties, but had the bearing of a younger man, thinner, with sloping shoulders. His face, which was smooth, almost oval, with a strong chin but soft jaw, was lineless and his hair was ink black, glistening. His mustache, like two lines drawn in ink, looked freshly clipped, and his eyebrows were furry and heavy, drawing attention to his small, dark, somber eyes.

We had seen that picture a hundred times. Mother had blown up the picture and framed it. And she had made smaller copies for us. The photo in the box that Sara had retrieved from mother's house was in black and white, but mother had had a larger version colored—she loved tinkering with pictures, cutting up a good likeness and superimposing it, gluing it, on another not quite as flattering. A good photo of Angeles's face would be cut out of one picture and pasted on another photo of Angeles that had not turned out quite as well. Pictures lost their true moment, their reality, but we all looked our best. The coloring of my father's picture gave it a strange, unreal look; father with pink lips.

What is this doing here? I said, picking up the picture, noticing the cracks where it had been crumpled. I can't believe she kept this picture.

She could never overcome him, Angeles said, no lo pudo sobrevivir was the way she said it—something she said often over the years. We knew that. We knew that his hold on her never loosened. That was a story we told ourselves over and over, until it became myth, the great romance, the horrible betrayal, undying love, like a song.

When was this picture taken? I wondered. Maybe in Mexico when he graduated, second in his class of one thousand men; maybe then, on the day he got his diploma and walked all the way from our apartment to the Basílica de la Virgen de Guadalupe, a long way, perhaps two, three miles, to kneel before the Virgen, the only time I knew him to have anything to do with the church. Or maybe the picture was taken later, after Mexico, when we were back in San Juan and he was doing his internship in a municipal hospital, before we moved to the east coast of the island and lived on an unpaved road near the district hospital where he did his residency. Maybe then.

We moved so many times for him.

Who wants the picture? I said, looking at Angeles. I already have it, she said, I have the original. Sara reached out and put it back in the box.

Why didn't he come to the funeral? I asked, relieved that he hadn't come.

He said he was very sad, very sorry, but he couldn't come. He said he was too old.

He was seventy-nine years old, and I hadn't seen him in almost ten years.

I saw him, Amaury said. They kept in touch. Amaury flew to

the island often. He knew him well. He's not doing well, his heart, you know.

Last I heard he'd bought a yacht, I said, unsympathetic. And he married her again, twice now. Married her, divorced her, and married her again. Seems he's not doing so badly.

Talk of our father came to me mostly in spurts, bitter remarks I couldn't resist and they raked Angeles and Amaury, who had been closest to him, who stood up for him, who had found in him in his later years a man I didn't know.

This was our second evening together, another night for the six of us after mother's funeral, and father was a specter. Typical, he was there but not there. Carmen refused to listen to this and left the room because, she would say, she remembered him too well. Sara and Olga had been so young, and their memories of him had filters that mother had created for them.

But you never cared for him, Amaury lashed out at me.

What do you know? I said, bristling because he had put a finger on a scar that ran so deep I often forgot it was there.

Let's go have dinner, Sara interrupted, seeing the cycle begin, wanting to break it before it was too late. There's a Mexican restaurant we like, she said. It has great margaritas. Now, it's nothing fancy. It's just Tex-Mex, you may not like it.

She was smiling her desperate smile, tight-lipped, on the brink of screaming, and she went about picking up the box of pictures and putting it away on a shelf, and smoothing down nerves.

The moment dissolved.

We piled into the cars, and took over the back tables at Felix's and ordered rounds of dripping, boat-sized margarita glasses rimmed with salt and stacks of tacos and enchiladas. Angeles didn't eat and I didn't eat, but Amaury had three, four drinks and shambled in his chair, the only person I know who can shamble while sitting, his left leg jerking up and down, like a dance, and his hands moving like my father's moved, quickly, pointing here or there, closing and opening, speaking their own words.

Watching him, hearing his voice, his jokes, I thought about father, tried to frame father's face in my mind, to hear his voice, to see him. I couldn't. But I could hear his tone the last time he and I had spoken. He had called me in New York. He was visiting relatives in Connecticut. His call surprised me. I had no idea he was nearby. My hands trembled. I could hardly speak.

I want to come down and see you, he said. It wasn't a question, it was a statement. I was silent. He repeated it. I wanted to get off the phone.

No, I said finally, like wresting a knife out of me, or into him, I didn't know.

No, I can't, I heard myself say.

What do you mean, he said, you can't see your father?

No, I said. I don't want to.

There was a brief silence. Then he said, That's too bad, I feel sorry for you. The words crashed on me, his anger filling my head. The words bounced in an empty chamber. I feel sorry for you. The phone went dead. I sat for hours alone, staring at a wall.

Our family moved to the rhythm of my father's life.

Mexico, San Juan, Fajardo. We were city people, with a car and a maid and our books and travels abroad, but this year, when I was eight, we were living on a rural road in the outskirts of Fajardo, where he was doing his residency in the district hospital and running a smaller municipal clinic nearby, delivering poor women's babies, making house calls in the middle of the night, and studying for the medical board exams before going off into private practice.

On the northeastern coast, Fajardo, the town of my father's youth, was becoming a big commercial center, a rough-looking place with a ramshackle shipping port that had once harbored pirates, a city with little of the charm of old Spanish-colonial towns, but with a spectacular shoreline of plunging hills and coral reefs that one day would be cluttered with packaged-tour resorts, honeymoon hotels, and million-dollar condominiums.

Small factories were opening around that time, shoe factories, garment factories, shops making small auto parts and electronics. New roads were being plowed through hills and flat coconut farmland. The countryside was being cut up into small plots to give the jíbaros a piece of land of their own for their bananas and pineapples, pigs and chickens and goats, the everyday fare sold in the open-air mercados and at roadside stands.

The road where we lived was nothing but a rutted dirt path off the Fajardo–San Juan highway, an unmarked turn by a gas station. We lived among the laundrywomen and field hands and the children who went to public schools in broken-down buses that left them off out on the highway.

Our house was set up on concrete blocks, a simple place with buckling floors and drafty wooden walls, not much different from the houses down the road where the field hands lived. Rain clattered like pebbles on the tin roof, torrents running down the grooves of the roof, seeping into the cracked walls. Chickens and stray dogs rooted in the damp ground under the house, and pigs, fattened for the kill, grunted in barbed-wire pens in the patchy mud yards nearby. The house was little more than a bohío, like the tin-and-wooden houses off mountain roads and on the edges of roadside towns deep in the island.

But we had a luxury the other houses on the road didn't have. We had a bathroom, an unpainted room with a cement floor in the back of the house. We had a shower, a single spout rigged up with wires, where water fell either in trickles or in sudden bursts, spraying the entire bathroom. The water was river-warm, but felt prickly cold on my head and my bare back, where it hit like icy pellets. I would jump in, sticking in first my legs, then my arms, then my face.

My parents rented the house because it was midway between the municipal hospital where my father was in charge and the district hospital where he had his duty shifts in the emergency room. The house was broom-swept every day and mopped, and it had a fresh coat of blue paint and yellow window slats, and a front porch with white rails. We had lights and running water and a field in the back where we put up a hammock. My mother had never thought she would live in such a place, but she said, pretending, that the house was like a little casa de campo, and she put up curtains, hung her Mexican tapestry, and bought rocking chairs for the rickety front porch.

For my father, and because she really had no choice, she had agreed to leave San Juan. But she kept her job there, traveling every day to and from Fajardo in a public car, an hour each way in busy traffic, jammed in the car with strangers. Angeles and I were transferred from a private school in Hato Rey, where Angeles awed the teachers with her way with numbers, and I was studying poetry and plays and getting into arguments over Nasser and the Suez Canal, and enrolled in a parish school in Fajardo.

Children get used to everything, my mother would say, because she liked to believe that she could get used to anything. San Juan one day, Mexico the next, Fajardo now. Fajardo was different. It wasn't Mexico, it wasn't anywhere she wanted to talk about. It was my father's hometown, where he had had his women and his old friends from the centrales, where his younger brother ran the family drugstore. He was married to a woman my father jokingly called la neurasténica, a bleached blonde who never left the house, who had to be put away before I was old enough to remember her face.

We didn't become part of the social life of the town, didn't set down to stay, didn't have children's parties and piano lessons. We lived mostly as if we were not there, far from our new classmates (I cannot remember a single one of them) and from the life and friends we had in San Juan.

My playmates now were the children up and down our road, the boys and girls, Rosaritos, Juanitos, who stopped by our house and waved from the road and called out for me to come out and play. But they never came inside my house and I never went to theirs.

I'd run out every time they came by, making bets on who could throw pebbles farther into a field, putting all the muscle I could into the swing of my arm only to see my stone wobble and drop just twenty feet away. I played baseball with the boys, bare-handed, with a hard ball and a stick for a bat. We ran footraces, the boys barefoot, road pebbles and dust blowing in our faces, my knees buckling, my ankle twisting.

Angeles didn't go out to toss rubber balls against the wall of an abandoned building, as I did when I got bored. She liked staying inside, dressing her dolls, talking to them as if they were children, and making costumes, sewing, cutting paper dolls, she could spend afternoons doing just that, sitting on the floor of the living room, alone with our brother at her side.

He was three then, maybe four, and rubbery and squeezable like her dolls, with eyes that pored over her face, that watched her as she cut through cloth and made her doll dresses. I could see then that he belonged to her, and she would take him by the hand and walk him around the room, teaching him to dance.

I usually knew what she was thinking. We had no secrets, but there were times when I watched her being very quiet and I couldn't read her face, but I knew it was something I wanted to know. I thought she knew everything. Some afternoons, she came out to play jacks with me and the girls of the road and she beat all of us every time, one by one, her hand faster than my eye (she learned from my mother), and she cheated at cards but was so sly I could never catch her.

How did you do that? I demanded, my hands clutched at my hips, wanting to know her trick, how did she do it? I looked down on her (I was then taller than she), threatening. She laughed, shrugged, and ran back to her dolls.

When I turned eight, my parents gave me an encyclopedia. They also gave me a doll and a pretty dress. They always gave us dolls and pretty dresses. I read the entire encyclopedia like a book straight through. I didn't play with the new doll, but I put on the dress and pretended I was a ballerina, thin arms arched above my head, legs stretched taut, head tilted like I had seen at the ballet in San Juan.

That Christmas I got a baby goat from Tití Angela. She almost never came to visit. She hated the one-hour drive from San Juan on the potholed highway, winding by the beaches of Luquillo and the rain forest of El Yunque. So when she came, it was a celebration. She was light, a nightingale flitting about in our airy rooms. Her voice, as usual, had the high pitch of excitement, calling out our names, and we ran to her car, not letting her get out before we jumped around her. She handed out her wrapped gifts with special notes to each of us and, gathering us around, would tell the latest stories from her world so far from ours. In the shade of the front porch, sipping their sugary black coffee, she and mother talked and talked and laughed, like young girls in their room. I stayed nearby, listening to them, trying to make out what they were talking about, but their conversation had a code of its own. There was always a big dinner, lechón asado or pasteles, or mother's paella. In the long evening of eating and drinking, after my sister, my brother, and I had been put to bed, a moment would come when my father, having his iceless tumblers of dark Don Q, his eyes watery from laughing at his own jokes, would turn to my mother, to her disapproving pursed mouth. He would stare at her, his eyes narrowing, fist tight against his lips, and pour himself another shot of rum.

Tití would titter girlishly, changing the conversation, finding a way to distract him, to flatter him with her attention while drawing mother away from him, from his glare. She had always put herself between them, between him and all of us. She would make him laugh, and the evening would wind down with fading chatter and the clatter of dishes and glasses.

But she didn't stay long, a day, a night. I would watch her get in her car, her thin ankles pale against her bright capri pants and strapped flat sandals, her hair in a silk scarf, her sunglasses giving her the aura (I thought) of a movie star. Too soon she would disappear from my sight down the road. I wanted to go with her, wanting the life we had had in San Juan, when she made us party costumes and cut our hair and baked us cakes.

I didn't know why she gave me a goat. But I kept it and kept the satin ribbon she had put around its neck. I named it Pepita. I tied her up with a long rope to a fence in a field behind the house. I fed her and gave her water every day and played with her, grabbing her and rubbing her gray forehead and stubby horns. Months later, when we moved to the pink house up the road, my parents refused to take her along and she was slaughtered, her long neck slashed with one stroke of a machete, her skinned carcass hung upside down. For a long time I went around by myself looking for her, calling out her name, listening for her cry.

The pink house was new, a cinder-block square with a flat roof, tile floors, and a carport. Out back there was a henhouse, and at dawn the roosters strutted, shaking their plumage, crowing us awake. Our maid—was it Lola then?—wore her apron and slippers, fed the chickens, running out after them with a handful of kernels of corn she cast wide on the ground. The fat hens with puffed-up chests and their chirping chicks came waddling in feathery flocks, flapping their wings, stretching their beaks, and pecking at her legs, their claws scratching for the kernels scattered in the dirt.

The yard had plantain plants, mango and tamarind trees with thick trunks and heavy limbs that I climbed when my parents were not around. Perched high off the ground on bending tree branches, I looked down on the tin shed nearby where orange and grape sodas were bottled. The bottles came from scrap, used over and over, with dents and fading letters. The cranking of the bottling machines and the whistles and loud talk of the boys stacking the bottles broke the afternoon silence, the quiet that spread over the fields after the lunch hour.

Our yard was wild with flowers. They grew in patches, in uncut grass, watered by the afternoon showers, blooming and withering with the seasons. A shallow gutter separated our front yard from the road, and across the way there was a big open field where the boys played ball, and beyond it, on the other side of an overgrown empty lot, stood the municipal clinic, a one-story cement building painted a mustard brown, rain-stained and dilapidated, where my father spent his mornings.

My father was a man of routines. Up at dawn, showered quickly and fragrant with aftershave cologne, he dressed simply, in a loose guayabera, or an open-necked plaid shirt. He didn't need a clock and never wore a watch. He didn't wear ties or jackets, and had stopped wearing the fedora he had worn in Mexico. His mustache was gone and his hair was receding, combed back flat on his head. But he still had a slight frame, the bony body of a swimmer, slim back, trim torso.

He learned to swim like the country boys, leaping nude from rocky banks into rushing rivers near Guayama, where he was a child, before his family moved to Fajardo. I never saw him in a swimming pool or diving from high boards, but in the sea he moved as if the water were air, his arms like paddles cutting through the waves.

On our Sundays at the beach in Luquillo, he tried to teach me to swim, lifting me at my waist and holding me on the open palms of his hands while I flayed and gulped salt water. Standing up to his stomach in water, his swimming trunks billowing, he rotated his arms back and forth, head down, showing me the motions. He had no impatience then, and on the afternoon when I first managed to keep afloat on my back for a single minute, he rubbed my head, the way he had done in Mexico when he let go of my bicycle and I rolled on alone.

Luquillo beach, a half-moon of grainy beige sand and soaring palm trees, their ripe coconuts heavy with juice and crusty bark, was crowded on weekends, packed with cars parked between the trees, fender to fender. Multitudes of children, loose from their mothers, raced in packs to the edge of the water, carrying inflated rubber tubes. Family parties gathered around the concrete tables on the beach grounds, slicing chunks of roasted pig, the charred pig skin dripping fat. Music came from everywhere, from the car radios tuned up to mambos and merengues, from the old men in straw hats with string guitars and maracas who strolled down the beach.

Mother sat in the shade of palms, on a towel spread on the sand, one hand shielding her face from the sun, the other holding a magazine or a newspaper. She rarely came into the water, and when she did, in her dove-white Esther Williams swimsuit, she would jump high with every cresting wave, laughing, holding on to us, her turban twisted tight around her pinned-up hair. Somehow not a drop of water splashed on her face. She couldn't swim and cared nothing for it. She didn't walk far into the sea, but stopped just as the water inched above her thighs. She didn't show fear, but she was afraid of the sea, afraid of what she didn't know.

Those days at the beach were for us, not for her. For us, she sat bored through four or five hours of sand on her skin and sun on her legs. She would bring egg sandwiches she made at home and her potato salad, which was crunchy with cut-up apples. At the end of the afternoon, she would walk each of us to the public showers, seeing that we stepped carefully around the shards of broken glass in the sand and the dirt that people left in the stalls. A few years later, she became a member of the Caribe Hilton Swim & Racquet Club, and she had us take swimming lessons. One day, while she sat in a lounging chair poolside, I climbed to the high board, and looking down to her, and to the water that seemed miles away, I dived headlong into the pool, shivering with terror, burning my skin and sinking toward the tiled bottom, knowing I would not make it to the surface, and when I finally did, she was standing in her belted white linen pants and espadrilles on the edge of the pool, applauding.

Sundays together in Luquillo, or anywhere else, in El Yunque (father's car huffing up the narrow mountain road to the peak of the rain forest, my father driving it at full throttle, one hand on the wheel, the other arm resting on the window) or at Las Croabas, the rocky coastline north of Fajardo, were like the family pictures mother glued to the pages of her photo albums, frozen moments a woman chooses to remember.

My father's footsteps began and ended our day. My mother always got up with him, their conversation immediately insistent, discussions in bed that seemed filled with urgency. Then came the shuffling of feet and the familiar sounds of my mother in the kitchen. She was boiling water for her black coffee, warming the cereal for my brother.

The first silver light of day filtered through my bedroom window, shining hard on my face through the mosquito net. Folding my sleeping rag, the same I had had for years, I climbed off the bed and, with Angeles in her swollen sleepy eyes, knocked on my parents' bedroom door for the morning kiss.

Water ran in the bathroom basin, the shower splattered on tile, and moments later my mother would come out in her robe and stand in front of her dresser, looking at her reflection in the mirror, lining her eyes, uncapping the tube of lipstick, screwing her earrings in pierced lobes, spraying perfume behind her ears, on the hollow of her neck. She dressed slowly, turning her breasts away from the mirror, strapping on her girdle, fastening her stockings to the garter belt. She pulled on the seams of her stockings until they were perfectly straight, brown lines running up her slender calves. Coming out of the bedroom, she raised her face to my father's, kissing him lightly on his closed lips, and he left for the day, banging shut the front door behind him.

He had the same breakfast every day—fried eggs and coffee—and left the house carrying his battered leather bag, which he had owned since his university days. He walked down the road to the clinic, where dozens of patients were already waiting with bundles of plantains and yuccas for him.

At noon, when his appointments at the hospital were done, he walked back across the field, his head lowered to the sun. Our maid had his lunch ready—pork chops, steak, rice and beans, plantains, an ordinary meal, staples of the Puerto Rican table. His tastes didn't vary, and he never ate the tomato and green bean salads that were placed beside his plate. He ate quickly, as he did everything else, barely tasting the food. He bit his tongue or the side of a lip eating so fast, leaving tiny spots of blood on his napkin. After his siesta, a half hour he rarely gave up for anything, he sat in the only armchair we had, his textbooks stacked by his side, and he would read, marking the pages, muttering, memorizing for the board exams. In the afternoons, he hitched up a footpath to the district hospital, a gray building on a hill where he worked mending broken bones, taking out appendixes, blood splattering on his white uniform, leaving maroon stains.

After he was gone in the mornings, Angeles and I had our breakfast, and mother drew up the grocery list for Lola. Six months pregnant, sallow around the eyes and thin as a bone, mother walked to the gas station on the highway to wait for the car that came by at seven every morning for the hour-long trip to her job in San Juan. Kissing each of us good-bye, she left the smell of her perfume on our hair and smudges of lipstick on our cheeks.

In our starched green-and-white uniforms, my sister and I were driven in a hired car that came every morning, with much crunching of tires and slamming of brakes, to our house to take us to school. The school was in the center of town, in a bluish concrete building, a rectangle with a paved courtyard. The classrooms opened to the courtyard, and nuns in their black habits, their head coverings pinned at the brow and their capes billowing, patrolled the playground and the hallways. Laughter and chatter were forbidden in the classrooms, and at recess the children were penned in the playground, the nuns watching like sentries. One day Angeles fell while playing, scraping her face and legs and splitting her lip. Blood dripped from her mouth and a front tooth came out in pieces. I was holding her, crying with her, but a nun grabbed her by a hand and took her to Mother Superior's office, blaming her for running too fast.

Around three in the afternoon, when the school let out, we were taken home by the same driver who picked us up in the mornings, a gruff old man who shoved the children into his car, packing us in tight because every head was money to him. He dropped us off along a route from the center of town past the new residential suburbs of square squat houses to the outskirts where we lived.

The house at that hour always seemed still. Lola was in the backyard, taking the dry laundry off the line to press it on the ironing board she set had up in the dining room. Angeles and I dumped our books on the dining table and sat across from each other, doing homework and drinking juice. Schoolwork was effortless for us, but just a little more effortless for her, and she could get hers done just a minute or two faster than I, the way she played the piano just a little better, as if she had been born knowing the keys, and the way she danced, her blouse off one shoulder, her hips loosened. Books closed, notebooks stacked, pencils sharpened, I jumped into the cold shower, and with my hair still wet and pulled back in a ponytail, I ran out to the ball field on the lot across the road. Several inches shorter than the boys, I was the only girl they let play. I was not a born ballplayer but I ran hard and threw the ball with heart. I practiced in front of my bedroom mirror, a mean look, a lift of the leg, my arm thrown back.

Life on a miserable rural road had little to offer my mother, who had her social airs and her work in the capital. Even when she was in the last months of pregnancy with her fourth child, she insisted on working, putting herself through a grueling drive every day, sitting in the back of a stifling car with other passengers and their smells. She was home from work at sundown, her blouse damp from the plastic-covered car seat, her skirt wrinkled. She called out for us and was full of kisses, her arms around us, asking about school, listening to the stories of our day and the catechism lessons we were taking for our confirmation. She didn't talk to us about her work, but I imagined an office in the Supreme Court, her desk piled high with those heavy books with frayed bent spines that she had inherited from my grandfather.

My parents had nothing to do with the people of the road but occasionally people my father knew came for the evening—doctors he worked with, and men from his days in the sugar mills, men he had dealings with in town. They came with their wives, and mother fixed her elaborate dinners (tablecloth, fine china, fine silverware). The men drank, and when mother talked to the wives about her work and her family, they looked at her with blanks in their eyes.

Few of my mother's friends ever came to visit. They lived in San Juan, and she didn't want them to see that she lived on a dirt road.

Thirty-two years old and married ten years, with three children and another one on the way, she was making more money than my father, far more than many of the women of her time, and she talked to us (during those late afternoons when my father didn't show up) about building her own house in San Juan, near grandmother and Tití. She kept up her connections, her membership in the women's clubs in San Juan and in the Colegio de Abogados. She shopped for clothes in San Juan and read the San Juan newspapers and talked about the theater and politics as if she lived in San Juan, in her circles. But after a day's work, she came home to a cold-water shower and the tiresome chores of the house, checking in on dinner, noticing the spot of dust on the armchair, the milk stain on the dining room table.

We were her little soldiers, obeying her every glance, fearing her mood those nights when dinner got cold, and she would sit on the porch, in her heels and her perfume, and wait for my father. I avoided her when I saw her like that, and avoided my father, too, when he came home late. We were in bed by the time the tires of his car rolled up the driveway and the car door slammed shut and the front door opened.

His footsteps were steady, deliberate (he never weaved or stumbled, no matter how drunk). I listened for my mother's whispery voice, hoping to hear laughter. One night they were quarreling in their bedroom, another fight I tried to ignore. But she was crying hysterically, her shrieks coming through the walls to my bedroom. I got out of bed and walked down the unlit hallway and stood at their door. He had grabbed her by her forearms and was shaking her. She was sobbing. He raised his right arm and the blunt palm of his hand came down and slapped her across the face. I screamed. He let go, and came toward me, ordering me to go to bed, and shut the door.

In the last weeks of mother's pregnancy, my grandmother came to stay with us, and for a while there was calm in our house. But I brought home a bad report card and my parents were livid. The nuns and Mother Superior, her pockmarked, potato-shaped face reddening with anger, had warned me and had slipped a note to my parents. I had a C in deportment, my first C ever, like a neon sign at the bottom of a row of A's. Talked too much in class, the nuns said, interrupted the teachers, disturbed the other students. My mother cried, shaking me by the shoulders, and when my father got home, she told him. He took off his belt, rolled it around his fist, and marched me to my room. He was a methodical man. The lashes came slowly, striking me across the back of my legs and thighs. One minute. Five minutes. I held tight to the pillow, the pain of the sting unbearable.

My grandmother didn't stand for it. They were seated at the dining table, the three of them, father eating, swallowing fast, lecturing. He liked lecturing.

Children are property, he said, a man's wealth. They obey their parents, never raise their voices, and never embarrass their parents. He pointed at me, but it could have been any of us, my sister, or my brother. No one interrupted him.

My grandmother rose from the table, very tall, very thin in her housedress. She gathered her things, her small bag, her purse, and announced that she was leaving that minute. Angeles and I ran after her and mother followed us, pleading with my grandmother to turn back, making apologies for my father, but my grandmother kept walking. Together we moved as one shadow down the dirt road, my grandmother straight as a pin, an elongated figure in the moonlight. She walked steadily, wringing her handkerchief in her hand, wiping my tears, and together we waited on the highway, at the gas station, until a public car on the San Juan route came by and she stooped in, a stubborn woman, graying and frail, giving me her handkerchief, with her embroidered initial, *M*. It smelled of talc and Maja soap.

School was out in May, and my new sister was born prematurely, weighing less than five pounds. My mother lay in a bed at the hospital for several days, her slender arms bruised from intravenous needles, the skin of her face brittle like wax. She looked exhausted, her hair matted, her lips bitten. The baby, smaller than some of my dolls, with shut eyes and a full head of hair, was hooked to tubes in an incubator, barely stirring. She was so little, so bony, I wanted to cry. Mother had a desperate look, but when she noticed us, Angeles and I, standing in the doorway of her hospital room, her face changed, the grimace turning into a smile, as if miraculously the pain had disappeared. We were still wearing our confirmation dresses, the ones she had had made for us, stark white, light as cotton frocks. She had wanted to be there in church with us, but the baby had come suddenly. She sat up in her bed, pushed herself up by the elbows, and spread out her arms, giving us kisses that smelled of hospital and sour breath. They named my little sister Carmen Monserrate, after my grandmother, and in a few days she was taken out of the incubator and they brought her home.

A few months later, my father finished his residency, and we left the road in Fajardo and my afternoons playing baseball with the boys, my games of jacks with girls whose names I would not remember for long, and those days when I dreamed I was a ballerina.

Chapter Five

The Doctor's Town

The house had gone to sleep, doors locked, porch lights out, and soft breathing was coming from the bedrooms down the hall. A low light burned in the kitchen. It blinked, going off and on, throwing ghostly light on the table. Angeles and Amaury were still there, whispering, occasionally laughing, breaking the silence like thunder in a dry night. I could hear them from my room, could hear the refrigerator door click open and shut, the bottle caps rolling on the floor.

They are still at it, still drinking, Sara said, pulling the bedspread over her bare legs. She turned off the bedside lamp and pushed the door closed with her foot and leaned closer to me, spreading a blanket over me. The air-conditioning was huffing at full blast as it always seems to be in Texas. I was freezing. It was two in the morning, and we had buried our mother that day.

Buried our mother that day. We didn't believe it. Why, it was just the other day, Sara started to say, and paused. She was crying. I could hear it, couldn't see it, but could hear it. I said, Better that she went this way, fast. She didn't get old and sick, she didn't waste away in a hospital. Better this way, Sara said. Yes, better. Those are the circumlocutions of grief. She didn't believe that either. There was no good way for our mother to go. There was never a right time.

People have to have lies.

We had to have lies. Sara had her lie, and I had mine. Or, to put it another way, Sara had her truth and I had mine.

That night she took me across the path of our mother's life as she had known her.

When you and Angeles talk about her, it's another person, she said. I didn't know that woman like you did. She was different here, Sara said. Different? I said. Her light had gone out, I said, cruelly. Sara shook her head. She wanted the mother she knew, not mine. She wanted the story to begin after father, she wanted it to begin when she was five years old, and mother remarried and came to live in Texas.

The way mother had told the story, she met Leon at a restaurant in San Juan. He was in Puerto Rico making arrangements for an Exchange Club convention. She was at the restaurant that evening having coffee with her friend Sorrito. He came over to the table, a tall man, at least six feet, with a strong chest and a flat stomach. He had gray hair, nearly white, and his face had deep lines from the corners of his eyes down his cheeks, but he was still handsome, still had the looks that could turn the heads of middle-aged women. He introduced himself and handed her his business card. He was in public relations. He asked if he could buy them a drink.

Mother said no but took notice of his drawl, which was very polite and low, as if he were tipping an imaginary Stetson hat, bowing slightly in the presence of ladies. He was wearing a well-cut suit in a place where no man wore a suit, and he looked at her as if he were dreaming.

She asked him to sit down and join them, and two minutes later she was taking out her wallet to show him the pictures of her six children. He smiled, saying the things she wanted to hear. But you are so young to have six children. She blushed.

Now her eyes were on him and she forgot that Sorrito, who was looking from one to the other, was catching the moment, sitting across from her, and listening to Leon as he told her about his own children. He had two, already grown and married, with children themselves. He was a grandfather, had been married once or twice, and was now divorced. Facts and dates. He was a Texan born and bred, and there was no doubt of that from the way he walked, as if entering a corral with horses to tame.

She saw him again and he met our family, all but me and Angeles. We were away in college. Months later I got a letter from her—Leon and I are getting married. You will love him as much as I do, she said. She was leaving Puerto Rico and moving to Texas. I couldn't believe it, my mother with another man, my mother giving up her job and the house she had finally built in Hato Rey. My mother in Texas, of all places. It didn't make sense. But I didn't tell her this. I told her that I was very happy for her, but I was only relieved. I could stop worrying about her, about her being alone and coming home from work and lying on her bed crying. Now she had a man.

Remember that old Cadillac they had when you moved to Texas, to Bryan? I asked Sara, grimacing. It rattled and groaned but Leon had to have his big car. Sara laughed. And that gas station they opened in Bryan, remember? Yes, Sara said, don't blame her, that's what Leon wanted and mother went along. She always went along, I said, no matter what she wanted. She was out there with him at that gas station in the highway the day they opened it, with all the little American flags announcing the opening, and she was handing out red carnations to the ladies. So like mother, I said. Well, that business didn't last long, the station went broke, Sara said.

Nothing lasted very long, I said.

No. How many towns did you live in? I asked, knowing them by memory. I had seen almost all of them on my annual visits around Christmas—Littlefield, Kilgore, Sweetwater, Abilene, Cleveland,

Alice (Alice!), Abilene. Each a stop on the trail, silos and cowherds, dry land, oil drills, heat, dust storms and ice storms, flat sky, long roads, but mother found something good in each of these places, glossing them up, building them up not so much for our benefit but for hers—a little college, a cute main street, a quaint tradition that made each town special in some way, even in the desolation of West Texas. They moved from east to west, from north to south, long distances in a state where a city a four-hour car ride away is considered around the corner. Leon worked for the chambers of commerce, seemed to change jobs almost every year while he looked for the next big opportunity, pulling up stakes, full of hope and good tidings. But he was past fifty and the offers became scarce and smaller.

Abilene was their longest stop. Sara liked Abilene, and mother liked it better than any other place. It was a bigger town. They built a house with the little courtyard and Leon had a good job and she had her office. She had somewhere to go every day, people to talk to.

Months after she had arrived in Texas, knowing not a single soul and speaking English like the foreigner she was, she took the Texas bar exam and passed it on the first try. She became pregnant with her seventh child soon after she married Leon. A forty-five-year-old woman, pregnant. We couldn't believe it.

I was spending some time with her in Bryan that spring, taking time to figure out what I wanted to do with my life, when the baby came. She had her suitcase packed for days. The evening she knew it was time, Leon was not there—he had gone away that very day on business. I drove her to the hospital. She checked in as if walking into a hotel. She seemed so calm, signing in, while I was a wreck, holding her by the elbow should she fall, but she was steadier than I was as we got to the elevator and the nurses took her to the labor room. I sat in the reception room—the only woman, the only girl—with husbands waiting for their firstborn, or for their fifth-born. A doctor came out and asked if my mother's husband was there. I got up and said, No, but I'm here. I'm her oldest child, and I want to be with her. He looked at me. He thought about it, and led me to the labor room.

She was lying mostly naked on a bed with straps. Contractions were coming fast, and the nurses came and went, seeming to me indifferent. She looked pasty under the hospital lights, drops of sweat broke on her forehead and above her lips. Her hair was matted, wet. I took her hand right away. She crushed it. Old, she looked old. Her stomach bulged like a tethered leather balloon. She twisted and moaned with every contraction. But she didn't scream like the younger women in the room. After a long time, they took her away. They didn't let me stay with her. An hour or so later, Leon Jr. was born.

You forget the pain, she told me, looking half drugged and exhausted in her hospital room. The flowers that come with those occasions had yet to arrive. But Leon was there finally, standing by the window, in his suit and jacket, totally at ease. He was there now and they were taking turns holding the baby. I got up to leave, and kissing her good night, I said, I don't know how you do it; I'll never have children.

I drove to her house and told my little sisters that they had a baby brother.

My mother had her license to practice law in Texas, a good husband, a new baby boy, and she handed out carnations at a gas station. But she had no job, no office.

It took four years and several moves, but finally, in Abilene, she rented an office and put her shingle on the door and opened her firm. Her office was plain, a single room on the second floor of a downtown mall of boutiques, real estate agencies, and doctors' offices, a row of buildings with facades made to resemble the Alamo and old Spanish missions. Her diplomas were up on the wall, our pictures on her desk, law books on a shelf.

She was over fifty, but to see her run up the stairs to her office was to imagine her twenty years earlier. She had such hopes.

You know she really didn't have that much business, Sara said, mostly poor Mexicans. They couldn't pay, and you know her, she didn't charge them. You know how people are here, Sara said. They thought she was Mexican, too, with her accent and her hands gesturing like Latinos do. She didn't have clients with money.

I knew.

Sara stopped. We could hear Amaury crying in the kitchen. I looked at the ceiling, thinking, Didn't mother know?

Yes, Sara said, but she pretended that she was just like any other lawyer. Yes, I said, she was so good at pretending, at seeing only what she wanted to see. But it was hard for us in school, Sara said. I know that behind our backs some of the kids called us wetbacks, at least in the beginning. Sweetwater and Abilene were the worst. Those places seemed to have a larger population of Mexicans, mostly illegals, and we were thrown in with that bunch, especially Carmen and Olga because of their darker complexions and a bit more accent.

That's when I started telling mother not to speak Spanish to us, especially in public, Sara said. I used to tell people that my last name was Slaughter, like Leon's. This started with me in Littlefield, she went on. Of course, I was young and silly, and also dumb, because at school my name was Lopez, so I don't think I was very successful in trying to become an Anglo.

God, I thought, I didn't really know.

Mother, well, she did all the things to fit in, Sara went on. She did all the expected things. She became a Methodist, she invited the ladies for coffee at home, and served them in her fancy little cups. The ladies smiled those fake smiles, picked up those little espresso cups and barely sipped the black coffee, and sat on the edge of their chairs. They were not used to the formality mother had, they didn't have espresso at home, and they never heard someone talk about faraway places they would never want to visit. And mother's accent, they called it charming, but you know what they meant. They didn't understand the first thing about us, about Puerto Rico, and here was mother, a career woman, divorced, with all those children but practicing law like the men and having lunch in the cantinas with Mexicans.

But she was happy, Sara said. At least as happy as she ever was in Texas, and after we got older and we started to fit in and have friends, we could do just about anything we wanted. She got home with her newspapers and sat in her chair and didn't pay much attention. Maybe she didn't expect the same things from us that she had expected from you and Angeles, she didn't expect us to get straight A's and stand out in everything. Our life was so different from yours when you were growing up. We didn't have the schools you had, the society rules, the fancy parties. So she didn't have to worry about keeping up.

She didn't hit you when you disobeyed her? I said, surprised. She didn't scream? She didn't make you get dressed up and go to parties in the clubs?

That's what I mean, Sara said, she wasn't the same as she was with you, with father. She and Leon didn't have that life. Leon would come home early and they talked over dinner—mostly mother talked—and, every now and then, when one of us did something she didn't like, like when Carmen and Olga screamed at each other because, you know Carmen, she wanted her own things and didn't want anyone touching them, and Olga made fun of her and they would get into a shouting match, then mother would get off her chair and come storming into our bedroom.

But nothing much came of it. Sara remembered one time when mother hit Olga. Mostly she shouted and slammed the door and went back to her newspapers. Then, Sara said, we got older and she got older and she would just shout, I'm tired of this, and Leon would come to our room and he talked or, if it was something really bad like when we screamed back at mother, he sat us down at the table and he would talk very slowly, you know the way he talks, saying the same thing over and over, that we had to obey our mother. Then he grounded us for a couple of days.

They never fought, Leon and mother, Sara was saying. (I was thinking, But how did she stand the boredom?) I never saw them fight, I said, echoing her. Of course, I was never around. Came once a year and it was always the holidays and mother wanted everything perfect, and of course it wasn't because we could not all be in the same room without somebody saying something hurtful, and Amaury and Angeles getting drunk. . . . I hated those visits, I said, especially when father came and we all had to pose like the Holy Family. And Leon was there, too, I said. It was so strange to me that Leon didn't mind father being there. He treated father like he would have treated any other guest, deferential and respectful. It was odd, I said, having the three of them together like everything was all right, as if everyone got along and we were a happy family.

Remember 1987? I said. I had gone to Abilene for Christmas, and there was father staying in a motel with Amaury. Mother was so nervous, setting the table, burning the yams or whatever it was, and we all sat together pretending that it was perfectly normal for the three of them to be together, that we were all together. None of us believed it. Angeles didn't, Amaury didn't. But mother wanted to believe it. We did it for her.

Sara didn't say anything. She saw trouble coming a mile away and turned the other way.

After a while, I said, Angeles handled it better. You know, the whole thing, mother, Leon, father, everyone in one room, opening gifts, hugging and kissing.

Angeles came more often, Sara reminded me, a reproach that I let pass. That's why we've been closer to her—we told her everything that was going on, Sara said. We would stay up nights talking about boys and, of course, about mother, always the same story.

Mother and I couldn't talk, not really, I said.

She knew that, Sara said. It hurt her you were so distant.

But we couldn't talk because there were things she didn't want to hear, I said. It was like that since I was very young. But that's not why I didn't come often like she wanted me to, I said. Sara said she knew I felt like a stranger there. I didn't say anything. I thought I made myself a stranger. I had made myself a stranger to my family for half my life. But I didn't say that to Sara. I said, It was depressing seeing her trying so hard to fit in, seeing her please father after all those years. . . . My voice trailed.

But she was secure with Leon, Sara said. She didn't worry with him. That was the important thing to her that you don't understand; she didn't doubt him.

Maybe, I said, but she was sad all those years.

No, that's how you saw her, Sara said.

The gray light of dawn came faintly through the bedroom window. Sara and I had been talking for hours, and the lamp in the kitchen had been turned off. Angeles and Amaury had gone to bed. Sara was still talking when I fell asleep.

In the morning, Sara brought me a cup of coffee, and I heard Tití speaking in the living room. She was leaving for San Juan in a few hours and wanted someone to write an obituary that she could place in the newspapers in San Juan. I wondered why she didn't write it herself, but she insisted that I do it.

"La abogada María Luisa Torregrosa Slaughter murió el 10 de septiembre en Edgewood, Texas, a los 76 años de edad. . . ."

I made it brief: one sentence of biographical background and the list of survivors. I had never written an obituary. What does one include? What does one leave out? I took the sheet of paper from the printer and gave it to Tití. I knew it said almost nothing about mother, nothing really about her life.

~

Miles inland from the northern coast, perhaps just ten miles if a ruler were put to the sky, or if the earth lay flat and barren, unobstructed by mountain or river, the island's core rises in waves of breast-shaped hills of coconut and mango groves and serrated peaks of volcanic rock and limestone canyons draped thickly in Spanish cedar, sandalwood, and pine forest.

From San Juan south on Route 1, before steel-and-concrete bridges were built over gorges, before hillsides were shaved and bulldozed to make way for the north-to-south autopista that in just ninety minutes now connects the capital to the southern coast, the drive to Caguas took an hour or more on a crooked, twisting two-lane road crowded with flatbed trucks carrying timber logs, sacks of flour, coffee and tobacco, pigpens and chicken coops.

Breaking away from Route 1, a narrower tar-topped road angled away from Caguas by the banks of the Río Gurabo. Route 189 may have been ten miles long altogether, a link to other country roads that bridged the scattered towns, villages, and aldeas of rural northeastern Puerto Rico. At a midway point on the road, where it flattened and straightened out for a few kilometers, with flowering flamboyán trees on either side, the town of Gurabo had grown from a settlement in Spanish times to a backwater town at the foot of a hill called El Cerro, a place of maybe five thousand people, little more than a gas stop for trucks, buses, and cars.

This was our new home, Gurabo, where we moved when I was ten years old.

The town had no great history, no claim to any place in the books. It had sprouted between hill and valley, like windblown seeds on pastureland, and was incorporated in 1815, with a swelling population of mestizos, mulattos, and blacks from the hills and the sugarcane fields, subsistence farmers mostly, squatters and mill hands, cane cutters with plows and machetes and squinty, sun-aged faces.

There were some comfortable people in the town, who had traveled, a few landowners, men with two hundred hectares of sugarcane or tobacco and herds of cattle, and some who had been to the vocational schools, who ran the drugstore and the food markets, families who read the newspapers and sent their sons and daughters to university. These were the families who lived around the plaza, the people who had maids and cars. But the great mass lived in the maze of barrios and dirt alleys, on half-paved streets and hard-clay roads that spread out in expanding quadrangles beyond the plaza.

We arrived in our old Chevy, all of us hanging out the windows, looking right and left, taking in the garbage piled up in alleys and the ramshackle houses built with planks of wood and rusting sheets of tin. On the main road, along the strip of storefronts, garment shops, beauty parlors, and bars, wiry men with hard faces, with thin mustaches and greased hair, milled in the doorways of bodegas, playing dominoes, smoking and gulping down beer, whistling at the broad-hipped, heavy-breasted girls in skintight shiny skirts strolling by. The road cut the town in half, the slums of El Cerro on one side, and the church and the plaza on the other. The San José Church, a typical colonial church with flaking pink paint and a bell tower, stood at the head of a tree-fringed plaza of lampposts, benches, and strung-up lights.

We turned toward the plaza and passed the movie house. Torn movie posters flapped off the front wall. Wooden houses with tin roofs and narrow porches, and houses made of cinder blocks, with arches and flowerpots on balcony ledges, lined the blocks around the plaza, and everything was painted in magentas and oranges, sky blue and turquoise and shades of yellow.

Our house fronted the plaza, a house with many rooms, with terrazzo floors and five terraces. It was built in the thirties, made of cinder blocks, bricks, and stucco and painted a light shade of yellow, almost vanilla, with dark-brown trimming. It was on the far side of the plaza, on a corner lot, in the shade of drooping trees. The house had been empty for years, after the owner was killed, stabbed to death by his drunken son, so they said, and the house had been abandoned, left to the spiderwebs and to the stories told around town of screams and blood splatters on the staircase and a woman in a black gown who was seen on certain half-moon nights in the upper balcony, her hair a monstrous tangle, a thicket of silver and black.

The house was a wreck. Weeds grew through the cracks in the carport, and leaking faucets had left rivulets of rust and mold on bathroom walls. Most of the tiles on the terraces were broken, tossed carelessly in jagged piles. The house was the only one in town with two stories, and it was the only house with a yard, with land around it. Plants of all varieties grew under the shade of mango and magnolia trees and scattered bamboo stands. Our treetops reached high, up to the top of the second floor, touching the sloping tin roof. The three terraces upstairs had no roof, no awnings, and when it rained they flooded, the water rising two, three inches on the unleveled, unfinished floors. When it stormed, the wind drove the rain, whooshing, wheezing, banging against the roof, knocking wildly against the shutters. The rain blew through the gaps in the terrace doors and the cracks in the slatted shutters. Water dripped down the joints of the roof planks, filling the tin pails the maids scattered in rooms.

My mother asked that the entire interior of the house be

repainted all one color, an earth tone she liked, a pearl cream. Instead, it came out a beige mustard color she immediately hated but did not bother to change. But the cobwebs were gone, the rooms aired and dusted, the faucets fixed, and the tile floors polished and buffed. Nothing else was done to the house in the four years we lived there.

The town called it the doctor's house.

In a few months after our arrival, my father opened his clinic in our house. He didn't need to announce the opening. Everyone knew. He was the only doctor in town. He put up the bronze-plated nameplate that my mother, who had envisioned the day he would open a private clinic in San Juan, had given him when he passed the medical board exams.

Setting up his practice took weeks, while he worked at the hospital and waited for the orders of supplies and equipment to arrive. He had prescription notepads printed, and mother had his diplomas framed and his textbooks put on shelves. He charged five dollars a visit, a pittance next to what he could have made in San Juan, but a fortune to the poor who came to his door day after day to see him.

His office was set up in a wing by the living room, in two large rooms closed off from the rest of the house except for the doors to the back terrace and to the living room, which he alone and his nurse were allowed to enter.

Six days a week the office filled with patients as soon as it opened, at nine in the morning. They came with bags of yautías and plantains, pineapples, corn, and peppers, what they grew in their gardens, and they brought him live chickens and river fish, and pots of asopao and platters of pasteles on holidays. The men took off their pavas, their straw hats, when he entered the room, and the women—old ladies with vague aches and pains, their arthritic hands clutching their bundles, and pregnant young women with babies dangling in their arms—held and kissed his hands. He remembered their names, remembered the ages of their children, and threw his arms around them when they came to him.

They think he can perform miracles, his nurse, Carmela, told me.

She said it countless times, her voice dropping a few decibels as if she were telling me a secret, on those afternoons when he was gone and she had locked up the office and I followed her to the back of the house, the maids' side, where my mother didn't allow me to go, and I would sit on the stoop with her, watching her smoke, her teeth stained, her breath sour. She would take out a crumpled pack of Chesterfields she kept in the front pocket of her white uniform, break a cigarette in two, jamming one half back into the pack, and light up, dragging deeply, shaking her head, commiserating with the poor souls who walked out of that office believing themselves healed.

He can perform miracles, she said, thinking about it. He's got the hands. I didn't know what she meant, but I liked hearing it, liked the way she said it.

We were las hijas del doctor, and those words had a clear meaning in that town. They set us apart. We were not allowed near the casino, the dance hall next door where women in rhinestones and slick red dresses mamboed through the night. We were not allowed to stay out past sundown, and we never went to the movies at night.

That first year in Gurabo, when I was ten and Angeles nine, in sixth and fifth grades, we were sent to public school. Years of parochial and private schools had spoiled us. We were such princesitas, turned out in ladylike dresses and clean, brushed hair, white ankle socks and new patent-leather black flats. We were obedient, we stood quietly in line and kept our voices low and listened to the teachers and did our homework without fail. We were not popular.

The sixth grade was the graduation class, the end of primary school, but my classmates barely knew how to add, knew nothing of history and geography, and paid no attention to the textbooks the school gave them. They shouted and dropped consonants and slurred *l*'s and *r*'s, and used words I had never heard in my house. I told mother the stories—the girls who smacked gum like cows chewing grass (we were not allowed to chew gum) and hitched up their skirts and wore red fingernail polish (never!) and put their hands on the boys (I didn't know how to tell mother about that). The boys yelled and hooted in class, making fun of the teacher, a heavyset, haggard woman who had wisps of graying hair shooting out in disarray.

She wanted to show me off, her prize student, and once she asked me to stand in front of the class and talk about Mexico, but my voice was shaking and I wanted to run out the door. The boys whistled and laughed and the girls turned their backs and eyed one another. I knew they were mocking me, running their hands through their hair and pulling on a lank strand the way I did when I was nervous. I heard whispers of "Blanquita! Blanquita!" The class broke out in laughter and I stood looking at them, trying not to cry.

Like the town, divided between the slums of El Cerro and the tidy homes around the plaza, between the families with servants and the families who were the servants, the school divided itself, light-skinned children pairing off with light-skinned children, dark-skinned students with dark-skinned students, blanquitos, morenos, negros, and we, Angeles and I, were the most blanquitas of all. We had maids who brought us to school and came to take us home; we had traveled far; we had gone to private schools; and we played with the girls and boys who lived around the plaza, the children of parents who were on occasion invited into our home. I understood only vaguely why the classroom made fun of me, and why the daughters of the seamstress next door averted their eyes when they first met my mother, why the parents my mother invited over for coffee came only once.

One morning, midway through the school year, I stumbled off my bed, and my father, taking a look at my face and peering at my eyes, picked me up in his arms and, with my mother gripping my hands, put me in the back of his car and drove madly, speeding all the way, to a hospital in San Juan.

I had hepatitis. The nurses came with long needles, and the doctors came with their stethoscopes, taking my father aside, speaking into his ear. I was secluded in a hospital room with a big window, a room large enough for a cot where my mother stayed. Flowers came and my cousins brought me stacks of comic books. Mother kept me company night and day and read to me from the newspapers not so much to tell me the news but to keep herself entertained, and the nurses washed me in the evenings and brought me the pills I had to take and the trays of blanched food I was allowed to eat, quivering boiled eggs and boiled vegetables. Everything had to be boiled and no one could touch anything I touched. I was contagious.

After the hospital discharged me, I lay in a bed alone at home for three months, and my hair grew to my shoulders and I read all the Superman and Tarzan comics and the classics mother brought me, imagining myself as Hamlet or the Count of Monte Cristo as I dozed off, books flopped open on my lap. My father came up three, four times a day from his office downstairs, and he would put his hand on my forehead, look into my eyes, rub my head. No one else was allowed to get close to me, but Angeles would stand on the threshold and tell me about school, which sounded far more boring to me than my days reading comic books and looking through movie magazines.

My skin, sunless for months, was almost transparent, it was so pale, but the filmy yellow had begun to clear from my eyes. My father let me out of bed for a few minutes each day, and in the afternoons when she came from work mother would take me to the front porch, holding me up because I no longer knew how to walk, couldn't move my legs without thinking about it.

I would sit on the balcony and watch the people on the streets and down in the plaza—the girls jumping rope, my friends flirting with boys, and Angeles biking at top speed on the bumpy sidewalks.

I was frightfully thin and had grown out of childhood, and the quiet that had always been in me, in that small place that children know but cannot explain, had become more silent, where I lived with books and with the friends who were the characters in the books and the voices I heard on the radio and the romance and adventure that lay beyond the mountains I could see from my bed, beyond the distant hum of a crop-dust plane that passed over the fields every day at the same time in the afternoon, at that precise time in the afternoon when time seems to stop, and the world seems still.

In those months in the back bedroom, with the smells of oregano and onions wafting up from the kitchen, fresh gardenias in my room, and my mother's perfume on my pillow, I turned eleven years old. The spring semester was almost over when I returned to school, but I finished the sixth grade with top honors, a bouquet of white lilies in my hands, resting on the lap of my white lace dress, a picture taken in the plaza in Gurabo, on a bench in front of a low white picket fence, on a day in May.

Mother gave birth that month to my third sister, her fifth child. They named her Sara after one of my father's sisters, and she had the same round face, small features, and light hair I had had as an infant. She was a good baby, mother said, smiled easily, and rarely cried at night. Carmen Monserrate, who had been born two years earlier, all bones and whimpers, had grown round, with pudgy arms and plump legs, but her face, with enormous oval eyes, even more sculpted than my mother's, and a nose so finely shaped it seemed chiseled, was a face already formed, the same one she would have at twenty.

Las nenitas, mother called them, and from that day on, from the day of Sara's arrival, they shared a bedroom, schools, clothes, maids. They were the last tier, the children who came in the middle age of my parents' marriage.

When mother became pregnant with her sixth child, almost immediately after giving birth to Sara, she was thirty-five years old.

In that twelfth year of my parents' marriage, we lived the way my mother had wanted, the way she had been brought up to live, with servants, with china and linen tablecloths—but the silver, kept in a velvet-lined box, was taken out only to be polished and the fine china lay untouched in the dining room cabinets, and there were no sit-down dinners or elegant cocktail parties. She bought a few pieces of furniture, in the blond hardwood style of the fifties, and she had a coffee table made with a heavy beveled glass top supported by a piece of gnarled driftwood, a limb of rough bark she had picked up on a beach. She brought her upright piano from my grandmother's house and had it fine-tuned and lacquered a glossy dove white, and she put it in the foyer.

On the Saturday afternoons when my father was away somewhere, she would play for hours, adagios, allegros, largos, De Falla's "Malagueña," Beethoven's sonatas, and, her favorite, "Für Elise." Her hands, which were strong but short, ran over the keyboard, her fingertips caressing the keys, her eyes closed. She played as she recited poetry, from memory, enraptured.

She had a new job, register of deeds for the Caguas district, one of the largest in the island. She had a dozen assistants, women who came to work in the government office uniform, navy skirts, white or pink blouses, and pored all day over heavy threadbare ledgers. The Registry of Deeds took up the fourth floor in a new building in Caguas, and while her assistants worked at metal desks in an open room, she had an office with a large window and floor-to-ceiling bookshelves crammed with law books. Her desk, elaborately carved, was cleared of papers except for the casework she was reviewing at the moment. Her signature went on every paper, on every record, a smooth signature slanted to the right, perfectly legible. Many times I watched her as she signed her name twenty, thirty times, her fountain pen held gently as if it were a plume, her eyes fixed on the handwritten scrawl on the pages before her. She ignored distractions, even me, restlessly walking around her office, pulling law books off shelves, waiting for her, teasing her, telling her she had an easy job, reading and signing, which seemed no work at all. She liked to tell me, with her slightly crooked smile, that she was paid for what she knew, not for what she did.

For at that time, and considering she was a woman, she had a big job. She didn't have the law firm she had wanted and she rarely went to court anymore, trying civil cases as she had done several times before the Supreme Court of Puerto Rico. But as the register of deeds, a political office, she was something of a figure in Caguas, a woman with connections and social position. Men came to her office—sultanito this, fulanito that—hat in hand, briefs under arms, lawyers and businessmen with cases to challenge, and she offered them coffee and a chair close to hers. She stretched herself taller in her swivel chair, her crossed legs sheathed in sheer hose and high heels, her mouth freshly lipsticked. She could twirl the conversation, argue any point with ferocious logic (my father said, not always with admiration, that she could make you believe white was black), and within minutes the men were agreeing, laughing with her, caught in those flashing eyes, in a face that seemed to gather all the light.

Mornings she was up before six, and Rosa the cook came up the back stairs, slithering up the narrow steps in bedroom slippers, her unwashed hair strung back in a ponytail. Rosa carried a coffee tray that, without looking at my mother, she set on my mother's dresser. My father was already up and in the bathroom, clearing his throat, the sink water running for a long time. I could hear him from my room. In their bedroom, my mother was dressing. She snapped on her girdle, then her garter belt, pulled up her stockings, screwed on earrings, brushed her hair. He would come out of the bathroom in his undershirt and pants, his fine hair raked back; his hands, when he embraced me in the mornings, smelled of soap, and were pink from the cold water.

They never had breakfast with us. In their room, there was their morning discussion, words I could occasionally overhear, mutterings from my mother. Their voices rose almost in unison when they quarreled, continuing, as if there had been no sleep in between, the quarrel of broken dishes of the night before, and the mood for the day was set right there—the slammed door, or the kiss.

Seeing her brooding eyes, I wondered why she stayed with him. Years later Tití told me about a time when, after one of my parents' fights, she asked mother, Why don't you leave him? Mother, pointing at her pregnant stomach, lashed out, It's this, if it weren't for this, I would leave him.

Of course, mother denied having ever said such a thing.

I had two views of her (at least two), the daytime mother, a lawyer in a world she dominated, and the other woman, my father's wife, subject to his will and enamored of him. I lived her contradictions, adjusting my vision of her, trying to fit in my mind the San Juan woman, the dancer and performer, enchanting, vibrant, and fearless, and the woman she became in his hands, an obedient wife, dutiful and submissive.

A woman is not complete without a man, she told me years later, when she wondered why I didn't marry.

The idea made little sense to me as a child, but later I began to notice around me women who served their husbands, sitting with heads bowed at dinner tables while the men carried on their conversations. Women who gave birth year after year, women who had no career of their own except being wives and mothers, who stayed home with the children and passed their days watching telenovelas and making meals. In school, in church, girls were taught obedience and, above all, to remain pure, and that marriage and having children were our destiny. That litany was deep in the traditions and social ways of the island as the gnarled roots of old trees. My mother was caught, trapped by tradition and her own fantasies of romance. She was María Félix, and he was Jorge Negrete in those weepy Mexican melodramas of insatiable passion and bitter betrayal.

Her life in Caguas was separate from her life in Gurabo. She drove out to work early in the morning, after telling Rosa what to prepare for lunch and dinner, after kissing us good-bye. Some days in the summer, when Angeles and I didn't have school, she took us with her, like she used to take us to the mercados in Mexico, and I sat in the front of the car with her, Angeles in the back, both of us expectant, children going to the city. In her old Ford, she made the twenty-minute drive in a trance, daydreaming, humming to herself, laughing at our chatter.

At ten o'clock she called out to one of her secretaries for an espresso, which she took at her desk, while talking to Gloria, her old friend and assistant, about Gloria's girls and husband or whatever happened to be on their minds that morning. Gloria was round-faced and stocky, looked much older than my mother, with breasts heaving heavily on her rotund stomach. She had known mother since childhood, and they had the familiarity that comes with knowing things that one never speaks about. It was to Gloria that mother confided, and I could tell when something serious was being discussed because Angeles and I were sent out of the room. I knew it had to do with father. Every problem, I already knew, had to do with father.

At the lunch hour, around twelve, we walked with mother to Gloria's house. Mother had lunch at Gloria's nearly every workday, and after lunch, mother took her little nap there, on Gloria's bed. And it was there where she went alone, closing the door, when she couldn't bear it anymore. Angeles and I didn't know then, but we knew in the way that children know. We went off to play with Gloria's daughters, girls our age, who were like us, the best friends of our lives, of our lives then.

Sometimes, in the late afternoon, mother took us to the stores, stopping at Delia's boutique, where she bought her dresses and hats and our clothes. A trim, tall woman who talked of Paris as if it were next door, Delia catered only to friends, and her store was a salon, something she had seen in Paris. She strode from a backroom and draped herself around my mother, kissing both cheeks, bringing out dresses, measuring and fitting, exclaiming, discarding one dress for another, announcing as she did to all the mothers who came to her store that she was putting on a children's fashion show for the ladies' club and that, of course, we had to be included. Mother flushed with excitement, red blotches traveling from her upper chest to her cheeks, every time she heard Delia say that, while Angeles and I sat quietly, glancing at each other, but smiling politely like mother had taught us.

Mother could not have enough invitations. She had cocktails at the Lions Club and the Rotary, where few women were permitted and she was a center of attention, and she had her lunches with women who would not be seen without hats and gloves, women who entertained themselves with banquets and sororities, who packed their daughters off to finishing schools abroad and organized the annual balls and the fashion shows and ran the charities.

Gurabo was almost a prison to mother (she did not tell us this, she told Tití); she had the house to run, the maids, father, the obligations of family, and, worse, she had my father's friends with their matronly wives, simple women of simple tastes, who read paperback romances and endured in silence their husbands' mistresses. These women never wore hats and gloves.

She insisted that my father join the clubs in Caguas, and he did, and they went to the balls and the banquets, but he was very much like his friends and their wives, a man of simple tastes. All he wanted was a place in the country where he could hang a hammock.

He bought it, had talked about it for months, each time my mother objecting—Why do we need a farm? Aren't we going to move to San Juan?—but one day he came home with the papers, the deed to the land. He wanted us to see it and packed us all in his car. The property, some one hundred acres, was nearby, on a hill on the outskirts of town. The hill sloped down to the main road. It wasn't a big hill. There were no palm trees on it, or groves of fruit trees, or a creek. It had a dirt road and dry pastures, fallen wire fences, and an old herd of cattle, their scarred skins spotted with sores. There were maybe fifty cows, all ribs and rumps lying here and there on bare patches, chewing dry grass. He had bought the farm, the cows, a shed where the cows were milked, and a palm-roofed house where the farm's majordomo lived with his family.

Trudging up the hill, mother sank her shoes in mud and in cow plops covered with flies, and she walked through stinking stalls to watch the cows give milk, Mario, the majordomo, squeezing shriveled teats in filthy hands. For us, who trudged behind her, and for my father, she suddenly played the great farm lover, recalling her days on horseback, fantasizing, paper in hand with the drawings she had made, that the hill would have her house on it, a house, she imagined, with fabulous vistas.

Como una casa de campo, she said, promising.

Now my father saw himself as a big landowner, un hacendero, a man of property with so many hectares valued at this much, and with so many heads of cattle and a majordomo of his own. He talked about retiring from his practice at forty-five and living up on the hill. He wanted to be like his friend Willie—fat, rich Willie—who did nothing all day, it seemed to me, but drink beer, ogle the women of the streets, and play dominoes in the casino.

With the farm, my father's routine changed. He left the house at five in the morning, wearing a wide-brim straw hat, the sort farmers wore, and rubber galoshes that came up to his knees. He talked about bales of hay and selling the dairy's milk in the town, but those sad cows never gave enough milk to sustain the farm, let alone make him rich. But the land was his.

Every morning he brought home milk tanks he tied down in the trunk of his car, the milk sloshing on the trunk's carpet. Rosa boiled it, and we drank it lukewarm with our coffee, milk clots floating and rising, like moss in a lagoon, leaving streaks on the glass.

I hated the milk, hated the farm from the first time I saw it, hated it because I knew my mother hated it, hated it because they fought over it. I didn't like the smell of Mario, and I felt sorry for the cows. And I knew, swatting flies off my arms, stepping around manure, and holding my nose in the cowshed, that the farm would keep us from ever leaving Gurabo.

Summer in the island was el tiempo muerto.

The zafra, the sugarcane-cutting season, was over, and the centrales slowed their production of sugar, molasses, and rum. The sugarcane fields lay fallow, scorched, and the men of the fields congregated in the town, trying to make a living, setting up roadside vegetable markets and piragua stands, crowding around the plaza and along the strip of stores in the main road. They came to find work and to the gatherings at the plaza, to the fiestas patronales, the street carnivals, and the holidays of flags and balloons, maracas and timpales. They came to the political rallies of Luis Muñoz Marín, the island's first elected governor and founder of the island's largest political party, who, in 1952, in one of those moments of political theater that would make him a legend, had walked up to El Morro to raise the Puerto Rican flag above San Juan Bay, establishing after almost five hundred years of Spanish and American rule the island's right to its own flag and anthem.

In the fifties, the years of his Jalda Arriba, the Operation Bootstrap that would transform the island from an agrarian to an industrial society, the banner of his Popular Democratic Party with a silhouette of a jíbaro in a straw hat over the words *pan, tierra y libertad* flew in thousands of rural homes and in every town of the island. In those years, he was at the height of his political power, his physical presence (he was a bulky, fiftyish man, with fleshy jowls and sunken, dark eyes, and a bushy, graying mustache) and bellowing voice brought thousands of people to the plazas, coming by mule or car, from the barrios and the slums, from the bohíos and factories, from the coast and the hills.

My mother, who had cried when Adlai Stevenson lost the presidential election in 1952, who could argue about politics, citing rhythm and verse and history back to Columbus, her voice breaking with excitement, who had politics in her blood and had made it a religion, was a socialist of the sort bred by the educated classes, by the criollo elite, Spaniards to the bone but born on the island, colonials, descendants of an old, dissipated aristocracy. She was sentimental about humanity, about the condition of the poor on the island (and everywhere else), and she was, like many in her family, a nationalist. By blood ties and political conviction, she was a Muñoz loyalist, still believing like many Puerto Ricans did at that time that he would bring independence to Puerto Rico.

But she would not go to his rallies, would not stand in the sweat of the crowd or wave the miniature Puerto Rican flags like the multitudes at a parade.

One day in the summer, Muñoz's caravan came to Gurabo. The workers set up the stage next to our house; lights were strung up on trees and around the plaza; flags were hung from telephone poles and balconies; and flyers with pictures of his craggy face were tacked on trees and storefronts. The town was papered with him, the skies exploding with firecrackers and floating balloons, the streets thundering with the noise of the crowd.

My mother, dressed as if she were to sit on the dais, in the floodlights, watched out for his arrival from our front porch, and he made his way, with the men sidled around him, and stopped at our steps, opening his arms for her, for his cousin's daughter. It was a minute, no more. Bending down toward her, he embraced her, swallowing her in his heavy arms, an old man suddenly, embracing an adoring young girl.

That night I did not go to bed early. I stayed up with her on the balcony, watching her mimic the words he spoke to the crowd, the same ones she had heard most of her life. An entire town sprawled around him, old women squatting on the grass in the plaza, fanning themselves; children up on the trees waving flags; bare-chested men and their women shouting his name as if the name alone would bring them wealth. Long after he had gone and the trucks had packed up, we could hear the chorus of people dancing and partying late into the night.

The next day, the town's sweepers came with the brooms and garbage cans to pick up the trash. The lights were taken down, and the town seemed empty—as it seemed every year when the carnival folded its tents and the roller coaster came down and the carousel stopped going around. Things went back to being what they were. The church bell rang on the hour, and the people went to Mass.

But the evening had left mother with something to talk about, a story she would tell Gloria several times over, reliving each moment with the same excitement she had felt leaning over the balcony, hearing the cheers of the crowd.

Chapter Six

Turning Points

Mother had been buried a day, twenty-four hours in the ground, and we were done crying, I thought, taking the cup of coffee Sara handed me.

Mornings are like that sometimes. You wake up empty, having left the pain to the night, and the sun shines, the sky brightens, and the world returns to the familiar, creating the illusion that we are safe now, that we are stripped clean, and we go about our business in slow motion, stirring the sugar in the coffee, lighting a cigarette, picking the cat hairs off the sofa.

It lasts a moment.

They are going tomorrow, Sara said to me. Do you want some toast?

I shook my head, looking out the kitchen window. It was going to be a hot day.

All but Angeles, Sara went on. She's staying for a week. Yes, I said, she came such a long way. Carmen is driving back home, Olga is flying to New Orleans. Tití had already left early that morning, so quickly I thought she had never been there.

Amaury woke up with that sweet face he had after a bad night, a look of remorse and innocence, a boy who had been bad, but he was good at making it up, throwing his arms around Sara, the way he had twirled mother, making her face light up. He rubbed his swollen eyes and put his hand on my shoulder. Nos tirámos una Angeles y yo, he said, sorry. Can't remember when I fell asleep, he said, laughing, did we keep you up? I kissed him on the cheek. He smelled of stale beer.

Angeles shuffled in, her T-shirt swallowing her, her hands shaking as she lit her first cigarette, but she was smiling. The ruptures, the cracks that were running in all of us, were not showing so early in the day. The words we'd flung the night before seemed forgotten, dried up like the tears.

Sara had cleaned the kitchen, and together we listened to the coffeemaker and got up for one, two, three mugs of coffee, saying nothing.

When are you leaving? Angeles asked me.

Tomorrow.

Why don't you stay longer? she said. I'm staying.

I can't, I said. I could have stayed longer. But what were we going to do, what were we going to talk about? I wanted my things around me. No, I was lying; I wanted to escape.

The day was long, nothing ahead.

The clock in the kitchen seemed to have stopped. The boys had gone off to buy beer. A tuna salad Rick had made sat untouched on the counter. Sara had been lucky with Rick—married very young, carefree and wild, Rick turned out to be a good husband, I thought as I put away the salad. Carmen looked rested as usual, as if she had had seven hours of sleep. Her makeup was on, her earrings were on, and as usual, she listened and said little. She believed her life of housewife and mother was so dull next to ours, but that was her choice, a life that was orderly and conventional, a life she had created to armor herself against chaos. It was the very opposite of our parents' life.

I remember what they were like, she would say, and let it end there.

She had married her high school sweetheart, a tall, serious boy, cheerful and attentive, who knew since he was a boy playing football that he would become an optometrist and inherit his father's practice. He gave Carmen everything she wanted, security, fidelity, an American family. She never had any other love, dropped out of college and they married and his family became hers. While he studied all those years, she kept an eye on their money and scrimped and managed to make a home even in that little trailer near the Texas A&M campus, taking occasional jobs to help him until they had their first child, a child they planned. She planned things down to the last detail. So she listened to us and made fun of herself—she knew she was a mall girl, who knew every bargain in every store within a fifty-mile radius, who set up bridge evenings with the wives and took cruises every year (at any dock, in Miami or San Juan or St. Thomas, she could name every cruise ship, pointing at the berth she and Bryan had shared and where they had gone and how much it had cost and where she got drunk—accidentally—on margaritas).

Carmen has an incredible memory, remembers everything, Sara would say. It's just that she doesn't take herself seriously like we do. She's the funniest one of us all because she knows herself and makes fun of it.

I knew that, looking over at her, feeling as I had felt when she was born, so small and scrawny, wanting to hold her. I didn't want any shattering in her.

Olga was sitting next to Angeles. Mi hermanita, she said, hugging Angeles. They had become so close when Olga lived in Honduras, when Olga was in high school and had left Texas to live with Angeles, to see something of Latin America, to get away from Abilene and mother and Leon. The first time she tried to leave she was three years old. Mother was pregnant with Leon Jr., and Olga couldn't put up with the idea that she would no longer be the youngest. One day she packed up a little suitcase and walked out of the house. Didn't get very far, just to the sidewalk, when mother came running and brought her back. But high school was different. Olga hated it. It was worse than fourth grade when she got into a fistfight because a girl had called her a wetback.

In Abilene, when she started high school, she was miserable. She was picked on because she had an accent and, just as bad, she didn't look like the other girls with their cheerleader smiles and pressed skirts. Olga walked around in flip-flops, jeans, beads. Those towns were really hick, she said, laughing now.

She was sixteen when she went to Honduras, and wound up finding the boy she would marry, a skinny boy who could just as easily party all night as talk about revolution, who became a doctor while she studied architecture at the University of Texas. As certain as she ever was about anything, Olga married Erick, and they settled in New Orleans and now they have two children, a pair of boys, and she and Angeles have the life they lived together in Tegucigalpa, which made them close in a way that one becomes only when you live with somebody. You know the secrets. I envy them that.

Let's go drive around, I said. I can't stand to stay here all day.

No one snapped up to attention. Herding a big family takes time, hours. Where should we go? Who drives? Which car do you want to take?

We drove around Dallas with no destination. The heat made the roads weave like reflections in old mirrors. We were sealed in the car, windows closed, the air-conditioning roaring, Sara driving, or was it Olga?

Let's stop at NorthPark, someone said. I'm not going into a mall, Angeles said, putting an end to that idea. Let's go by the museum. We drove around Highland Park and the lakes and down Greenville and up and around McKinley.

Expressways that didn't end, mansions that seemed as quiet as mortuaries, sprinklers rotating on lawns, curtains drawn against the sun, people going about their business downtown, but my mother was gone.

The world should be still. Didn't they know?

. . . Y no saber adónde vamos/ni de dónde venimos . . .

I heard Angeles say that, so quietly I could hardly make out the words over the hum of the air-conditioning.

Rubén Darío? I said. Yes, mother liked that, Angeles said.

How do you remember? I said. I heard her reciting it many times, she said.

What does it mean? Carmen asked.

I said, Not to know where we are going / nor where we came from. . . .

Thirty years mother had spent on these roads, in these cities without music, without her music, without her poetry. When was she happiest? I wondered.

Were we ever? Maybe when I was eleven, that year and the next, maybe then.

When I was young I imagined the years beginning and ending in summer, perhaps because those years seemed to revolve around that time of year when the days ran one into the other, when there was nothing but time for the gathering of dreams, piñata parties, and picnics in the far hills, legs sunburned and scraped, running hard from the sudden afternoon storms.

That summer when I was eleven, when I played softball in the plaza and twisted the middle finger of my right hand, and rode bicycles with the boys far into the fields and raced with them in roller skates, and lost each time to Angeles in games of Monopoly, that summer comes back on days like this, somnolent, barely stirred by a seaborne breeze, the sun bleaching the sky, almost white with heat.

Mother was pregnant. My father had bought a new car, a two-tone beige-and-olive-green Pontiac Catalina, with shiny chrome and fins, fancy as a Cadillac in that town. We hired more maids. Rosa made our meals; Estrellita took care of Carmen and Sara; Luz cleaned the house; Lorenza, the lavandera, came once a week to take away the dirty laundry, bringing it back folded in a cloth bag she carried on her back. Mother made lists: the grocery list for Rosa, the laundry list for Lorenza, and the housekeeping list for Luz.

The maids lived in a small windowless room behind the kitchen, in the well under the back stairs. Their door was usually closed, but I could hear them at night with their radio, and talking and laughing on the kitchen steps. Angeles and I were not allowed back there, night or day, but on those afternoons when Carmela the nurse was having her cigarette or Rosa was showing me how to make a cake (she battered the mix with sugar, butter, and milk, and I scraped the bowl, licking my fingers), I could hear them talking about their men and the women in the barrio.

Once, when they didn't know I was in the kitchen, I heard my father's name and their snickering. Servants' talk. I ran out of the kitchen.

They said father was un mujeriego. That he liked women. What does that mean? I wondered. I wanted to tell Angeles, but I didn't, any more than I told her that the maid in Fajardo had told me that father had another daughter, a girl older than I, who looked like me. I didn't believe that either.

My father was filling out in his middle age but he was still a man of looks—he liked to say he felt like a boy of eighteen, said it anytime he had a few drinks—and he was spending more and more time out of the house. His dinners sat on the stove.

Long after we were in bed and the maids had gone to their room, mother paced around the house, biting her nails. Her stomach was getting bigger, but even though she was pregnant for the sixth time, she had a slim figure, and her robe, an open throw over her long sheer nightgown, clung to her body's shape, to her swelling breasts and the slopes of her thighs.

In my bed, in the dark, under the mosquito net, I waited half asleep, watching the light of the moon and the streetlamps casting moving, ghostly shadows on the walls. Under our closed bedroom door, a spill of light came from the den, where mother rummaged, pulling a book, any one, from her bookcases, maybe reading a sentence, trying to distract herself. Some nights the phone rang, a patient calling for my father, and my mother said that my father was out on an emergency. At midnight, at an hour that I always thought of as midnight, his car swerved up to the carport, the tires scraping to an abrupt stop, and the door clicking shut. From the hall downstairs he called out to her and her light step came closer to the other side of my door, beside the top of the stairs. She moved quietly down the long stairway. Low voices downstairs, whispers, and then my father's voice would wake up the house. Her cries followed him as he climbed the stairs, the leather soles of his shoes making the sound of his steps heavier and slower. Sometimes I shut him out, shut them out, but there were nights when she cried harder, and I got out of bed and went to him, asking him to stop. After so many years of pleading, I finally gave up, I don't know when, and tried not to hear.

At the end of that summer, for reasons I didn't know, Angeles and I were sent to live with our grandmother, and we returned to the private school in El Vedado where we had gone when were five and six years old, after returning from Mexico. We were back in the house on Pérez Galdós that many years later we would remember as it was then—the living room with the cane-bottom rocking chairs, the glass cabinet with grandmother's blue-and-white china, our narrow beds in the room that still had Tití's dresser, her mirror, her smell (Joy de Jean Patou), and grandmother's old Singer sewing machine.

Over the five years since we had last lived there, little had changed in that house. My grandmother's flowers still grew in the planters in the front yard; the bougainvillea climbed up the walls; the guava tree in the backyard, near the outdoor sinks where clothes were washed, had grown taller and we could pluck ripe guavas off the branches.

The neighborhood, the horseshoe-shaped street, now had a supermarket on the corner, and we had new neighbors next door, a house of sand-colored stucco almost touching our wall. The traffic was heavier, and Eleanor Roosevelt Avenue seemed narrower, a racecourse for cars and buses, and for people trying to cross to the other side. There were more taverns and bodegas, more food stalls, more taxis. Little boys sold cigarettes on the street. Women in mesh slippers smoked lazily on the steps of shacks built around food-and-drink stalls tacked up with Camel and Carta Blanca signs. Music blasted from radios round the clock, mambos and plenas, merengues and boleros. Pérez Galdós itself, a street that in the late forties, when my grandmother had her house built, was mostly vacant, now had houses, large houses, with grilled balconies and arched porticos, car garages and grassy yards hosed down in the late afternoon.

There was construction all around the neighborhood. The cranking of cement mixers and the shouts of construction workers woke me in the early morning. A big shopping mall was being built several blocks away, and on the dead-end streets that paralleled our street, a new subdivision was going up. Everyone seemed to have a car, and residential areas were being laid out like so many grids of tract houses, all square, all with flat roofs and carports, that people could buy with small down payments and government loans.

San Juan was spreading, barely able to contain its million people. It was already a city with several commercial centers and suburbs, rich and shabby neighborhoods cropping up side by side, ranch-style homes walled from overcrowded government-run caseríos of low-rise buildings and concrete yards.

The emigration that began in the thirties and forties to New York and other American cities had crested in the mid-fifties, and within the island itself more people were moving, leaving the small farms and remote villages for the bigger towns and busy port cities. Manufacturing was taking the place of sugar as the island's biggest source of revenue, and Muñoz Marín's plan to modernize the economy had become a blueprint for the salvation of small countries. Sociologists wrote about it, scholars came to study it. Abroad and at home, Muñoz was described as a hero of democracy in the Caribbean. He was no Batista, no Trujillo, no Duvalier. He was invited to the White House. He spoke at the United Nations. He published policy papers in *Foreign Affairs* and lectured at Harvard. It was the spring of his reign as governor, and the bohemian poet who once wrote about la patria and revolution while living the artist life in Greenwich Village had become the master politician, balancing the poor against the feudalists, balancing the island between colonianism and freedom. So they said.

The island became a refuge for intellectuals and artists from Franco's Spain and from the military dictatorships of South America. The Spanish poet Juan Ramón Jiménez, a Nobel Prize winner, exiled himself to Puerto Rico, and the cellist Pablo Casals, a Catalán whose mother was Puerto Rican, made San Juan his home, starting the Casals Festival of Classical Music, bringing to the island celebrities from the United States and Europe, names we knew only from the papers and the movies.

Tití Angela was a guest at the inaugural concert, and it was all she could talk about for days—her meeting with Don Pablo, who was eighty, and his twenty-one-year-old wife, Martita, and the stars who came for him, the stars the government flew in to advertise the festival and the island to the world.

Marilyn Monroe was everywhere, in all the newspapers, on television, arriving at the concert in a flood of flashbulbs, curtsying in front of Don Pablo. Puerto Rico was an island of farándula and what could be more farándulero than Marilyn Monroe embracing Pablo Casals.

Tití and Jacobo were now living in the apartment above my grandmother's. They had moved there after their son was born, and in the evenings, dressed for a reception or the movies, they stopped by—Jacobo chain-smoking and telling his macabre jokes.

Grandmother laughed every time even if she didn't understand the joke, fawning over him, charmed by his attention. We all laughed with him. Tití now had her own child and her newspaper column and no longer had time to make our dresses or bake our cakes, but we were still her girls and she took us to Saturday matinees, sitting through Disney movies with her eyes closed, dozing off, and she took us to the Caribe Hilton to swim and to the Chinese restaurant she and Jacobo liked, and to the Mallorquina in Old San Juan and the Swiss Chalet, where the waiters wore tuxedos and the menu was in French.

In those days, when she was known even to strangers by her given name, Angela Luisa, she and Jacobo were adornments in any room, movie characters, like Nick and Nora. Tití had the quick wit, a sarcasm that came couched in a girlish voice, and he had his lean, craggy looks, his years as a political journalist, the books he had written . . . and his reputation with women. I see her always in pedal pushers and pastel-colored silk blouses, in sunglasses and billowing scarves, and I see Jacobo in a dinner jacket, bow tie unclipped, cigarette in one hand, a glass of whiskey in the other, his dark hair ruffled, his face creviced, creased.

Jacobo died that year, in 1955. In the months before his death, his hands trembled uncontrollably, his fingers yellowed by cigarette stains, and his eyes sunken in dark purple sockets. The day he died, after days in a coma in the hospital, nights when Tití did not sleep at all, lying exhausted in a chair by his bed, no longer hearing the steady drip of the plastic IV bag or the rumble of his breath, they brought her home.

Angeles and I were standing on grandmother's porch. My mother was with Tití, and my father was there, and José Luis and grandmother. Somebody was holding Tití up, almost carrying her along. She had lost weight in those last weeks, and her face had no air in it, no color. Angeles and I were not allowed to go to his funeral. We were too young. It was a big affair, they said later, with hundreds of people and flowers and eulogies.

Tití was thirty-four years old.

Jacobo left the mess of his life to her. He had a former wife, grown children, his money scattered. She had his books, and his plaques on a wall. She had their three-year-old son. Her life at the newspaper, he had left her that, too. It could be said that he had made her, created her, and as diffident as she was in public, she would give him all the credit.

After the funeral, she took a leave from the newspaper. She stayed in their apartment sorting out death from life. She woke up and took her Equanil. She went to bed at ten with her glass of Ovaltine. When she came out of seclusion, a seclusion that did not exclude us and a parade of friends coming and going, bringing casseroles and flowers, she went back to work, to her newspaper office in Old San Juan, with the dirt-streaked windows and a view of San Juan Bay and her clanking Remington typewriter, and her morning breaks at the coffee shop at the Plaza San José, having churros and hot chocolate.

Our days on Pérez Galdós flowed with the ease that my grandmother seemed to make of everything. She woke us on school days, a slight knock on our door. Breakfast was ready, our clothes were laid out on a bed, and when the school bus came, she waited on the sidewalk in her housedress, her thick stockings rolled up and held by rubber bands at the top of her skinny calves. She stood there until we were out of sight. We were no longer five and six years old—we were ten and eleven—but to her we had not grown a day.

Some days she didn't leave the house, spent hours chattering with neighbors, arguing with the maid in the backyard (grandmother was as particular as my mother about housekeeping, the laundry, the dust on the furniture). She pruned her small garden and listened to the radio whenever my uncle's show was on.

Grandmother was in her mid-sixties then, she had few friends from her past, and her circle was getting smaller, dying. But she had her sisters and her children and her grandchildren. Shh, José Luis is on the air, she would say to me every time, moving closer to the radio, turning the knobs. She clipped the articles he wrote and the pictures of him that appeared in the papers. He was her favorite, my mother would say, shaking her head, saying nothing else, only raising her eyebrows. I was too young to know. José Luis had been a heartbreak to his parents, had dropped out of university and had married a woman who didn't come from their class. Their marriage had been such an affront to the family that none of them showed up at the wedding. But that had been years ago, and now she was welcomed in the family, and no one talked about that, not in front of us, no more than they talked about my uncle's drinking. But I found out.

One day I was walking down Eleanor Roosevelt, and I heard a voice, his voice, call out my name. I looked into a dark doorway. He was seated in a bar, his hat squashed down over his forehead, his face hardly visible in the dark of the tavern. I walked up to him, and he put his arms around me. It was the middle of the afternoon, and he was drunk, weaving on the stool. I moved free from his arms and he made a coin appear out of nowhere, from behind his ear, and put it in my palm. I clutched it and walked away. I didn't tell grandmother, I didn't tell anyone.

All the years away from my family, living in Mexico and Fajardo and Gurabo, and now, this year in Pérez Galdós, I was surrounded by them. My life was teeming with relatives, my mother's, my father's.

Almost every day, grandmother's younger sisters, Pepita and Isabelita, came by the house, big women with arms and laps I wanted to hold on to. Isabelita came in her black car. The driver helped her out of the backseat and carried the packages she brought with her. Gifts for Angeles and me, trinkets she had picked up in Italy, or in France, or at a department store in San Juan, little bottles of cologne, mantillas, dolls. Isabelita was the youngest of grandmother's sisters, and she lived in a two-story house that had fountains, curving staircases, and grilled balconies. Looked like a mansion to me. Her husband had owned sugar land, and they had cooks and chauffeurs and they traveled to Europe and rented houses in Spain. Their three children, two boys and a girl, inherited the beauty of her face—blue eyes, chestnut hair—and grew up with tutors and bullfight seasons in Madrid, boxes at the Milan opera, and fast cars. Going to her house was like going to a hotel. We played dress-up, put on makeup, went to the theater, slept late in the morning, and had breakfast in bed.

Pepita lived down the street from Isabelita in a simple house like so many in the middle-class neighborhoods. She had none of the money Isabelita had but she had the same light laughter, as if she had not known a day of pain. Very blond, with bushy hair, and a face with laugh lines around the mouth, she used to say she had two blessings—a devout son who excelled in his studies and went off to Temple to study medicine, and a brilliant daughter with a gift for the classics, who played the piano like a prodigy.

But her daughter, had been born a cripple and as she grew older she had violent spasms and seizures that slowly, over many years, shattered her mind. She lived closed off in a bedroom done all in pink with lace curtains and books stacked up on shelves and sprawled by her bed. Every time I saw her, I was scared. I didn't know what to expect. On her good days, she remembered me and chattered about books and spoke easily. Angeles never seemed afraid of her. They played the piano together, Angeles keeping up the pace, and they giggled when they ran their fingers down the keyboard, ending with the usual flourish, hands open and out toward their audience.

But suddenly a convulsion could come over her, shaking her entire body, and her tongue would twist and her hands would jerk like lobster's claws. She had a mad laughter, and when she laughed like that, like a wild animal, her face looked not beautiful, not womanly, but virginal, like the face of saints who die miserably when young and are portrayed in church in a godlike glow.

I saw less of my father's family, but for a time on Pérez Galdós, my father's mother, Josefina, lived there with her youngest son, Ernesto the veterinarian, a finicky bachelor in his twenties. My mother called her Doña Pepita. We called her abuela (there were so many Josefas, Josefinas, and Pepitas on both sides of our family, we had to invent nicknames for all). Abuela was stocky and compact, not quite five feet tall, round-faced like my father, and double-chinned. She had been a widow for years and lived no place in particular, hopping from daughter to daughter or son to son. In the summers she went to White Plains, New York, to stay with her daughter Sara, and to Saranac Lake for her tubercular lungs. Now she was staying with Ernesto in an apartment barely big enough for two, but she had a proper living room and a kitchen and she had a balcony looking out to the street.

At least once a week, Angeles and I went up to her apartment on our obligatory visits. After giving us wet kisses on our foreheads and listening to our recitation of our school days, she hoisted herself up from her chair and limped to the kitchen to bring out a tray with two glasses of juice and a tin of chocolates, candies, and cookies. Careful not to spill crumbs, with napkins on our laps, Angeles and I sat stiff and attentive like grown-ups. Angeles rushed to her side, helping to lift the tray, but abuela shooed her away, easing herself into her chair, her black dress falling down to her calves, her eyes watery behind bifocals, and her paper fan stirring the air around her. We were used to abuelita, who let us do anything we wanted. But abuela had rules, where to sit, how long to stay, when to be quiet, and when to speak, snapping at me every time I picked up a magazine while she was talking.

Even when seated, she held her cane. Her limp wasn't so noticeable, but my father said she was in pain much of the time. I wanted to know that story, how she got the limp, but that was a question she would bristle at, too personal, too intimate.

My father's brothers and sisters were big talkers, loud talkers, but they didn't drag the past around with them. They rushed through things, through meals, through children, patting this one on the back, snapping at that one. These were not people to sit back on a rainy afternoon and tell stories, but, of course, they were—all Puerto Ricans can sit back on rainy afternoons and tell stories.

I just wasn't listening.

Every Friday that year, my parents drove up from Gurabo to take us back for the weekend. Seeing their car round the corner, Angeles and I ran out to the sidewalk, a little anxious, a little afraid. With them there was always a quarrel ending or one about to begin. But mother's smile was a surprise, a relief, and climbing down from the car, she wrapped her arms around Angeles and me, holding us tight against her.

Sometimes they brought Amaury, Carmen, and Sara and stayed in San Juan for the weekend. We had Sundays at Ana Celia's, my father's oldest sister, in El Condado, where the rich lived in colonial-style houses partly hidden from the street behind high walls and big gardens. Ana Celia, stout and fleshy all over, big-breasted and boisterous, who inherited her money when her first husband died, had her servants cooking all day, making paella, pasteles, and lechón asado. The cooks kept the kitchen doors closed, but before we had stepped up to the main door we could smell the cumin and the adobo, the smells of the island, of the fiestas and Christmas and New Year's.

They were always the same, those family visits.

Father and his brothers stood by the bar, and the women sat in a sort of circle in the sunroom, having their tall glasses of watered-down Cuba libres, talking about the children, who got good grades, who had a piano recital, who was graduating first in her class, while we banged on the piano, ran in and out of the house, splashing in the garden fountain. Usually someone drank too much—an uncle, my father—and arguments started. It was a scene I knew by memory, one of the women would break down in tears, her children would come to her side, downcast, embarrassed, and the party would dissolve just as the sun was dropping into the Atlantic a few blocks away. The children were rounded up and kisses were thrown and everyone picked up their bags and got into their cars.

The red-and-white school bus of the Sacred Heart arrived at our street around four. Every afternoon after school, I waited for it. The bus brought Julia home. She was the girl who lived in the apartment building on the corner; she had short black hair and played the piano and read *Hamlet* out loud, wearing black tights and ballet slippers and a scabbard, like Laurence Olivier in the movie. She was a year or two older than I, and much taller, with broad shoulders and heavy legs and skin so pale you could see the furry hairs on her forearms. Almost every afternoon, we sat on her terrace, a wraparound porch open to the rain and the streaks of the fading sun. I sat on the floor while she read aloud from her parents' books, dialogues from plays by Calderón de la Barca, passages from *Don Quijote,* and Shakespeare's sonnets. She danced to Ravel's "Bolero" and to *Swan Lake,* lifting her arms in the air, going in circles, and she taught me the difference between a Bach fugue and a Mozart symphony. She talked about books and characters as if they were alive, and the sun would fall away from the terrace, leaving it in shadow.

At the stroke of six, abuelita came out to the sidewalk and called out my name, but I paid no attention. Angeles was home already. She went out to play for a little while, she went to the swings, played with the kids up the street, hopscotch and rope, and bicycled around the horseshoe-shaped street. But she liked to stay with grandmother, listening to her stories, watching her cook, and sewing clothes (when abuelita died, Angeles asked for abuelita's scissors—she still has them). I spent the afternoon with Julia, stayed until it was sundown and her parents came home and my grandmother was calling me again, clapping her hands, and then, only then, when I heard her hands clapping, did I run down Julia's stairs.

We made plans, Julia and I. We wanted to go to school together the next year, after the summer away from each other, and she planned to become a ballet dancer and I would become an actress, just as I was in the seventh grade, a star in a comedy, my audience (my mother and Tití) on its feet, roses laid in my arms, kisses on my cheek.

The future at the age of eleven—no, I was now twelve—seemed so certain.

But one night in May, in the last days of the school year, my mother, who was eight months pregnant, stooped to the floor to squash a bug with her slipper, and suddenly she felt a thick liquid trickling down her thighs and then a gush. She was bleeding. My father could not be found, and she bled on the floor until the maids managed to lift her onto her bed. When they found my father, in a bar, he came running up the stairs and bundled her in his arms and drove her, flying madly in his car down the dark road, to the hospital in San Juan.

Angeles and I learned about it the next day, at grandmother's. My father arrived alone, looking drained, his eyes bloodshot. It's your mother, he said, embracing us desperately. She had an accident, she's in the hospital. Grandmother covered her mouth, stifling a cry, and held us to her skirt, putting her hands on our heads. Father sat down. He had pindrops of blood on his shirt. I had never seen him so pale, so worried, his voice a mumble. He choked back tears.

I wasn't there when it happened, he said. She could've died.

But mother was alive, the unborn baby was alive, and that was the end of our year at Pérez Galdós. Angeles and I went back to Gurabo after mother left the hospital, and every night in that last month of her pregnancy, my father stayed home at her side, keeping a vigil. In June, she gave birth to a daughter, Olga, their sixth child, their last.

After our school year with my grandmother and my afternoons with Julia and those starstruck fantasies, I spent the summer in my bedroom, going one by one through my mother's bookshelves, reading poems, novels, plays, García Lorca, Rubén Darío, Oscar Wilde, Tagore, books with cracked spines, their pages loosened and crackling with age. She had books she had never opened, their pages still stitched together. There were a few shelves of books she had boxed over and over and carried from one move to another, books from her university days—Cervantes, Ortega y Gasset, Unamuno y Jugo, collections she had inherited, or books she had bought second-hand. Some of the passages were marked-up, underlined with a fountain pen, and some of the words in the poems seemed familiar to me, because I had heard my mother say them.

"El dueño fuí de mi jardín de sueño / lleno de rosas y de cisnes vagos . . ."

I thought I understood them all, but I hardly understood any of them. I turned the pages, reading passages she had underlined, saying them under my breath. I could see myself standing by a piano, an elbow reclining on the edge of the lid, my wrist turning, my hand unfolding, fingers playing notes in the air, like my mother. I dreamed the words, saw their shape, listened to the way they moved.

I heard the words in my mother's voice, the chords she struck, the shape of her mouth, her moist eyes, her fluttering eyelashes.

"Verde, que te quiero verde."

She would take the five words, her body poured into them, her voice a tremor, and Lorca's words would fall from her mouth, slowly, petals on water.

I started to stay up late, keeping the night-light on long after mother had sent us to bed, punctually at eight o'clock. Under the mosquito net, with the tiny cup of light the lamp shed on my pillow, I read page after page, until Angeles, who couldn't sleep with any light on, threatened to call mother.

The light off, I would lie awake, eyes closed, waiting for morning and the next page. I could hear Angeles's breathing. She was sound asleep. The stories I read became the life inside me, separate from the one of that summer, separate from my family, from my friends, from the afternoons with the boys in the plaza, and the Saturday matinees.

You live in the clouds, my father said often.

I knew what he meant. When he called out for me, I went to his side, and he ruffled my hair and rubbed my back, but my mind wasn't with him. I stared into a distance that was invisible to him. I was wandering in my head, in a world he could not enter.

On the evenings when he came home early, we had dinner together. We sat around him, eyes on him, giving him the attention he expected from each of us. Angeles and I sat side by side; Amaury, eight years old, a rather timid boy, sat across from us. The three young ones were in bed already, in their room—they would not have these memories. Angeles and I didn't speak until our parents spoke to us, but sometimes the three of us, being children still, would start talking at once. When he was feeling expansive, my father cracked a few jokes he had heard somewhere (he told jokes badly, but we laughed), and he let us do whatever we wanted, go to a movie, go to the plaza, stay up watching TV. He was easier then than my mother.

Dinner was not a drawn-out affair. My father asked about school without listening to the answer, since the answer—we like it, we got good grades—was usually the same. Whatever we had to say got lost at that table. Once, when he was toasting their anniversary, making a solemn occasion of it, I interrupted, trying to say something funny, smirking. He stopped and glared at me and sent me to my room. So we knew to gauge the mood, the tone, to laugh only when he did.

Mostly, he and mother talked, argued, while we pretended not to hear, but noticing that she was barely eating. We were not allowed to leave the table before them. We had to sit, hands on laps, our eyes going back and forth from one to the other, seeing the look on my mother's face when our father, finished with his meal, wiped his mouth, dropped his napkin on his plate, and pushed back his chair, hurrying out of the house.

He never said where he was going, and mother didn't ask. Some nights he didn't come home at all. But every night she waited up for him.

I didn't go to school that year with Julia, we didn't go back to grandmother's. Mother wanted Angeles and me home with her, and in August we began school at the Notre Dame Academy in Caguas. American nuns ran the school; they were tomboyish and smooth-faced, with rimless spectacles and stiff black wimples pinned tight around their foreheads. In those flowing long habits, they seemed to flit from classroom to classroom, their rosaries tucked at their waist, their faces flushed. During recess the younger nuns hitched up their skirts to play ball, running the bases drawn in chalk on the concrete playground. They jumped rope, squealing and giggling like girls themselves. But there was nothing tender about them. They liked to think they ran the best school between San Juan and Ponce, and we were all expected to speak English in class, read textbooks in English (I soon knew more about the American Civil War than I knew about Puerto Rico's fight for independence from Spain). We did the home-work in English and recited the Lord's Prayer and the Pledge of Allegiance.

I was in eighth grade at twelve the youngest student in my class. Angeles was a grade below me, but she was far ahead of her class in math and reading, in all subjects, and she was no longer a shy girl with pleading eyes. She had my mother's swift tongue and my father's belligerence. We had arrived at that age when sisters hate each other, even Angeles and me. We fought constantly, over the bedside light, over girlfriends and boyfriends, over things not spoken—scratching, punching, and clawing at each other.

Wish you were dead, I told Angeles a dozen times.

She usually won. She could stand more pain than I, and when it was over, she threatened to tell mother. It didn't matter what it was that she was threatening to tell, the thought of mother's fury was enough to stop me.

I believed Angeles told mother everything.

They were so much alike. They looked alike, the long, sweeping eyelashes and arched eyebrows, the same plum mouth, etched cheekbones, black swimming eyes. Angeles had a deep, low voice, and other children made fun of her, mimicking the way she spoke. She had the voice of a woman and the knowing eyes.

With the years, her eyes would reflect the sorrow of all our secrets. But when she was just a girl, she seemed to absorb us all. She took care of Amaury, playing with him and telling him stories at night, the two of them giggling in his tiny room, and she happily took care of the little girls, running after them, feeding them, when the maids had a day off.

Angeles was always the first to know everything.

Now, at Notre Dame, our life was changing again, stretching away from our friends in Gurabo and from our summer days of bicycling and picnics at the farms of my father's friends, when we played spin the bottle and a boy first kissed me. Soon we had other girlfriends, daughters of my mother's friends in Caguas. We joined the clubs that they joined and invited the boys they invited, and we danced under the moonlight on rooftops strung with lights and ballrooms decorated with paper lanterns and balloons.

We were no longer little girls in sailor blouses. By the time I turned thirteen, toward the end of the seventh grade, I had been to seven schools and had lived in half a dozen houses. There was little of the child left in me.

We were becoming señoritas, in my mother's image.

I already had a boyfriend, in the way we had boyfriends then, in that society of chaperones and virginal sex, when you became sweethearts by looking only, sideways glances in church, hearts drawn on the back of schoolbooks.

He was a freckle-faced altar boy, with light greenish-brown eyes that were as round as bulbs, with sleepy eyelids. His name was Roland, a name his mother took from a novella about princes in dungeons. Limber and lean, he was lightning in skates, and that was the first thing I noticed about him. That, and the way he looked at me in church. I liked his liking me. He had lived in Gurabo all his fifteen years, but he had city manners, and mother liked that. He brought me corsages and boxes of candy that his mother bought at the drugstore, and I scandalously let him hold my hand in the dark heat of the movie matinee, his hand cold, bony. We grew up dancing together, his body bent to mine, his sweating temples against my cheek, his feet barely moving, he was such a clumsy dancer.

There was no thought in him that there could be anyone else but me, and he talked about going to the university and becoming a doctor and having many children. He saw it all very clearly, all straight lines. I saw nothing.

Our summers together, when I was twelve, thirteen, and fourteen, would soon pass to that part of my life that I was leaving before I knew I was leaving it. He was becoming smaller to me in those years when I was at Notre Dame. He was the boy I knew in Gurabo, a sweet comfort, a face too familiar. But there were other boys and bigger parties in Caguas, boys in jackets and ties who drank rum and Coke and moved their hips against mine and breathed words into my ear.

I felt their hot faces, their lips on my neck, their eyes on my breasts.

I must have been in ninth grade then, thirteen. Everyone in my class was suddenly bigger, older. Girls in full bloom. Boys with shaved faces and manly voices. I had had my hair cut. There were faint lines on my brow and the slightest deepening of the hollows below my eyes.

My body, small and light, had defined shape, curves. It fitted softly, flesh malleable, almost liquid, into a boy's arms.

We knew what boys wanted, their eyes on our bosoms, their hands on our lower backs, pressing us against them. We hid our desire—never calling it that—beneath ruffles of crinoline and taffeta, feeling a flush on the neck. Romance came to us that way, furtively, with flowers, with the movements of the hips to the limbering guarachas and swooning boleros, in the books we read under covers, in the brush of hands and the flirtations of a single dance.

The secrecy of it, its false innocence, was a sweet seduction.

I kept the handkerchief with Roland's initial under my pillow, I kept corsages other boys brought me, I pictured myself being lifted into an embrace and held softly like air, and I imagined the words that would be written for me, the words I would write.

I saw my mother's languid face in emerald earrings, my father's hand on her waist, the two of them going out on New Year's Eve, she in silver chiffon and lace, he in a black tuxedo. He smelled of shaving lotion and cologne, she of eau d'Arpège, and they danced until dawn, a little drunk, a little crazy, and she played the piano and recited lines of poetry to him.

"Cuerpo de mujer, blancas colinas, muslos blancos . . ."

Theirs was the romance I knew, opera and zarzuela, poetry and music, the bruised love in my mother's eyes, the wretched mouth.

Looking at her, watching them, seeing the shards that they made of our lives, I renounced, not knowing it yet, their romance, the union they had made, the surrender of woman to man. I wanted only the illusion.

In those years my father was drinking more and more, coming home late, slamming doors, calling out to my mother, demanding his dinner, pounding the dining table with his fist, throwing his dinner against a wall.

Their fights were predictable.

Tienes telarañas en la cabeza, he shouted at her—you have cobwebs in your mind—laughing sometimes, and sometimes shouting.

We saw in the morning the pain in her eyes. Of him we saw less and less. He was up and gone to his farm before we were up for school, and had closed his office for the day and left the house by the time my mother, Angeles, and I returned from Caguas in the late afternoon.

But my mother waited for him day after day, sitting in that chair on the front porch, in her heels and her perfume. She didn't eat with us; she simply sat there until she climbed the stairs to her room, changed into her nightgown, and wandered around the terraces, silent.

One night, in the middle of a fight, mother grabbed her car keys out of the ceramic bowl on the piano, ran out the front door, and drove away. She left in her robe, in the rain. My father was standing in the living room, the wind was blowing in, and mother was gone. We stood holding each other, Angeles, Amaury, and I. She was gone a day, two days. She was in San Juan with my grandmother. My father called her, went to see her, took my grandmother flowers, and cried in my mother's arms.

They had been married fifteen years.

The hours away from my parents became a world within my own world. I longed for the school week to start, the pace of the school day was familiar, comforting, from math to science to geography to English and Spanish, from trigonometry to anatomy to Greek history and the history of the American colonies. I ran through the textbooks at home, finishing them before the class was through the first chapters. I memorized Portia's soliloquies and Marc Antony's and Othello's. I recited them with such melodrama, words rehearsed over and over in front of my bedroom mirror, imagining myself in armor, a sword sheathed at my side, a flag raised in my hand, just as I had, when I was eight, imagined myself a ballplayer and a ballerina. School was theater, and music, poetry, writing. It was my stage, my audience.

Our class was small, maybe twenty students in the classroom. I sat midway on the far right row, along the windows opening on the yard, behind a girl I didn't know, a slender girl with limp brown hair and a soft, dimpled face with light coffee eyes. In the playground, she usually sat alone, reading. She seemed to have no close friends. I noticed her the first day. She was almost a head taller than I.

She tucked in her skirt when sitting, legs closed together, firmly planted on the floor, and she stacked her textbooks and notebooks on the left of the top of her desk, neatly aligned, her pencils sharpened, lined up. She wasn't pretty, didn't have the kind of beauty boys whistled at. But she walked with a certain grace, like an older woman in a Chanel suit, tall and high-necked, carrying her books in the crook of her arm.

Her name was Gabriela. She didn't speak often in class, but when she did, her voice cut through the noise, crisp and commanding. I glanced up every time at the sound of it, and followed her with my eyes when she walked to the front of the class to present her recitation. After she was done, with a smile I took to be only for me, she bowed her head ever so slightly.

I knew so little about her. She lived in a new suburb, a subdivision of wide streets and big houses set back on large lawns. Her house was the color of caramel, with large windows and climbing vines. She didn't seem to invite classmates over, but once, toward the end of the school year, she had a pajama party, and a dozen of us stayed up most of the night, putting curlers in our hair, talking about boys, dancing, spilling Coke on the rug. She and I sat in a corner away from the other girls. I told her I was going away after the summer to a boarding school in Pennsylvania. She said she would write me every week.

We became inseparable.

I began to look for her in the school yard and keep pace with her long strides, and I ran to catch her at the end of the day. We spent afternoons after school on her porch, sometimes reading to each other and listening to the music she liked, piano pieces that she played. We invented stories about the writers that we dreamed we would be someday.

One day I was talking about her and my mother stopped me.

Looking alarmed, she said, You talk about nothing else. You talk about her like she was your sweetheart.

I felt something horrible. She was accusing me of something I knew she thought was frightening. I said nothing. And she never brought up the subject.

Ninth grade ended shortly after my fourteenth birthday. I heard that Gabriela had moved to San Juan. I didn't see her again.

That summer before I went away to school, a hurricane came through the island, the winds tore into the roof of our house and the windows rattled and shook and blew open, and my mother went about with the maids nailing wood planks to the windows and the doors, and when it was over the next morning, she was still sitting on a sofa, waiting for my father in her white nightgown.

Chapter Seven

In the Land of Snow

For years my mother kept letters and yearbooks of my life in boarding school. I once came across them at the top of a closet—a box of letters and two leather-bound yearbooks. They were deep blue with embossed letters, and I hadn't looked at them for several years. I noticed them on the high shelf of the closet of the guest bedroom in her house in Bryan, Texas. I climbed up on a chair and dragged them down. There they were, with all the things from me that she kept: notes, cards, dried flowers, pictures.

I rifled through the letters, but I didn't read them all the way through. There were so many of them, a young girl's letters, in studied handwriting, the loops made just as I had been taught in Catholic school, the sentiments so sweet. No other word could be used for them. I asked for money, I talked about the winter, I mentioned classmates and teachers and the movies I had seen in the cinema on Saturday, the only day when the school permitted us to go into town, a teacher always keeping us in line.

Tonight, at Sara's house, after we had driven around Dallas looking for nothing in particular, we brought out my mother's boxes again, as if they contained the key to the puzzle of our lives, as if somewhere in there the answers were spelled out and we could then understand not only us but our parents. More than anything we wanted to know what she had treasured from us, whose pictures she kept, which letters, because perhaps we could then understand her.

We needed to make sense of our lives together and our lives apart, and her death. None of which could possibly become clear that night, just two nights after her burial.

We flipped quickly through the scrapbooks, stopping here and there, telling the back story, trying to remember the place and the year. There I am, age two or three, in the ballerina outfit, looking away from the camera, seated on a stool with one leg crossed on top of the other, quite unladylike; that's me on the lawn of the University of Puerto Rico, age two, looking at a book; here we are, Angeles, Amaury, and I, on a grassy square across from our apartment in Mexico City, Angeles and I wearing ribbons in our hair and round-collared dresses; abuelita in her rocking chair, surrounded by all her grandchildren in her house on Pérez Galdós; Angeles and I, in identical dresses, holding Carmen and Sara in our living room in Gurabo; Angeles and I at the party mother gave us for our twelfth and thirteenth birthdays, a party in Caguas. We are standing at the table with the birthday cakes. Our friends from Gurabo are there and our friends in Caguas, names and faces I had forgotten. Angeles, her hair curled, is looking down, not smiling; I am standing next to her, smiling, with my hair pulled up and my eyes lighted by a flashbulb.

That is the last picture of our childhood, I thought.

My mother had sent me copies of most of the pictures when I was so far from her. "I thought these pictures," she wrote, "would bring you fond memories of your childhood. . . . Please keep them safely. Hope you cherish them as much as I do."

Through her last years, when I saw so little of her, the pictures came periodically, on my birthdays, on Christmas holidays, sometimes without any special reason. I glanced at them and bundled them in a manila envelope, not to look at them again, not until she had died.

Now, in Sara's house, the years flashed back, like scenes from an old movie, with every page we turned.

Angeles was laughing. She pointed at a blurry picture of me on a horse. Boarding school, the stables, the only time I got on a horse in my life. I was bundled up for the winter, and my face was pudgy, chubby. I looked like a stuffed doll.

You loved that school, Angeles said with her malicious grin. It was coming, I knew.

I thought it was a jail, she said, not bitterly, but as if stating a fact known to all mankind except me.

I know you thought so, I said, annoyed that I had loved something she had not cared about at all.

She had been enrolled in the school my second year there, forced to go by mother. Angeles didn't want to leave Puerto Rico and live in a strange place where she didn't have her family around her. She hated it instantly, the way she could hate—from the minute she arrived.

I paid attention then to her misery, and was angry about it; and now, too, when gray had come to our hair and we had lives that had been lived so differently, I paid attention again. I always paid attention to whatever she said.

It's because you hate everything American, I said, teasing her.

No, she said, laughing. It was a jail, all those girls piled up in the dorm, all those rules—get up at this hour, go to bed at that hour, get up for breakfast—and those boring hours in study hall. All that niceness.

Nice, the damning word.

I read over one of the letters I had written my mother. It was too nice. Nice. I talked about the weather and the hockey games, and the

Halloween dance at Valley Forge, but mostly I asked for money, twenty dollars a month (I was very precise about this) to buy movie tickets and ice cream and toothpaste. Reading the letter, I had to laugh with Angeles. It was so . . . innocent. I didn't tell mother half the story.

My mother had talked since we were children about sending Angeles and me to school abroad, to France or Spain or Switzerland. She imagined us in the Alps, speaking fluent French, learning the courtly manners and cultured diction of the Europe she adored. She imagined visiting us in Paris or Barcelona, and she spoke of El Prado and the Louvre and the Left Bank. But when the time came, she didn't have the money to send us to Europe, which was too far. She would send us instead to the United States.

I was going first and Angeles would follow. We would finish high school in the United States and return to Puerto Rico for college (the college years were the dangerous years for girls, she said, they needed to be home). That was the plan. She pored over magazines advertising private schools in Massachusetts, New York, New Jersey, and Pennsylvania. She sent away for brochures and studied the pictures and the requirements and asked me to read every one of them.

All of them seemed alike: great brick buildings with gables and spires and immense lawns covered in snow, girls on horseback, prom dances with boys in military uniform. I had no idea what a prep school was, had no notion that it was special or spectacularly expensive. But I knew that I would be two thousand miles away from my family, in a place I could barely imagine, living with other girls. Like a big pajama party, mother said, building it up. Like a big pajama party, I told my friends.

I was enrolled at a small school in Pennsylvania, a Protestant school that my mother chose precisely because it was small, two hundred students, in a very small town. She didn't want a coed school, and she didn't want a Catholic school. She believed we had had enough of Catholic schools. She wanted to broaden our lives, she kept saying, to give us the social polish that came from having gone abroad, like the daughters of her friends in San Juan. She painted such a picture that I was happy to be going. That picture was all I knew and I tried to see myself in it, in a wool coat and mittens, walking in the snow. It was like a movie I had seen, with lights reflected in the snow and Bing Crosby crooning in the background. It didn't occur to me to be afraid or to imagine the loneliness I might feel, taken away from the life I had lived, from everyone and everything I knew.

Why did you like it there? Sara asked.

Now, looking back, I'm not so sure I did like it, I said. But it changed my life. Being there began to change the way I saw our lives in Puerto Rico.

What do you mean? Sara said.

Well, I think I began to realize we were not what we thought we were.

What's that? Carmen asked.

Don't know exactly, I said, but I started to think I wouldn't go back home, that I wanted another life. I think that's when I started to leave home.

~

I left the island with my new trunk and suitcases filled with cardigans and plaid skirts for the northern cold, for a place of apple trees and stables and hockey fields in a small town near Philadelphia that smelled of hot pretzels and melting chocolate. I left with my mother and Tití on a Pan Am flight to New York City, the plane packed in the back cabin with hundreds of islanders, mainly laborers and campesinos joining relatives and looking for luck in New York, carrying their shopping bags and cardboard boxes.

Unlike them, we had seats in the front of the plane, and friends of my mother's from her university days were waiting for us at the airport to drive us into the city. We had matinee tickets to Radio City and evening tickets to *My Fair Lady* and room reservations at the Waldorf-Astoria, a table booked at the Peacock Alley and seats reserved at a flamenco show at the Waldorf's Starlight Roof. My mother had treated this trip like a law case, and had seen to every last detail. My entire family came to see me off at the airport.

There was such a commotion.

Everyone at the airport seemed to be talking at the same time. Somebody was taking pictures. Suitcases were weighed and labeled. The terminal, at the new international airport the government had just built on the outskirts of San Juan, was crowded, stifling, every passenger with his noisy caravan of relatives and friends seeing him off. I kept looking at the boarding sign, distracted, clutching my boarding pass. Finally they announced the flight, and I rushed to my relatives, saying good-bye to aunts, cousins, my brother and sisters, and abuelita. In her soft cotton dress, she smelled of Maja powder and the cologne she sprayed on her handkerchief, her kiss leaving wet smears of tears on my face. My father held me a long time, burying my head in his hands. Angeles stood back, waiting to be the last, with the saddest face, those black eyes dark with what she didn't say, and a fleeting kiss on the cheek.

The flight was long, from morning to late afternoon. Nothing to do but pace up and down the aisle, follow the stewardesses back and forth to the galley, watching them load and unload the trays, their hands steady, not spilling a drop while the plane rocked and bumped. They had sprayed hair, like glued straw, pinned up and bundled under their peaked blue caps, and when they handed out boxes of Chiclets they wore smiles that seemed as if invisible tape was holding back the corners of their mouths. To me they looked like Doris Day, all blond, all athletic, and tall. They puffed the head pillows and spread the gray blanket over my legs, hoping I would sit still. I couldn't sit still for very long, last-minute scenes playing over and over in my mind.

Roland had said, You'll change. You won't be the same when you come back.

No, I said, so sure. It's just a big pajama party.

I kept my mother and aunt awake, babbling about nothing, just to keep my eyes from drifting toward the window and the terrifying depth of gray blue outside as the plane cut through cushions of clouds.

New York came slowly, after the brown coastline of the mid-Atlantic and the bleak coal-tinged skies of the New Jersey flatlands. The city seemed to rise out of nowhere all at once, filling the sky, its buildings like immense gravestones, rectangles and spheres, puncturing the low-drifting clouds of that late afternoon. The plane flew directly over Manhattan, slowly dropping altitude, its shadow crawling on the roofs far below. We swerved away, leaving the skyscraper city behind, its jagged profile to our back, and we landed.

My mother's friends were waiting there, and they drove us through some of the most dilapidated neighborhoods I had ever seen.

That's where poor Puerto Ricans live, I heard Mirta say. Mirta lived with her husband, a doctor, on Long Island. She seldom came to the city, to this part of the city. I stared at boarded-up buildings, garbage piles, the litter of Harlem. I had seen the barrios and caseríos of the island but nothing was as ugly and forlorn as those streets in the Bronx, as miserable as those people sitting on stoops.

My mother kept shaking her head, Why do they come here? In Puerto Rico, they have sun and trees with fruit and the sea, people don't go hungry, and there's no cold weather.

Then we turned down Central Park and the city of the movies, the one I had seen on TV, which I had imagined since I was a child, appeared before us.

We had three days in New York, and we walked everywhere, down Fifth Avenue, up Madison, to the stores with names I had known since childhood. I was speaking English to everyone—the English I had learned in the island's Catholic schools. Sure of myself, I spoke to the bellboys, to the waiters and the concierge. I made reservations at restaurants, I gave directions to cabdrivers. I no longer had to imagine New York like *The Naked City* or black-and-white postcards of dark streets in gloomy night fog.

It was there around me.

I saw a life I wanted, cafés and beautiful women, theater, books, music.

We arrived at my new school by bus, a daylong trip from New York through Newark and Trenton, barren cities, wastelands, blackened factories and warehouses of broken windows, treeless streets, muddy skies. We traveled by fields of corn and autumn-orange farms, the land of the Amish in Lancaster County (I was studying a travel book, and mother was providing the captions: Those people in the distance in black frocks riding buggies, those are the Amish). The bus dropped us off in Lancaster, and we hired a car to take us out to the school. The town of Lititz had one traffic light, and it had an old inn named after a general, with fieldstone fireplaces and creaking wooden floors and braided rugs. There wasn't much else to the town. A movie house with a large lobby and a fading maroon carpet, an ice cream parlor attached to the town pharmacy, a pretzel factory. The Moravian church, built of dark gray stone, granite, and large panes of stained glass, was the most imposing structure in town.

There were no neon signs, no buses or noise, and nothing painted in coral shades, nothing in the sea blues and canary yellows of the homes in the island.

The homes were painted gray or vanilla, with butterscotch shutters and olive green and gray blue doors; the store signs were hand-painted and hung on whitewashed poles or nailed with brass tacks to brick facades. What my mother called picturesque. Linden Hall had a weathered white sign perched on two carved poles with the school's name and the date it opened, 1746, America's oldest boarding school for girls. The sign was designed, or preserved, to make it look historic. The lettering on the sign had the serifs and curlicues of old script, with a touch of gold leaf. The church and the school edged the town square, the church surrounded by green lawn and shedding trees, with the school standing like a bookend at the far end of the green.

The school had three-story buildings set close together in an L shape. They looked like big homes I had seen in American movies, with shutters, paned windows, porticos, gables, slanted roofs. Fifty acres of cut grass surrounded the buildings, a campus of sloping lawns, apple orchards, trellises and rose gardens, clipped hedges, and pebbled paths. Coal was burned to keep the school heated, and by early fall, with the leaves beginning to drop off, the smokestacks came to life, venting rolls of steam, spitting charcoal chips.

The school went from grades six to twelve, and had no more than two hundred students, girls who came from the steel towns of Pennsylvania and the north and south shores of Long Island, from the suburbs in Westchester, New York, from places I knew from watching *I Love Lucy,* suburban towns where mothers drove paneled station wagons and made peanut butter sandwiches, where fathers wore felt hats to work and carried briefcases and took the train at the commuter stations in Larchmont, New Rochelle, Rye. They came from Connecticut, from New Jersey (Cranbury, Saddle River, Hopewell), from Delaware and Maryland; they were the daughters of pediatricians and optometrists and lawyers and stockbrokers, families with split-level houses and columned redbrick colonials, with cleaning ladies and washing machines, and mothers who played bridge on Wednesday and golf on Saturday, people who sent their children to summer camp and country day school.

The day I arrived, my roommates were already settled in, their *Webster's* dictionaries and textbooks on the shelves, their clothes in their closets, their desks (the two by the windows) arranged. They jumped up when we entered the room, introducing themselves, shaking hands with my mother and my aunt, inquiring politely about our trip with the feigned curiosity of girls taught to please adults. My mother was charmed, laughing and telling her stories.

Linda, the tallest, smiled and nodded, trying to understand my mother's English, but said little, picking lint off a sweater on the back of her chair. She had a soft body, heavy around her waist. Her light brown hair hung limp, pulled off her forehead with bobby pins. She came from a small town in New Jersey, and carried that kind of shyness. Sandy, my other roommate, was totally different: blond and tan, with a big smile that showed off straight, glowing teeth. She was a girl who knew she was pretty, who got the boys and was always voted president of her class. She had lived all her life in a town of clapboard homes, placid neighbors, and Sunday school, near the Wye River, on the Eastern Shore of Maryland. She spoke with exclamation points, charged with excitement.

My mother and Tití planned to stay a few days in Lititz, and before dropping me off at the school, they had installed themselves at the inn, in an enormous room where the wood-burning fireplace was already lit, delighting my mother, who wanted to ward off the chill of September.

The first couple of days, girls continued to arrive in Buicks and Lincoln Continentals. There was laughter and banter, girls running up the stairs two steps at a time, sliding down the banisters, banging desk drawers, slamming doors. There were parents everywhere, flocking into the dining hall, gathering in our rooms, parading through the dorms, having tea with the headmaster and the dean. On the third or fourth day, the school had a picnic to welcome parents and students—hot dogs and hamburgers and potato chips, and homemade cakes mothers brought. My mother walked about introducing herself to the teachers, starting conversations with the other mothers, while Tití, her silk scarf wrapped around her neck, her sunglasses poised on her head, stood quietly with me under a tree.

My mother nearly always could find something to say, but in her heels and flouncy skirt, she looked out of place around women in plain khaki skirts and tennis shoes, women whose conversation ran to children and homemaking. My mother pretended not to notice, turning to me instead, exclaiming, Nena, es tan bonito! La gente es tan fina! It's so pretty! The people are so friendly!

My room was on the third floor of the main building. We dressed and studied there and slept in an attic with dormer windows and linoleum floors. Our beds were separated by thin wooden partitions. We had no bedside tables, bed lamps, or rugs, nothing but a single bed on a metal frame. The brochures had not shown this, and I thought I saw a disappointed look on my mother's face while she and Tití made my bed, saying nothing. I thought of Angeles and our bedroom back home and the pictures on our walls and the bedside table with my books.

On the first morning after my mother and Tití were gone (as they were leaving me, my mother was crying, leaning out the car window, forcing a smile, and I turned my back on her, running off to my room), I woke up before the bell rang. The sky was still dark, and the windows had a frost on them. I lay in my bed, the silence pressing down. I got up and made the bed and, with my arms around me to keep me warm, I sat on the rim of the bed for a long time, not knowing what else to do.

The bell rang at six-thirty every morning. We shuffled out of bed, and the girls ran down the stairs to the bathroom, dropping pajamas on the floor, shaving armpits, pushing one another into the showers. I moved slowly around them, keeping on my pajamas until I was in the shower stall. I knew right away that was an odd thing to do around girls who thought nothing of walking around naked no matter what their shape—flat chests, heavy breasts, large thighs, big bottoms. We had cheerleaders, athletes, party girls, girls in glasses, girls who stuttered, girls in braces, and girls who cried a lot, smoked in the dorm, and skipped classes. These were girls who had paper routes when they were kids and now spent summers as camp counselors or bagging groceries or playing guard at the local pool, not so much because they needed the money but because keeping busy and filling their résumés with hobbies and extracurricular activities was what people did in America.

The school had few foreigners. One was a senior from Colombia who had grown up in Washington, D.C. She was stocky, with a broad face, tightly waved copper-colored hair, and wide hips; her father was an official in the Embassy of Colombia. She was eighteen years old and already engaged. There was a girl from Hawaii, part Polynesian, maybe Japanese, with a wiry, pin-thin frame, who rarely spoke to anyone but sprung easily to the head of the gym class. And there was a tall peroxide blonde with Anita Ekberg lips (thick, pouty), who was the daughter of an American oilman working in Saudi Arabia.

I was an American foreigner, more foreigner than American. I spoke

English with an accent, so charming, they said, even as they made me repeat everything I said. My clothes didn't quite fit me, a Peck & Peck aqua sweater that became too tight, tweed skirts that seemed too long. I had no tartan skirts and no knee-high socks, Peter Pan collars and circle pins, like my roommate Sandy wore with a charcoal gray crewneck thrown around her shoulders or knotted at her waist. I had my virginal innocence and island insularity, and listened in shock to sixteen- and seventeen-year-old girls, just two or three years older than I, who smoked and drank and had sex with their boyfriends on weekends. These girls didn't hide in the closet to change clothes or put their hands on their mouths when they spoke, as I did.

I sat on the edges of conversations. I watched them, and I watched myself trying to become like them.

The girls had seen Carmen Miranda movies and had heard *West Side Story,* and that's what they thought life was for Puerto Ricans—song and dance and gang wars. Once, I danced the mambo for them, and they crowded around me wanting to learn. But it was impossible because they couldn't move their hips. I didn't tell them that, that the music was going somewhere their feet couldn't follow.

So I became the Carmen Miranda of the sophomore class, Chita Rivera in *West Side Story,* fitting the picture they had of me. I knew the history of their country, but about all they knew of mine was Columbus and *West Side Story*—and not much of Columbus at that. They had no reason to give it a thought. Are the beaches pretty? they asked, and in a short time I learned to expect nothing else, and by rote, I recited the few facts they seemed to care about:

My father is a doctor. My mother is a lawyer. I have four sisters and one brother. The island is an American commonwealth. I am fourteen years old. I have a boyfriend. His name is Roland. What an American name!

I wrote home every week, and every week I had a letter from my mother. She had such a fluid slant, the handwriting I had seen so often when she signed the documents in her office. (I wondered, did she write her letters to me sitting at her desk, with the sun shining through the window behind her?) She always wrote the same thing, about everyone we knew, and everyone was well and they all missed me. Occasionally, she sent me clippings—Tití at a function, my mother speaking at the Colegio de Abogados—and the inconsequential news of the island. She wrote about Castro and the revolution in Cuba, and what a great man he was, but we got no newspapers at the school and to me Cuba was a dreamy image of those nights we spent in Habana when I was a child.

The weeks passed and the months of autumn came, and the sky took on the gray of the north and the cold came through our windows, and the radiators were turned on, their pipes boiling hot, and soon there was snow. I no longer needed to translate from Spanish to English in my head before speaking and writing it. I didn't think and dream in Spanish anymore. I hardly spoke it. I rarely spoke about Puerto Rico or my family, and there were fewer mornings when I lay in my bed with the silence pressing in on me.

There was a strict schedule to the days, school weeks filled hour by hour—chapel at 9:40 A.M., biology at 12:25 P.M., study hall at 7:30 P.M., lights out at 10:00 P.M.; candy bars in the canteen at 3:00 P.M.; Saturday afternoons at the ice cream parlor and matinees in town; church on Sunday. We had a couple of scandals that year: One senior was expelled (the girls said she was pregnant), and a freshman was kicked out (caught smoking). But mostly no bad news entered our world, only occasional stories of parents divorcing and breakups with boyfriends. I sent my mother pages filled with stories of my daily life, my classmates appearing like stars, taking on such importance, especially the girl who joined our class after the school year had started.

We were on the hockey field the day she arrived. I was sitting in the bleachers, bored, forcing myself to watch the team play, when the roar of excitement broke above the clack of hockey sticks.

She's here! She's here!

The girls broke into a run down the field to the dorm. There she was, a reedy girl no more than five-foot-three wearing a light brown wool suit. A dozen girls crowded around her, jumping up and down, calling out her name, Jean, Jean. She was trying to talk, laughing. Her suitcases and trunks lay half opened on the floor. She had been in boarding schools most of her life, at Linden Hall since she was thirteen. She had grown up traveling, living in foreign countries, and now her family lived in Buenos Aires, where her father ran an American company. She spoke French and Spanish, the Castilian Spanish of textbooks, had fluffy reddish brown hair cut short, a smooth face she lathered in cold cream at night, freckles on the tip of her nose, and wan skin.

For days I watched her, the way she made notes with her pen, her shoulders bent under her desk lamp.

The snow came in November, crystal light and tender, melting instantly when it brushed the ground, the roof, the windows. The girls were calling for me, and I ran to the porch and stood bareheaded under the flakes, wiping them off my face. I remember everything in slate gray and vanishing flecks of white. My first snow lasted late into the night, and for days the campus was a gentle watercolor, draped in white, covered in ice. I walked through two-foot piles of snow, following no tracks. I stumbled into ice holes, my mittens crusted, my overcoat freezing wet, my long scarf flying off my neck in a wind that came raw through brittle tree limbs. I threw myself against the boulders the snow had made, and the girls baptized me, pushing me down in the snow and laughing.

My eyes followed Jean, tramping ahead of me in earmuffs and furry hat, moving easily in her black boots. She pulled me along, her hand gripping mine, her face blistering in the cold wind. We walked huddled across the hockey field and down to the dorm, stomping the crust of ice and snow off our boots, throwing our coats and gloves on the floor, her hand playfully rubbing the damp from my hair.

She used to tell me about the houses where she had lived, the lawns and swimming lakes in Connecticut, the river where she learned to dive, throwing herself from a broken-down pier; and when she was older, ten or so, the apartments she lived in abroad, drafty places of tall French doors looking out balconies on cobblestone streets.

We have places like that, streets like those, I told her.

We have cobblestone streets—Calle del Cristo, San Justo, Caleta de las Monjas, Fortaleza—streets of narrow sidewalks where my mother walked behind me, pushing me along, telling me to straighten my back; where we stopped for susurritos in the afternoon at La Mallorquina and shopped at the Padín department store; where we went to the ballet at the Teatro Tapia; where Tití's newspaper stood gray and tall on a corner, a view of San Juan harbor below it, below the fortress walls. These were streets of blue stones, made from the ballasts of Spanish ships, streets bearing the hooves of horses that walked on them when San Juan was a garrison, before the garrison was a city, when it was nothing much more than a mosquito swamp surrounded by forested mountains.

Jean liked my stories and each time I embellished them more.

The houses my classmates lived in (so silent, I thought) had lawns—flat lawns, short lawns, narrow lawns, sloping lawns, rolling lawns—but no drafty windows and tall arched glass doors opening on grilled balconies. There were no cobblestone streets, no vendors of piraguas. No one came out on the roads, and there was no noise, no clattering of wooden cart wheels on pavement, or the scraping of leather soles on sidewalk.

Everything seemed enclosed in glass.

The town where I spent Christmas was built in the coal foothills, crouched under the perennial hanging cloud of a steel mill's steam, soupy yellow in the morning, sunburned orange at sundown, but mostly watery gray. Even in the spring, even when the rain washed off the sky, there was a film of gray. It was not a pretty town.

In the old parts of town, where the steelworkers lived, the houses had aluminum awnings, small scrubby yards, tarpaper roofs, fake brick fronts. The steel mill's executives lived on the hills, up a narrow road that twirled and dipped high above the town. Judy lived up there, on the side of a hill, in a beige-trimmed brick house built on several acres bordered at the bottom of the hill by a thicket of trees and a trickling creek. Nearby there were colonial-style homes and multilevel ranches made of brick and wood siding painted in dawn blue, gray-blue shades with occasional green and marigold shutters. Drapes were hung at the windows, blocking the light. These were big places with big cars and big garages, houses with carpeted stairs and parquet floors, wood-paneled basements with liquor cabinets, bar counters, dartboards, and pool tables.

Scotch was what they drank at these houses.

Judy was a senior, three years older than I, with a little girl's voice and protruding upper teeth that had been strapped into braces since she was a child. She had a long frame, slightly swaybacked, as if she had learned to walk balancing trays in each hand. But she stooped a little, conscious of her height. A run-of-the-mill student, straight C's and B's, she called herself a daddy's girl, spoiled like girls who are the only daughters of men of power and money; and she was madly in love with the six-foot, red-haired navy cadet who wore dress whites and a buzz cut in the picture she kept at her desk.

I saw right away she had a plain turn of mind, small ambitions, a warm, disarming femininity, the sparkling eyes of the airline stewardess she would one day become.

I barely knew her when she invited me to her home for Christmas. I had known that I couldn't go home—it was too expensive a trip—but I had no idea where I would go. I had envisioned garlands of lights, the church bells, and the feasts of my Christmases in Puerto Rico—and dancing all night, drinking Cuba libres and going to midnight Mass.

Strings of Christmas lights framed the brick buildings of Judy's steel town, but there was no dancing all night, Cuba libres, or midnight Mass. We went to Methodist church services and choir programs in school auditoriums filled with parents and children singing "Joy to the World." We went caroling in the hills, and went shopping in stores loud with the jingles of Christmas.

On Christmas Day, under the ceiling-high fir tree Judy and her mother had trimmed with popcorn and cranberries, draping lights around it and throwing angel hair over the branches, Judy's parents had stacked gift boxes wrapped in shiny paper with big red and green bows. On the mantel, they had hung Christmas stockings with each of their names. The swanky silk drapes in the living room had been pulled open, and the wind hissed and lashed at the windows. Judy's father, in a plaid flannel shirt, carried fire logs up from the garage, poked at the ashes, rubbed his hands, letting splinters fall on the rug. He was a tall man, in his fifties, I thought, with sunken cheeks and a professorial look in his black-rimmed glasses. Judy adored him, going up to him and kissing him lightly on the lips. He sat in his lounging chair, in stocking feet, smoking a pipe, with a glass of Scotch at his side, two fingers, no more. I never saw him angry, never saw him drunk, never heard him arguing with his wife. The first time I met him, that Christmas, he kissed me on the cheek and kept his arm around me. He wanted me to know that this was my home and asked me to call him uncle.

That was a Christmas different from all others I had known, quiet in the house and outside the house, as if we were inside a snowball, with a fire crackling in the fireplace and a football game on TV.

After the holidays, we went back to the routine of school. The winter settled in, with the ugly months of January and February. I cried a lot that winter. I was not crying out loud so much as stopping myself from crying. I didn't know why. I wasn't homesick the way the girls talked about it, longing for their mother's cooking and friends back home. Jean would ask me if I missed home, like she did, like all the others did.

No, I lied. I was trying to push the island away. It was becoming smaller, the noise fading, the voices muted. I wrote to Roland, but my letters were an obligation. His letters to me seemed very distant, the words meaningless. I couldn't see what he was seeing.

You are changing, he kept saying. No, I said, I'm not. But I wasn't telling him the truth either. I told no one the truth.

Easter finally arrived and with it the first signs of spring. Flowers poking through the cold earth, birds on the branches of trees still barren of leaves. The school went on holiday, everyone scattering.

The train from Lancaster rattled to a stop at Penn Station in Philadelphia. Our car was filled with schoolmates going away, to see boyfriends and parents, to the Caribbean, to Florida on spring break. Judy was on the train, on the way to Bermuda with the other seniors. This was her last spring at Linden Hall, two months before graduation, before she signed up with Delta and packed up for West Palm Beach, where she would rent a poolside apartment with sliding glass doors and a barbecue grill. On this day, on the train, she had no idea that in a few months her navy cadet would leave her for another girl. She had no way of knowing that her father was having an affair with the woman next door, and that her mother, fleshy but prim in her blousy dresses and weekly hairdos, would have a breast cut out.

That spring, at nineteen, Judy was the happiest girl, in love and engaged to her navy man, blowing kisses at me as she stepped out of the train car with the herd of seniors running up to the Thirtieth Street taxi stand to catch a cab to the Philadelphia airport. They were going to Elbow Beach, the pink beach, doubling up in ocean-view rooms at the Princess Hotel, parading in new bikinis by day and low-cut cocktail dresses at night.

The train started up again, on the way to New York. I was going on to Long Island. I was staying with one of the girls in my class, in the two-story house where she'd grown up, a plain house with the stairs in the middle, parting the living room and den on one side from the dining room and kitchen on the other. They had a deck out back and a motorboat at a pier on the canal. Spring had not yet come to Long Island, and the wind off the ice blue Atlantic still carried the late-winter chill.

The first couple of nights we went bowling with girls and boys she had known all her life, the kids she had grown up with, drinking beer, smoking. I said little, and I didn't bowl. The ball was too heavy, the shoes too big. One night they fixed me up with a date, a bulky high school football player, who took me to the drive-in and put his arms around me and his hands around my waist and bent hard over me and opened his mouth on mine. I got sick that night and spent the rest of spring break in bed in the guest room. There was nothing anybody could find wrong with me, but I wouldn't eat and I wouldn't leave the bed. Alone for hours, I read and cried.

A week later I was back in school, and in the senior dorm, Judy was unpacking in her room, lobster red from the Bermuda sun, her light hair sun-bleached blond. In the room next to hers, with her skin burned black from the day she fell asleep on the sand in Elbow Beach, Barbara was laughing, her laughter ringing down the hall.

I had met Barbara months before, in the infirmary. There were just the two of us on a floor of beds. I think it was Barbara's voice I noticed first, before seeing her face. She was humming in her bed. She came around to me, barefoot, in baggy pajamas, her hair tousled. Who are you? she said. She was a senior and lived in Maryland. She seemed many years older than I, the lines on her forehead deeply marked. Her skin, darker than mine, a deep beige, had the infirmary pallor. She was ragged thin. She clutched a damp handkerchief in her hand. Her fingers were long, tapered, more graceful than she was.

She was not pretty. She was much too ancient in her face for that.

One day, not long after we met in the infirmary, I was walking down a hall in the music department. I heard someone playing a piano and singing behind a closed door, the same chords gone over and over. Someone was practicing "Un bel di," an aria I had heard on my grandmother's radio. I had not heard such a voice, not so close to me, not so powerful and so sad. I stood outside the door for a long time, turned the knob, and tiptoed into the room. Barbara was at the piano, and stopped immediately when she heard my steps. She looked up at me, saying nothing, went to the record player, and slid down a disk. The needle jumped over worn grooves. She looked through sheets of music and with the scratched record playing, she began to sing. Her voice rose, fluttering, took hold, and spread out. She was singing "Summertime."

We began to talk every day. In the mornings when the students waited in the hallway to go to chapel, she walked by in her choir robe, stopping at my side. We talked in study hall, passed messages back and forth, pieces of paper doubled up and mashed inside our hands. We ran into each other at the mailboxes, in the canteen, in the library. We talked in her room, a messy room with a view of the sooty furnace building.

Barbara was the first Jew I had known, and she thought that separated her from the other girls. It made no sense to me. I knew nothing about being a Jew. She looked like everyone else. We talked about that and the way I grew up, and she held my hand when I cried talking about the island, how far it was, and how different. She had a boyfriend, a college boy who came on weekends and to the dances the school held every season. I had Roland and the boys who came for the mixers, busloads from Pottsville and Valley Forge and Lawrenceville, boys who couldn't dance, who plunked one foot down and dragged the other foot like a chain and wore thick glasses and stared hypnotized at a point right below my neck, at my breasts.

But she and I didn't talk about that, about boys. She talked about voice lessons and music and wanting to study opera and going away to Oberlin the next year. I went to her home several times, and went out with her brother, who had the awkward manners of a fifteen-year-old and the pudgy body of a boy who has yet to build muscles. At night, Barbara and I stayed up talking for hours, until she fell asleep, her arm around me. Her parents took to me like a daughter, like I was Barbara's little sister. We went to the Colts games, her hand on mine in her coat pocket, in the drive to Baltimore. We had big dinners and bigger breakfasts, gefilte fish, smoked salmon, matzo balls. Her parents seemed like people from the movies. All the parents seemed that way to me, like Loretta Young and Doris Day, like Gregory Peck and William Holden. Perfect specimens.

When Barbara was not alone in her dorm room, I would sit in a corner farthest from her desk, out of the way of half a dozen seniors who liked to get together in Barbara's room, fixing their hair, putting on makeup, and playing 45-rpm records, dancing to Bill Haley and the Comets and Elvis, and sighing to Johnny Mathis—girls dancing close together, longing for their boyfriends. Music bounced off the walls in those late afternoons, until the housemother rang the bell for dinner.

The day Barbara graduated, her shoulders sagged and her face looked ridiculous under the hard-board hat and tassel. But she was happy. She was going to Oberlin.

After Barbara had left with her parents and balloons drifted on the lawn at the feet of empty chairs, Jean came looking for me. Taking my hand, she ran with me just as we had that first time in the snow.

The next day I took a plane in Philadelphia and flew home.

"Walk on with hope in your heart. . . ." Barbara had sung that for me so many times I thought she had invented the song. That summer, we wrote nearly every day, and in later years we occasionally saw each other, but we grew further apart until there was nothing left of our talks at night and she no longer sang. Not a note. She dropped out of Oberlin, her voice had failed her, she said, and moved to California.

Many years later, her brother called me. Barbara was dying. She had cancer. I spoke to her on the phone. She could hardly talk, and we said words that had no meaning, polite and strained, like two strangers.

Chapter Eight

The Crackup

Sara and I sat in the backyard, her dog running around us, the air still hot.

The boys had returned with six-packs of Corona and a bottle of Tanqueray, bags of ice and bags of groceries. Sara was pointing at the new shrubs she and Rick had planted to edge the paths around the patio. She had a way with plants, and would make them grow even during the long Texas droughts. She even knew their Latin names, and in the winter, when the freeze came, she and Rick moved dozens of planters to the nursery they had made in the garage. Flowers didn't die on her.

We heard shouting coming from the kitchen. Amaury's voice. Carmen came out to the backyard, almost running, her short steps almost tripping one on the other. Her thin shoulders were shaking, and mascara was running down her cheeks.

What happened? Sara and I asked at the same time.

He's drunk, Carmen said. We knew who she meant right away.

But what did he say, what was all that shouting about? Sara said.

By this time Olga was also with us, also crying, but angry, too.

It was a chorus.

Finally we made out what the screaming and crying were all about. Nothing was clear, as it never was when all of us got together and someone screamed and someone cried. He was mean to Carmen, Olga blurted out. He can't do that to my sister.

Olga could start a war with a single match, and this was a match.

Okay, okay, I said, what did he say?

He made fun of me, Carmen said. I could imagine. He had been doing that for years, laughing at Carmen. She was easy to poke fun at, she was so conventional, so square, so proper, so . . . well, white, gringa, definitely not like Amaury.

He's just like father was when he gets drunk, Carmen said. Few things scared Carmen more than father. She couldn't bear the sight of him.

Get out of here, Olga screamed when Amaury came out to the yard.

I was just teasing her, he said, laughing; she can't take a joke.

Angeles was right behind him and pulled his arm and led him back into the kitchen, coaxing him, as she had since he was a boy, protecting him.

I could picture him at eleven years old, in his shorts, crying in the bathroom the day mother told him she was leaving father.

He's been like that for a long time, I said. I didn't know exactly what I meant, and the girls certainly didn't know.

Carmen and Olga left the yard, holding each other, looking for their children, for their husbands. Rick is used to this by now, Sara said; he knows our dramas. He just stays out of the way. Sara and I went back to our chairs. The sun had set, the house was quiet again, the TV news the only sound reaching us through the closed sliding doors.

When did you know? she asked suddenly, out of the blue.

Know what? I said.

About our parents, she said, about their separation.

I was the last to know, I said. I was away at school, remember, and mother didn't tell me. All she told me was that you were all leaving Gurabo and moving to Caguas. But I thought father was moving, too. Well, that's not true. I've known since I was very young it was a disaster but I never thought she would leave him.

You found out when you returned home, Sara said, amazed. That was some homecoming.

How did you find out? I asked her.

I don't remember, Sara said after a long while. Then she said, One day we moved to Caguas, but we didn't really know why. We were too young to know. But Angeles knew, she was the first.

Yes, I thought, she is always the first to know.

Sara picked up my glass. Do you want some wine or a gin and tonic?

Wine, I said, and could you bring me my cigarettes?

I watched her walking so straight, so high-chinned, to the kitchen.

The sky was gray blue, lights had gone on in the house, in the houses around us, and the air smelled of summer dying. Rick lit up the grill. They were going to charcoal some steaks, he said. How do you like yours? he asked me. Rare, I said, and Sara reappeared with my wine and my cigarettes and sat down.

Angeles knew first, I repeated. I know the story.

She was standing in a corner on the main road in Gurabo, waiting for the car to take her to school, when she saw father, saw him in his car with a woman. She knew at that moment that what she had heard around town was true. I can only imagine what she felt because, you know, she won't talk about it, I said to Sara. All I know is that in the afternoon when mother came home from work, Angeles told her.

How did she do that? I wondered. How does one say a thing like that to one's mother?

I had a picture, something I created, of Angeles in her school uniform, standing alone in that corner, her heart racing, her heart breaking. But I had no details. I had only that story, that image. For most of my life, I believed it.

But, of course, it wasn't the whole story.

Nothing between my parents was exactly as it seemed.

Angeles didn't tell me what happened that afternoon when she went to my mother. Not for many years, not until our mother was long dead, and then one night she told me, but even now I don't really know.

~

We move slowly through the years that are endings, circling them in our memory, and we return time and again to them, searching for the exact moment when the end of childhood came, when a passion died, when a marriage ended.

It was the summer of my fifteenth year, and I was arriving home after nine months away. Nine months that seemed years. The journey from Philadelphia was long. Six hours, a stop in Miami, restless dreams during a light sleep over the sea, my eardrums aching. My family strained to catch a look at me in the crowd of passengers lumbering down the landing stairs and across the tarmac. They were pressed against the gate, and I was walking slowly, feeling the sudden change in temperature, the salt air heavy with heat, wet steam rising from the concrete pavement.

They had all come.

My father was there, holding me tight, strumming my back, as if he could bring me closer to him. Angeles had lost the skinny flat body, and her face was no longer childlike but grown-up, filled in, with a defined shape; my brother, now eleven years old, with his sullen face, the face my mother liked to believe looked just like Tyrone Power's (for her, nothing less than a movie star) was too timid, too much of a stranger, to come bursting into my arms. Tití was there, looking not as tall or as blond as I remembered, and grandmother stood at her side, in a familiar flowery shirtdress she wore on special occasions, her hair pulled back in a bun, her face more angular, her eyes more pronounced, but her lips had shriveled with age and her hands had wrinkled, her wedding band now too large for her thinning fingers. Everyone was talking at once as they always did at family gatherings.

My mother, even before putting her arms around me, had teardrops floating on the rim of her eyes. She clung to me, her fingers holding my wrist. Everything seemed the same, the arrangements of family, their exhilarated greetings, those exclamations, but I could see in my mother's tired eyes that something had happened. I felt sealed off, as if the distance I had gone and the time that had passed had rewritten the language, the script by which I saw things and the sense I had of myself in the presence of my family, in my country.

Words in my family were used to hide, or to dress up, or to wash out layers of lies and illusions only to reinvent them all over again, each layer building one on the other, metaphors, similes, beautiful lines thrown away. So, of course, we were a happy family, there, at the airport, at that moment.

The afternoon had faded by the time we arrived home, which was not the house of seven terraces in the small town where we had lived for four years. Gurabo was gone; Gurabo was not to be remembered. We buried places.

Mother had rented a two-story house in Caguas, just two blocks from her office, close enough so she could come home for lunch. She no longer had to drive her old Ford on the patchy tar road to Gurabo, driving at ten miles an hour behind sputtering trucks loaded with loose cords of sugarcane; she didn't have to daydream through the dreary routine of her late afternoon drives when, too distracted to know if a truck was heading her way, she would shift the gear and, her mind wandering (her eyes open, her eyelids lowering), forget until she was right up against someone's fender that she was behind the wheel. Now, living in Caguas, she walked to work and she walked home, her car parked in the driveway behind the locked metal gate of the house.

The house had no front yard, only a thin patch of grass along the front wall. The street was a few feet from the front steps that led up to a portico, a very small square porch. In this house, there were no terraces with cracked tiles, no terraces at all, or hovering trees grazing the roof, and no dancing hall next door, as there had been in Gurabo, with the night-and-day drifts of men playing dominoes and bulbous women swinging their buttocks.

Mother showed me around the house when we arrived after the ride from the airport. Her voice had become higher. She was nervous, flushed, her hand on my arm. Angeles and I shared a bedroom as we always had. This one got the best sunlight, on the second floor, looking to the street. We had our same plain single beds, the same night table, and the same flower-print vanity table that I think had once belonged to Tití.

Downstairs, in the living room, the maid was bringing trays of drinks, and we were all gathered: grandmother, Tití, Roland, all of us waiting, expectant, my homecoming having to be celebrated, toasted in some way. Mother had plucked flowers from the courtyard, narcisos and violets, and had placed them in a glass bowl. I could see her doing this, looking at the flowers from every angle, looking for perfection, arranging and rearranging, but I didn't appreciate then that she did those things.

She did it for you, Angeles said later, only for you.

My father cleared his throat and raised his glass and said something about my becoming a woman (or maybe I have this confused with another instance, another equally momentous pronouncement of his, or maybe I just can't remember a word he said). Soon he was rustling each of us, the way he did his good-byes, approaching each of us one by one, giving me a peck on the top of my head, the hard glaze in his eyes showing maybe regret, maybe love. I didn't know, but I did know that our life was no longer the same life we had known for fifteen years. Something had been crushed. That was in his eyes.

I don't remember much about that night. I was lying down next to my mother in her bed, very still and silent, my eyes on the far wall. She was telling me why my father wasn't there. She was crying the way she used to when I was younger and he didn't come home and she wandered around the house in her nightgown. I couldn't see her tears but could feel them the way you feel rain before it comes. Finally, she said, Your father has another woman. I watched the shapeless shadows on the wall, the reflection off the streetlamps falling in jagged angles on the window shades. I felt everything quieting down, the lights of the street flicking off, the cranking of passing cars, everything slowing, and breaking piece by piece by piece.

I said nothing. I didn't move. I didn't reach out to her. I don't even think I cried.

They were divorced in a matter of weeks. There was no hearing, no court case. Without a meeting between them, the papers were filed and signed, and my mother dropped my father's name. His pictures came off our walls, and she began to refer to him rarely by his name, but as "your father." She would come home from work, gather the afternoon newspapers, and lie in her bed until dinner, reading the news or staring at nothing.

After the divorce was final, my father came to the house, walked into my mother's bedroom, where we had been waiting for him, my mother and the three of us, Angeles, Amaury, and I. He looked shrunken in his baggy pants, his upper arms thinner, and his face looked sallow. He stood at the door of the bedroom. We looked at him and quickly looked away and turned to mother. She said nothing. She wasn't looking at him.

He said he had come to ask each of us a question:

Who do you want to live with?

He knew the answer, but he had to ask. And each answer, each the same, the one word, whispered, penetrated some awful place in him, and his hurt spread across the room. I felt a pity for him, for that man so small.

For the rest of the summer he came on Sundays to pick us up. Without knocking, he opened the front door and walked in as if he lived there, joking with the maid, asking for something to eat. Occasionally, not every Sunday, he went upstairs to my mother's bedroom. We could overhear them arguing. His voice had lost no volume. It cut through walls. There were Sundays when he went up and we heard them talking under their breath, and sometimes there was silence. He would reappear downstairs in varying states of agitation, and reached out to embrace each of us again, glum, demanding, or, in his good moods, doing a little shuffle, a little dance, telling jokes. Only Angeles laughed at his jokes, even when he was mocking her voice. He made fun of her big lips, her pigeon-toed walk. We sat around him, nodding at his stories. In these stories, he was at times a wealthy man of land and ranches, or he was a small-town doctor, a man with nothing but his good name. He was not yet forty-five years old, but he had his last will and testament prepared, he said, his properties and assets in order, the dairy farm, the hill, and the other acres he owned. He used money as a weapon, threatening us time and again over the years that he would drop us from his will if one of us displeased him. We, of course, believed none of it.

On his visiting days, he took us to the beach, driving us to Luquillo, the only beach he knew, where he had spent days of his youth, where he had taken us when we lived in Fajardo. But he no longer went into the water.

He waited for us under a palm tree, not in swimming trunks but dressed in his street clothes, a short-sleeve shirt and long pants, his tie-up shoes sunken in the wet sand. He hunched beneath the palm fronds, leaning against the tree trunk, drinking the milk of a ripe coconut. He was restless, walking to the edge of the water in his shoes, leaving heavy prints, and waving us out, calling out our names, signaling that he was ready to go, just as we had gotten our suits wet. More often on those Sundays, we went to see his family. We made the rounds, going from house to house, from El Vedado to El Condado, a ritual of family obligations, little kisses and hugs from our assortment of aunts and uncles. My father, in high spirits with his family, drank all afternoon like the men in the family did. He didn't get drunk, but ordered the wives around, the maids, the children. I didn't like him then, didn't like that he was loud and vulgar, that he didn't seem successful the way I had wanted him to be. I didn't like the smell of defeat about him, the ordinariness about him.

In the late fifties, in the island, divorce was still unthinkable, the sort of thing that didn't happen in good families. Men had their mistresses and their bastard children, as they did in other Catholic countries, in Spain, in France, in Italy, all over Latin America. Soap operas were built on these stories. The wives feared the scandal of divorce more than the infidelity of their husbands and looked the other way, performing their public roles as wives and mothers, ladies of the house, their place in society secure. They let themselves become old women while they were still young, their sexuality neglected, their sham marriages papered over.

My mother, who had pursued boys in her youth, who had betrayed and been betrayed, who had known about my father in a way that a woman knows, could no longer pretend that nothing had happened when he flaunted his affair, and she would no longer suffer in silence. When she found out, when she could not deny it anymore, she left him.

That was the version my mother told. There were other stories, other versions that I heard years later, but the basic facts were invariable. She filed for divorce—irreconcilable differences, said the papers she signed, not adultery. She was not going to put that word to it.

We lived splintered lives, Sundays with father, the rest of the week with mother. But they didn't talk to us about it, about the divorce, and we didn't talk about it to one another. We were locked in silence.

Mother went to work, read her newspapers, and in the evenings she gathered on the patio with her friends, drinking espresso and nibbling on cheese. She had plans, she told them, plans to move to San Juan, plans to send Amaury away to military school—he needs men around, she said, and the discipline—and she had plans to send Angeles along with me to Linden Hall in the fall.

After a while, life seemed normal, a whirl of parties, dances, boyfriends. There was the Ecuadorian who sent me handwritten notes vowing eternal love, and I had Roland when no other boys were around, his voice breaking, his eyes brooding, saying I had changed, that I had become like American girls. I laughed him off. He took me to parties and brought me orchids that wilted on my wrist. Nights passed with the rhythms of mambo drums and twirling conga lines, the perfumed sweat of pressed bodies, the words of songs he hummed in my ear.

But I knew he was right. I had changed. Everything seemed smaller to me, his ambitions, his presence, the towns, the island itself.

Some days stretched endlessly, afternoons when the house felt empty, nights when I could hear my mother crying, afternoons when Amaury locked himself in his room, refusing to come out until Angeles came to him. He didn't want to go away to military school, he wanted father back. Angeles held him and sometimes she cried with him. I felt helpless, I just wanted to go away, and many mornings I walked alone to the cathedral in the plaza and sat for a long time in a back pew, saying the rosary, or doing nothing at all.

One day just like any other, I took out a pile of letters and other things I had written and burned them all. I dumped all the papers in the backyard, tearing them into pieces, struck the match, and watched all of it burn down to a heap at my feet. I watched the pieces of blackened, ashen paper float up and fall, crumpling on the ground. I stomped on all of it. Anger came like that, but I didn't know it was anger, didn't know it was desperation.

I got letters almost every day, letters from Barbara and Jean and Judy, from the girls whose lives seemed so unreachable to me, living as I was in a place they could hardly pronounce, on an island they saw as a postcard. I didn't speak to them about my parents' divorce. I couldn't tell them that my father had another woman, someone who was only five years older than I. I couldn't tell them that I had seen her once or twice walking in the plaza in Gurabo, her breasts bulging out of low-cut blouses, her legs bare in stiletto heels. I was a child then, but I noticed. She strode slowly, swaying her lower body, and as she passed, the men whistled and craned their heads, watching as she disappeared at the end of the street.

She had the skin of almonds and black hair down to her waist, a woman from the barrio, with the body, full, loose, fleshy, that Latin men want to own.

I didn't know who she was, didn't know her name. I found out later that she had been my father's mistress for years and that everybody in town had known about it. Those lonely nights of my mother's, when she waited for him, their late-night fights, the pain in my mother's face, the violence in my father's, all that now had a name, a face.

By the end of the summer, my mother was planning to move us again, this time to San Juan, farther from my father and the gossip about him that made the rounds. She was sending Amaury to junior military school in a remote town in Tennessee, a place no one had ever heard of, and he was suited in gray uniforms and caps, a boy made to look like a man. Angeles didn't want to go to Linden Hall, but mother had her mind made up. The three of us—Angeles, Amaury, and I—would be gone.

On this trip to the United States, there were no days at the Waldorf, no Radio City Music Hall or stroll down Central Park. Mother didn't come with us.

Angeles and I flew straight to Philadelphia. Angeles was miserable, sulking. She seemed so small and lost those first weeks in school, and I avoided her, angry that she didn't want to fit in, that she didn't want to be the American girl I thought I had become. We no longer fought like children, with nails and teeth and knuckles. We fought with words.

She lived on the floor above me, and being a grade apart, we had different classes. Days went by when we hardly spoke to each other, not even to read each other letters from home. I wanted to see her happy; I wanted her to fall in my steps. I wanted her to make me look good in front of my friends. But she knew immediately she didn't want to become one of them. They're silly, she said, dismissing me with them. She didn't want their lives, their boyfriends, their school. It's like a convent, she cried out. She got sick, lost weight, and spent holidays in homes that were like graveyards to her. She wrote letters home, longing to return, consoling my mother and pleading with my father, begging them to reconcile, forgiving him. We argued about that, too. She was forgiving; I was not.

Soon that fall, my mother started writing letters full of father. He was courting her, bringing her flowers, taking her out to restaurants, telling her he had left the other woman and that he wanted mother back, for all of us to be together again. I thought, How can she believe him? But I didn't tell her that.

It was winter, January, when they came to the school, a big surprise. We were called to the headmaster's office, and in the parlor stood my father in a suit and tie, a hat in hand, and my mother in a black overcoat. He had one arm around her shoulders.

We didn't run to them; they gave us no time. Their arms were around us instantly. They had remarried and flown to New York, had a room at the Waldorf, went dancing and drinking at the Stork Club. They were young again, my mother exclaimed over and over. But they were not. He was portly, with a scowl even in the picture someone took of them at the Stork Club. She looked coquettish but older, with her hair curled and shorter. They stayed three days with us, in the town's inn, and there, my father announced that I would not be returning to the school for my senior year, that he wanted me and Angeles back with them. I looked at my mother for help, and she looked not at me but at him. I saw she agreed with him. I knew I had lost. But I fought back, and finally he promised to send me to any college I wanted if I finished high school that summer in Puerto Rico. All

I needed were a few credits that summer to finish high school a year in advance. I could skip my senior year and go straight to college.

I want to go to Columbia, I said. I'm studying journalism.

Fine, I'll send you there, he said.

We had dinner with Judy and her parents that evening. They had driven from their coal town just to meet my parents. My mother came out in a fancy ruffled blouse and black skirt, high heels, earrings, her face blushed. She was meeting new people, she was going out, and nothing made her come to life more quickly than that. In a dark suit, my father looked very much the successful surgeon, opening the door for my mother, speaking in a soft tone. They ordered drinks and my father, his jacket still buttoned, making himself taller, more important, spoke about his plans to move to Spain to specialize in cardiology. That was the first we had heard anything about this, but Angeles and I knew, with one glance at each other, that this was my mother's idea, her price for taking him back. She wanted a complete change, a new city, a new country, a bigger profession for him. She wanted complete oblivion.

I didn't believe it for one minute. I could never see my father in Madrid, but my mother dreamed it, planned it, and spoke about it with the conviction she could bring to anything she wanted.

Worlds fall apart like that.

The school year ended, and gone were my walks with Jean and our talks about moving to New York together and becoming writers. She still had another year at Linden Hall. Angeles and I returned to the island to yet another new home, an apartment half the size of our earlier houses, on an ordinary street of middle-class homes a few blocks from Pérez Galdós, close to grandmother's house.

The apartment was a way station. It didn't have my mother's touch, no garden, no bookcases, nothing to suggest we were settling down there. A porch was our escape from four walls. But I liked the apartment, liked that we were back in San Juan, that Tití dropped by in the afternoons to have her beer, and she and mother sat together until dark, the canvas awning over the porch flapping in the breeze that came with dusk.

There was little left of my parents' marriage. Even after his second marriage to my mother, after all the flowers and promises to her and to us, he had returned to his mistress. He came to the apartment a few nights, but he was not really living there; his suits hung in the closet, but that was all he we had of him. There was no more talk of moving to Spain, and late at night on those evenings he spent with us, the arguments between them had the wretched hopelessness of endings, lost arguments relived and lost over and over again.

Mother was a woman nearly destroyed. We were caught, their six children, trapped in their madness, and that took longer to kill than their marriage.

Marriages end with a flip of a pen and papers put away in a lawyer's office, but passion takes much longer to die.

The unraveling would take all of us with it.

By midsummer I had completed the credits I needed to finish high school. I was done with summer school at the University of Puerto Rico and received my diploma, not one I could frame and hang on a wall but an ordinary piece of paper. Now I could go on to college. I had sent away for several college applications, Columbia, New York University, Maryland, having no idea that the schools had already chosen their freshman classes, that I was too late.

It didn't matter in the end.

One night, when the time had come to send in application fees and I was asking my father for the money, he interrupted me, laughing at my plan to go to school in New York. Tienes la cabeza en las nubes, your head is the clouds as always, he said.

My mother was standing a few feet away, in the doorway, standing in the wings. She glared at him, and said all she could mutter in anger. But, Amaury, you promised her. He didn't bother to answer. Her face was a mirror of mine, in a rage.

He turned to me. You stay here in Puerto Rico, he said, and go to the university. He was standing by the dresser, looking down on me. It was the same high-polished dresser they had had most of my childhood, with the wide drawers and gold handles and the mirror with the beveled edges.

You're a woman, he was saying, all a woman needs is to learn to cook and get married. I heard the words and ran them slowly through my mind. All a woman needs is to learn to cook and get married. I sat straight up on the edge of their bed and stared back at him. I hated his voice, his mouth, his face. I hated the island.

I'm not staying, I said.

For weeks, mother and I looked at brochures from small, inexpensive colleges. She discovered a women's school in South Carolina we could afford. Look at that campus, she said when the brochure arrived, so pretty. I knew almost nothing about the South and had met no southerners, but I had read the books, seen the movies. It was no place I had ever wanted to see. New York had been my dream, living in a garret in Greenwich Village, writing poetry in the cafés, and trying out for parts in off-Broadway plays. But when the letter came from South Carolina, telling me I was accepted into the freshman class, I ran around the apartment, shouting with joy, holding the letter like a trophy, my ticket off of the island, and freedom.

All that time, Angeles was reading Marx and flirting with boys much older than she and drinking at parties, and Amaury was playing drums and guitars in his room—Elvis singing at full volume. He was not going back to military school. The parties didn't stop because my family was falling apart, and Angeles and I were being fitted for the gowns we would wear on the night of our debut in San Juan. We had practiced for this all our lives, parading in girls' dresses at children's fashion shows, dressing up in costumes, giving parties big and small, raising our gloved hand just so, wearing girdles and seamed stockings, dancing easily in heavy, hoop-skirted gowns and high heels.

Angeles had the face of a model, oval, strong cheekbones, and fine black hair that she liked to pull back into a twist or let loose around her face. Ah, Rita Hayworth! On the dance floors, she moved as if she had no bones, so limber, her legs and hips flowing with music. I was sixteen, she was fifteen, but she seemed the older of the two of us, with a woman's face and a womanly frame, as if she had skipped clumsy adolescence like she had skipped so many grades.

On the night of the debutantes' ball, we looked like mannequins in long dresses of many layers, gowns that bounced and floated off the dancing floor. The hotel ballroom was festooned with candelabras and chandeliers and tables laden with flowers. Tití, the master of ceremonies, chosen for that role because she was well-known, stood at the bottom of the long stairway, introducing each of us as we came down, chins up, backs straight, the trails of dresses flowing behind us, the tiaras glinting. At the bottom of the steps, boys in tuxedos waited, their arms stiff at their sides. Roland was waiting there for me, surprisingly handsome in his tuxedo, and my mother, in a jade-colored chiffon dress that made her look slimmer and younger, sat with other mothers at the chaperones' table. She looked radiant to me, more so than all the debutantes, in her dangling emeralds and long gloves.

We danced all night and drank champagne and watched the sun come up over the Atlantic. By morning, the ballroom was strewn with withered orchids and roses, confetti and broken glasses.

The next day the newspaper had an article about the ball with a picture of two dozen girls standing in rows, the picture so small we couldn't see ourselves in it, but mother found us. Angeles looked composed, serious, a strand of hair falling on the side of her face. I had my face turned to her.

The season of parties was over, and I started working at Tití's newspaper, *El Mundo,* rearranging her files and sorting the mess of magazines and pictures that lay all about her office. After weeks of this, she gave me an assignment, a story on a new theater company. I did the interviews and spent a day or two writing the story. She didn't say anything when she read it, marked up a word or two and was done with it. I didn't dare ask if she liked it. The next day she came by our apartment with the newspaper and handed it to me. I looked through it quickly. I found my story and my name above it, the byline seeming much bigger to me than any other words on the page. I looked at the words I had written as if someone else had written them, but they were mine.

Tití came by every morning in her car to pick me up and, driving through the traffic jams to Old San Juan, we talked about the newspaper and her column, but mostly she was lost in thought, and I wondered about her life. I wanted mine to be like hers: interviews with the governor and artists and movie stars, afternoons secluded in an office with the bay breeze fluttering the stacks of paper at my desk, and my fingers clacking the keys of the typewriter.

But I didn't want to live in Puerto Rico. I didn't want to grow up in her shadow and in all the other shadows of my family. I didn't want to see the darkness that came to my mother's face when my father's name was mentioned. I didn't want to marry and have children.

Days flew as they always did in August. The storms came with the season, and I broke up with Roland at the top of the stairs to the apartment, when he leaned over abruptly and kissed me on the day I was going away to college.

Part Three *A Scattering of Dreams*

"Think of the long trip home.
Should we have stayed at home and thought of here?
Where should we be today?"

—Elizabeth Bishop, "Questions of Travel"

Chapter Nine

A Boy and His Drums

So you don't want to come with me to the airport, Amaury said, turning to me. We were in the kitchen, plates piled up with grilled steak and Carmen's potato salad. She made it exactly like mother had, with boiled eggs and crunchy bits of apple—the best potato salad in the world.

Now he was angling for me, but I ignored him. He laughed, the mock laughter he used to show his anger. And he was hurt, I knew. I could hear it in his sneer.

Being with me is too much for you, eh?—and he kept pushing.

He did that to me anytime we were together, saying exactly the thing that would set me off. It wasn't what he said precisely, but the way the words fell on me. Even his compliments—you are so successful, we read your articles—came out badly, a beautiful rose handed to me, but the thorns of its stem prickling. Not that poetically. The rancor was there, the resentment, envy, and the distance we had traveled separately, by different routes, to different destinations.

I could hear my father in his voice, in his tone. Tienes la cabeza en las nubes, just like father used to say to me, you have your head in the clouds. Amaury was glancing over at Angeles, checking to see if she approved, as if proving a point to her, See, she thinks she's too good for me. Angeles glared at me, and I knew she was thinking, why couldn't I soften up on him? Everybody else looked the other way, talking to one another, ignoring Amaury's little drama.

In this family we were experts at that. We refused to see the blood.

I let it go. Then I said, with a forced smile—the one I had when I wanted to make friends, when I wanted to paper over pain—It isn't that, it's just that I leave in the morning and you leave in the afternoon. I was lying. He knew that was not the reason; they all knew.

He got up from the table, went to the ice cooler, and dug up another beer. His hands wet from the melting ice, he grabbed the bottle and gave the cap a twist and took a long gulp. His limp was usually worse, more noticeable, when he was drinking. He dragged his bad leg just a little and stood with the leg thrown out, as if it weren't connected to his hip and didn't belong to his body.

Like his mind and his words—disconnected, like his life. But I knew so little about his life. We had lost track of each other, like only sisters and brothers can drift apart, separated by the distance the heart puts between us, the years, and the things we hide from each other, but we were never totally apart, never completely severed.

He's your brother, mother reminded me every time she asked me to call him to see after him.

Just because he's my brother doesn't mean I have to like him, I blurted out once, a slap. I was thinking about the words I had said the last time I had seen her, in New York, two years before her death.

I remembered the words and studied him. He was taking another gulp of beer, the bottle almost upside down, his head turned up to the ceiling. He's gotten old and tired, I thought, wanting to rush up and embrace him. But I didn't.

He had a wife, a Puerto Rican he had met in New York in the early 1980s. I had seen her only twice. The first time I met her, in New York, during my mother's visit in 1992, she didn't wait a second to throw her arms around me, her body like a rubbery cushion, and, surprised, I patted her back with the tips of my fingers, that gesture of tentative affection. Taking a beer, she sat back on a corner of the sofa, smoothing her skirt (I could tell, or guessed, she had made up her face and coiffed her hair for the occasion). She laughed loudly when she spoke, and was all endearments—mamacita, amorcito—toward all of us. But, I thought, she's tough, hard, and demanding. Her skin was the color of light coffee, and she had a broad, fleshy face, puffy under the eyes. Her two children came with her—a sullen boy who looked at us shyly, his eyes peering at the floor, answering in monosyllables when we addressed him; and a hefty girl with frizzy big hair who was as brassy as her younger brother was timid. She stumped into the room and shook her body inside her tight skirt and thrust out her chest. They were not Amaury's children, but he treated them as his own, pampered them, stood by them in and out of trouble.

We saw one picture; Amaury saw another. Tamara was a woman from small-town Puerto Rico who had grown up in the New York barrio like thousands of others, struggling in a city segregated by color and race, but she had pushed herself up. Amaury was proud of that—she has a master's degree, he boasted, one of the best teachers in the Bronx. She's good for him, mother would say, takes care of him, keeps him under control. Eventually, they left the projects in the Bronx and moved out to Queens to a house in a quiet neighborhood. But we still wondered, What was that life he was living, the years they lived in the Bronx? How could he have lived like that? He knew we thought that, every one of his sisters. This came up usually when he was drinking. Even with Angeles. One time with her, when I was not around, he started ranting, You'll never accept me, all of you think you're too good for me. They were in a car, and Angeles, who treated him almost like a son, who had brought him up to her way of thinking, who had bailed him out of trouble time and again, who had been there for all his falls, stopped the car and walked out.

Now, in Sara's kitchen, I watched him standing with his beer, making jokes, swaying just so. He's spent, I thought.

After a minute, I left the kitchen, found a magazine, and sat alone on the sofa in the living room. He turned to follow me and stopped at the sofa, set the bottle down on the big coffee table where Sara had a bowl of drooping flowers and a stack of gardening books. He took the far side of the sofa, sat on the edge, head down. I offered him a cigarette and pretended to look at the magazine, flipped a few pages, waiting. His eyes drifted off my face. I used to smoke these, too, he muttered, but now, with my stomach, I'm not smoking anymore. I looked at him, concerned. Your stomach? I asked. Yes, they say it's an ulcer, so I had to quit. Good, I said, but what about drinking? He shrugged.

We didn't know how to talk to each other—not like Angeles and he talked with each other, not with that ease, with that comfort. That time comes, too, when you forget the language of family, and it had come to him and me a long time ago, when we were children. All we had now were greeting kisses, tight embraces that promised something, a buoy at sea, and memories we could not know were different one from the other, or the same. I knew so little about his life. I had lost him so early.

~

When he was ten, maybe older, he got his first set of drums. He wanted to be Gene Krupa and pounded on those drums for hours. Rock 'n' roll star, that was Amaury, that was what he saw in his mirror.

He was in a military school in Tennessee, where young boys

would grow up to be men, drill sergeants, captains, men with mettle, with stiff spines, taught manly discipline, made to endure physical pain with whiplashes and wooden paddles breaking splinters on their bare backs, forced to stand at attention for hours on the parade grounds, trembling in the cold wind of winter.

Mother had sent him there after the divorce, thinking a boy needs the company of other boys and firm discipline. She was too buried in her own grief to deal with this boy of hers who, after our parents separated, would hide in the bathroom crying, muffling his own loss. She had no idea what to do with him, not really. Sending him off to a military academy was her answer, so off he went, barely out of shorts, with his bony body and his big watery eyes—a picture shows him in his gray uniform, saluting, his face on the verge of tears. He hated it, hated the barracks, the barren grounds, the distance from everything he had known, and the sneer on the face of the bigger American boys when he spoke English with an accent. He despised the school like nothing he would despise in his life. Luckily, he found a place in the school band. He became their drummer, his boy's fury held between two fingers. He had been left partly deaf by a fall from a horse when he was eight and he could not read music, so music was nothing he learned, it was all there in his mind.

The drums saved him, gave him a dream.

A year later he returned to Puerto Rico, refusing to go back to the piney hills and the one-stoplight towns of Tennessee and the barren barracks where boys gnashed their teeth and cried into their pillows at night. Discipline was not one of the things he had learned, and mother, not knowing what else to do, sent him instead to the private school where Angeles was finishing high school, a few blocks from mother's new house.

In the first year I was gone to college, my mother had a house built on a lot she bought near Pérez Galdós, after her divorce from my father. Now she had the house she had wanted for so long, using the blueprints she had drawn and redrawn. It was a simple quadrangle, its exterior painted light sienna, not quite beige, not quite almond, a soft shade in a row of yellow and pistachio-green houses. She had checkered black-and-white tile floors, built-in cabinets lacquered in pitch-black, a courtyard of dwarf palms and climbing blue, pink, and lavender bougainvillea. We had deep sliding glass doors to the patio and a flow of air and light that left no corner without sun. The piano, the white-enameled piano, was in its place in the living room, and the glass-topped table with the driftwood base anchored the sofa just as it had for so many years, moving from one house to another.

Her friends, the Glorias and Sorritos and Mirtas, and Tití came in the evenings, had their beer on the patio, and made girlish talk and plans for weekends at Caneel Bay. But the ravages of the last years with my father was written on her face, and her frame, always slight, was frail. She was so thin that doctors ordered her to leave the island and spend months in Madrid recuperating, which she did, spending one summer eating tapas night and day and fainting at the bullfights.

So much changed from summer to summer. I was a sophomore in college and Angeles, who was sixteen, was in her freshman year at the University of Florida. She didn't last long there. For her, it was another prison. She didn't fit in, she didn't want to fit in, she didn't want to be an American, she didn't dress the part, she didn't act the part. She stayed out nights, she drank, she flirted, she skipped classes, yet somehow she managed excellent grades. But she hated being there, and finally she exploded one day in class, when a professor made a sly, insulting reference to Puerto Rico. She jumped up and yelled at him, Mierda! That was the end. The professor banned her from the class and her course credits were taken away. She left the university and returned to Puerto Rico.

She was in between colleges the summer after my sophomore year, partying and drinking, a girl so strikingly lovely that when she was fifteen she had made her debut in a movie, a melodrama set in the hills in western Puerto Rico. It played briefly in the movie houses around the island—there she was, with that long, wavy hair falling on her shoulders, and her seductive eyes flashing innocently under her long eyelashes, her name in the film credits, her picture in the papers. Angeles, teenage movie star!

Amaury, who had lost his sweet boyish shyness, spent the summer days out of the house, driving around the city with friends and, when he was home, locking himself in his room in a tantrum, banging the drums for hours. That was his escape. His anger and hurt ran through him, but he didn't talk about it. He no longer cried over the divorce of our parents; his sorrow had turned bitter, had become part of him, unspoken. He was not a bookish boy, school was a hardship for him, and my mother's lectures only angered and embarrassed him. He could never be as smart as Angeles and me, he said, he could never measure up. But music freed him. He was Elvis then, a shock of black hair falling on his forehead. He practiced, hitching up his hips, dancing with Angeles in the living room.

In those years after their divorce, we still had our Sundays with father, but now they were more infrequent and he no longer took us to the beach as he had when we were younger. And he didn't take us on the rounds to visit uncles and aunts and cousins. He was heavier, heavier every year, growing fat around the middle, his stomach bulging against his shirt, popping like a balloon over his waist. His eyes, too, had changed. They seemed smaller, narrower under heavy eyelids, and swollen pouches underneath. The years of hard drinking were sculpted on his face. But he had not lost his bad temper. When he drank too much, his mockery, a sarcasm laced with humor, was still directed at my mother, but she made it a point not to be present when he came to pick us up or to bring us back to her house.

You're just like your mother, he would say to Angeles, his words cutting, insinuating, without saying what exactly he had in mind. Seated next to her, I imagined something dark and secret and awful—an unmentionable affliction that only he knew or suspected, or maybe the insanity that he liked to say ran in our family. He laughed saying these things, and Angeles, going along, protecting herself, cleverly avoiding a fight, a provocation with a frown or a question, laughed along. But I could barely look at him.

All I wanted was to escape from him, from them. The tension in the house, even when mother was not there, was like the humidity in the air, like secrets they had that I knew nothing about. The time away from home had left me a stranger, had left a hole I could not fill, an emptiness that kept me separate from the people I grew up with, separate from my own family, and the island. The island was my family, what I had known, and now the island seemed very small, isolated, too crowded, backward, noisy and dirty, always living in dreams, believing its own lies.

Angeles and I smoked, drank. That alone made us different from other girls our age and from many of the women in the world in which my family lived. But Angeles got away with it, got away with her peculiarities, as mother would politely put it, like the artists in the family, the prodigals, so many of them in our family, and that made her one of them. Her passion for family, for the island, and for her Latin blood, something she displayed with audacity, without any timidity, drew them to her. She was one of them. She stayed within the circle, she played dangerously, daring everything, but she didn't go away from them, she didn't stray too far. I was different. I pulled away. I had lost track of most of my old friends, knew almost no one my age, and felt no connection with anyone I met. Half my mind, more than that, stayed hidden, shut down. I talked to no one but Angeles about my life away from home.

You're changing, you've changed, she said one night. I knew. I already knew I was leaving my family, and the island with them, as if the people and the place were one and the same.

You've become a gringa, Angeles would say then, poking fun, the worst thing she could think of. Some nights, when she came home from her parties, we would stay up talking. Around that time she was reading Marx and the Latin American leftists, convinced that the United States had sacked Latin America, and that Puerto Rico had sold out, that the governor, Muñoz Marín, our grandmother's cousin, was a worm, un gusano. Because she could outthink me, because I knew that she was right, I listened, but politics didn't interest me the way it consumed her, and my life in the United States had nothing to do with Marx or Castro. I had become an American, I told myself, with my American friends and my American attitude, looking down on the island, with my head full of big ideas. I wanted to go to New York, I wanted to become a journalist away from the journalists in my family; I wanted to write books and poetry but not like other Latin American writers. I wanted to write in English, to read books in English; I wanted a larger world. I was reading Thomas Wolfe, Faulkner, Eliot, Dostoyevsky, Sartre, Camus. I saw myself on the Left Bank, in Greenwich Village, and I went around muttering, with Dostoyevsky, "My liver is diseased." I was bored with Jane Austen and Charlotte Brontë and Chaucer, the required books in English class my sophomore year, the year I was seventeen and punching holes with my bare fist into the glass panes of the college doorways.

It happened suddenly, this punching into glass doorways.

Happened only a few times, just around the time I stopped wearing my nice blouses and started wearing my roommate's brother's khaki shirts, around the time when my handwriting changed into a scrawl and I scowled in class. You're a sane Norman Mailer, my philosophy professor told me, and I took it as a compliment, as if his saying it made me a writer, the way the boyish khaki shirts and messy handwriting made me different. Some days I skipped class and stayed in my room, reading, writing, daydreaming. Sometimes I longed for home, I worried about mother now that father was gone and remarried, but I never wanted to go back. There's no unthreading the tangles. Was it the divorce of my parents, the awful sense of abandonment? Was it a mere phase of growing up? Was it anger and loneliness? I didn't know, but eventually I stopped talking about my family as if I had sprung out of nowhere. My world at times seemed dark to me, unknowable and forbidden.

A girl in the dorm became an obsession, the way other girls, when I was younger, had become obsessions, and that was frightening and exhilarating, as it had always been. I didn't know why this happened, these obsessions that took me completely and shook me and then left me saddened, lonelier. But for the time they lasted I had a mooring, a drama of my own invention, a fantasy. I wrote her bits of poetry, I gave her books, I read to her aloud, and she devoured the attention, holding me with green eyes that seemed created just for me. I had that curse, seeing only what I wanted to see, painting others the way I wanted to see them, infusing them with a love they did not feel. I saw my own lies and believed them. One evening in my dorm room, an evening like any other, the room crowded with girls talking about boys and girls, loves and sex, one of the girls said, teasing me, You like girls, don't you? I stared at her, stunned. I leaned back on my bed, closer to the wall.

I shook my head, and she kept smiling, teasing, and I kept shaking my head. No, it's not like that, I said, and I began to cry. I cried all night.

Angeles didn't know that. But she knew something.

She was seeing that summer that she was losing me, or worse, that I was rejecting them, and at times it seemed that all that remained between us were our memories and a simmering anger and the bedroom we shared—our lavender bedroom in mother's new house, the bedroom with the gallery posters mother had chosen.

I can't come back here, I said one night. Angeles lay on the bed, leaning against her pillow, hunched over, and said nothing. She lit a cigarette.

We all have problems, she said. Amaury is wild. He's lost. I drink, and you, you have a problem, too. She said it softly, tenderly. I knew instantly that she had figured it out.

What problem? I asked, afraid she would tell me.

You know, she said, but said nothing else. Then she said, Maybe you should see a shrink.

I shook my head.

Can't live here, I repeated. I imagined the scandal I would become, imagined my mother's reaction, my family's shock. I couldn't live with that. I didn't fit in. I didn't fit into any of my mother's dreams for me. Marriage, children.

I spent most of that summer away from the house, like a guest passing through. I worked at my aunt's newspaper during the day and worked at a theater company at night. Mornings I rushed to get into Tití's car for the ride to the paper. We took off in mid-morning for the coffee shop across la Plaza de Armas; we had long lunches at La Bombonera and La Mallorquina; I tagged along to the receptions where women fawned all around her. There she was, taller than nearly anybody else, with the mayor of San Juan; there she was, holding a bouquet of flowers or yet another prize, award, or encomium that she would hang on her office walls.

I loved those times in the island, the barroom discussions with Oscar the Chilean director and Helena the Argentine actress, the same one I had interviewed for a school assignment when I was thirteen years old, only now she was rounder and more regal, fierce in her beauty. Her theater company had been going for a few years, but it still had the raw nerve of an amateur company, and with that came the fights backstage (Helena's temper was frightening, her small body shaking, her blue eyes devastating). Everyone screamed, everyone slammed doors, everyone threatened to quit. On opening night, when everyone seemed to fall apart just before curtain time, I ran back and forth, checking off the prop list—phone, glass, bell, book, slippers, gun (it was a murder mystery set in Juan-les-Pins). Raising the curtain brought instant calm and we had nothing but perfect timing, no missing props, no flubbed lines, and always flowers and kisses when the curtain fell and the applause rose. There was total immersion for me in those nights at the theater, and in the newspaper, as if I were someone else.

But that ended, too, with the summer of 1962. I was leaving for my junior year of college, and this time I would stay away for a long time. I didn't know that then, but I would be the first one of us to leave the island, to leave the family. I had no way of knowing that my departure was the beginning of the dispersion of our family away from the island, a scattering none of us had ever foreseen.

That's when Amaury started a rock band, in the sixties, and that's when he was caught stealing cars.

He stole them not to keep them or sell them, but just to drive them, to feel the wind, to feel the speed, to do it because he believed he could get away with it. It was easy. He had it down to a science.

He and a couple of friends would drive to El Condado, the most affluent residential area of San Juan, and cruise up and down Avenida Ashford, along the beach hotels and the mansions, looking for Porsches, Triumphs, MGs, anything shiny, convertible, and fast. Hop out, someone on the lookout, and wire up the Porsche and take a spin, and then, to make a point of it, he would park the stolen car right in front of mother's house, right on the street. Amaury would tell this laughing, still laughing about it years later.

One day the police called my mother. Amaury had been caught. He was at the police station, in detention.

Sometimes mother could surprise. She didn't scream, she didn't cry, she didn't say, as she usually did when we did something unforgivable, What will the neighbors say?

She went to the police headquarters, the lawyer that she was, and got him out.

He was fourteen years old, foulmouthed, quick with a joke, and just as quick with the remorseful kiss on her cheek, his arms lean and longer than they should've been for his height, holding her. Mami, mami . . .

His life and mine were threads, the knots mother made to hold us together pulled apart, the threads running out. We came across each other once a year in my summers home, but we rarely talked seriously as he and Angeles did. I had been away from him, in boarding school and then in college, as he was growing up. To him, I was a stranger. And after those summers, I saw him less frequently, occasionally at Christmases at my mother's, but even those brief visits became more and more rare for me.

In the sixties every boy wanted to play in a band, every boy was Elvis or Lennon Jagger, letting his hair grow wild, pulled in manly ponytails, girls swooning at his feet. When my mother remarried and moved to Texas, Amaury went with her. He was fifteen years old, living in the small town of Bryan with my mother and Leon and my younger sisters, when the Beatles arrived in the United States. But Amaury wasn't taken with the Beatles. Not with Ringo and his ringed fingers and floppy hair; not with McCartney and his baby face and soft love songs. He didn't sit up to watch them on *The Ed Sullivan Show*. He was driving cars full-speed down the highway between Bryan and Houston. He was getting drunk on beer from the 7-Eleven and tossing cans out the window, and smoking marijuana when he could find it.

He had no drums in Bryan, in mother's house. So he did what he could to let air into his head. He raced cars on the highway. He pushed down the worn pedal on the used sedan he had bought with money father had sent him, and shot straight through the highway, hands off the wheel. It was sweet! He got tickets, let them pile up unpaid, and he was flunking in school.

What am I going to do with him? mother asked me when I came to visit that spring of 1964.

He needs help, I said. He should see somebody.

No, she said, I won't have any child of mine . . . Oh, God, I'm such a failure, she said, chewing her nails. She cried; she twisted her face into a grimace, as if hitting her chest with her fists, mea culpa, mea culpa, mea maxima culpa.

It's not your fault, I said automatically. What else could I say? There's nothing wrong with going to a shrink, I said, but it made no difference to her what I said.

No, she said, wiping tears, sniffling, now resolved, more angry than sad, we don't need that to solve our problems. She had conveniently forgotten that Angeles had been going to a therapist for years (against mother's will), but I didn't say so.

One day not long after that conversation, she was straightening up Amaury's room when she found a stack of girlie magazines in a drawer. She was beside herself, horrified. I doubt she had ever seen such pictures. She threw out the magazines before she told me. She didn't even know how to tell me, how to talk about it. She knew how to cope with the girls, but this was something for a father, for a man. When Amaury came home, Leon ordered him to the kitchen. I was in the living room, trying to hear what Leon was saying. I could see him, arms across his barrel chest, bifocals firmly on his nose, Leon cleared his throat and spoke very distinctly, like a math teacher to a class of slow students, he told Amaury that either he lived by their rules or he had to leave their home.

Amaury bolted, ran up to his room, slammed the door, and refused to let me in when I followed him. Finally, he opened the door to me and sat on his bed. He was half crying, half shouting. I patted his hand, helpless. He was right and mother was right. I'm going crazy here, he said, Leon is so straight, so white-bread and dull, and this town is dead, there's nothing to do. I knew what was coming, he wanted to go back to Puerto Rico. The next day he was on the phone to father. Father talked to mother, and she agreed, it was best for Amaury to be there with father. A plane ticket arrived within days and he was gone.

I didn't see him again for several years.

Old San Juan had the life he wanted, late nights, late mornings, and it had the club Gatsby, a popular joint in its time, and there he met his first girlfriend, a go-go dancer with lush blond hair and a figure to go with the hair, with the boots and the skimpy outfit. She fell all over him. He was seventeen, eighteen, wiry, with rock 'n' roll features, the lean body, the leather pants, hair grown long, falling in waves, like Jim Morrison's, eyes that sent lightning bolts, but he had still the gentle manners of a boy who worshiped and feared women (his mother, his sisters), afraid to touch them. He had finished high school in San Juan, had started a new band with a couple of classmates, and was getting noticed in the nightlife columns of the local newspapers. They called the band The Living End, and Angeles had created their logo, curlicues painted across Amaury's drums. The Living End was soon a headliner, playing at sorority balls, at the hotel clubs, and in the all-night bars in Old San Juan, when Old San Juan was the drugstore of the city, junkies and pimps and drug dealers on every corner.

We were big, Amaury liked to believe even years later. We were in demand, could choose the club, the night, the music. We filled those places.

He was living in an apartment in Old San Juan, a palace with four bedrooms and two bathrooms, the way Amaury remembered it, and he had gigs and soon girls all over town. First, there was the go-go girl, and then there was Millie, and then Sally, an American who worked as a waitress in San Juan. For girlfriends he didn't lack. But he was a monogamist, never two-timed any woman—I am not like father, he would say laughing. They just came to him, and they were beautiful, all of them, blond, morenas, black.

But not one of them really took his heart.

That belonged to the music, to the band, to the school of brothers that they were.

The big break came, New York.

Nights in Harlem, in clubs so dark you couldn't see the audience, clubs with names he could not remember, and long nights in a barren, heatless loft on West Fourteenth Street, women, waitresses, singers, barmaids, marijuana as plentiful as water. Drugs—it was the sixties. Sex, drugs, and rock 'n' roll, that was his life. You know, he said, you stay up all night, sleep a couple of hours wherever you happen to fall, and go to work in the docks in the morning. He got a job in a factory downtown, loading up boxes, just to make sure he had some change on him.

The band was just on the verge—marquees, big money, a record contract. Close, so close to making it. And then, just a year or so in New York, it happened. Capitol Records wanted to sign them. The big, big break was right there, he could touch it, just on the horizon, across the country. They had to go to Los Angeles, do the meetings, meet the bosses, sign the papers.

It was a sure thing, their manager said.

There was a house in the Hollywood Hills ready for them, the manager said.

Amaury and Sally put their load into a new Triumph that Amaury bought for the trip. They crossed the nation, the universe. Stopped at the sights. Slept in roadside motels. Drove into Los Angeles, the neon sprawl, craned their necks looking up at the famous Hollywood sign—H O L L Y W O O D—like thousands of dreamers and suckers, often one and the same, had done for years. They spent a night or two at the house in the Hollywood Hills, but that was temporary. They got a place in Hollywood, a run-down two-room apartment, and Amaury got a day job, another factory job loading boxes, nine to five, breaking his back.

The day came for the meeting with the recording executives. It was a big record studio. The band, all five of them, the boys and the black singer, were swept up an elevator to a carpeted office. They sat in the reception room for a long time. The Beach Boys were there (the Beach Boys!), waiting just like them. Finally, they were called in. They were ready to sign on the line.

The man at the desk looked them over. A big desk, window behind him, Los Angeles below, laid out into eternity.

We've discussed this thing, he told them, and we've decided you're not for us.

Silence, footsteps outside the door muffled by carpets.

You want to play Puerto Rican music, and clearing his throat, the man went on. Your singer, she's not right. Amaury thought, She's black! That's what he means. I'm afraid that won't sell here, the man said. He's not even looking at us, Amaury thought. Now Amaury heard him say, If you could change your singer and play American music, maybe we could have a deal.

Silence. But, Amaury finally said, we were told this was a deal.

The man looked at him and said, Maybe you want to check somebody else, other record companies, but we can't do this. We didn't know . . .

Amaury heard nothing else. The words evaporated. He didn't believe he had heard what he had heard. They stood up, all five of them, The Living End, and one by one, they walked out.

It took no time for the band to break up. How true that name, The Living End, turned out to be, Amaury said later. For a while, in L.A., the band had gotten some work in strip clubs, in gay clubs, in places down in the Valley. But after a few weeks, each had started going his own way. George played the piano in clubs. Carli went back to San Juan. Amaury had no money to return anywhere. He and Sally stayed awhile longer—he working at the factory, she waiting tables—but his spirit was broken. The split in the band finished him, and he took Sally back east, and eventually they left for Puerto Rico.

The year he broke his left leg in a dozen places in a car crash on Avenida Ashford was the year, 1972, he gave up the drums, Sally, and all hope. He was twenty-four years old.

He had had a ten-year joyride, and it ended right there, at two in the morning.

He was drunk, driving alone, and his car, a big old guzzler he had borrowed, drove straight into a huge tree. Still conscious, he put the gear in reverse and pushed the pedal, but the car, instead of moving back, slammed the tree again. His arm was caught in the wheel, one leg was crushed against the door, but he tried again to reverse the gears and again he rammed the tree. He fell into the windshield, like a bird shot from the sky, his body sprawled, twisted, bleeding.

This is what happens when you drive drunk, he said when my father arrived at the hospital, making fun of father, who had driven drunk too often, making a point while lying in so many broken pieces on a gurney on the way to the operating room. He was half out of his mind. The operation lasted six hours. Mother arrived from Texas. She called me (I was living then in North Carolina) and told me that Amaury had had an accident but that he was going to be all right. His head was not injured but one leg may be shorter than the other. She sounded calm, the way she became, her nerves stilled, when the worst news had to be delivered. When he was eight years old he fell off a horse and fractured his skull, his ears bleeding. She came home and ran up the stairs to find him almost dead, but even so she didn't scream or cry. I didn't see him that time either (where was I?). At the time of the car accident I was a thousand miles away, listening to my mother's voice, trying to imagine her at the hospital, trying to imagine my brother lying unconscious on a hospital bed. There was no way for me to really know the moment, the scene. I didn't see the pulp, the bandaged body or the scarred face. Nor did she tell me about it.

He walked on crutches for a year.

What a slide I had, he said later, many years later. I had hit bottom. A bottom that you can't imagine.

Everything about his life has a glaze about it for me. Years overlap, cities, girlfriends, clubs in San Juan and New York, in Los Angeles, day work in the factories. Mother would have preferred it if her son had liked the law, or even medicine like my father, or architecture like Angeles, or newspapers like Tití Angela and me. While I was off making money, buying a house and getting promotions at newspapers in the United States, he was broken down, in debt, unemployed.

It's the small successes that kill you, I thought. He wasn't just talking about the band and I knew it. It could have been anything. Those little successes feed bigger dreams and you think you can make it to the top, better, higher. You think you can go on forever. But you're always afraid in the back of your head that the last gig will come, and you won't even know it.

The bottom came fast for him. He was no longer a boy drummer, a half-deaf drummer, a bandleader. He was not quite twenty-five years old. Now he was facing the United States Army and Vietnam. The draft came calling. There was no way he was going to Vietnam. That would turn him into a head case. My father, who was familiar with the mind games the draft board put the boys through, coached him, rehearsed him every step of the way. Amaury was to pretend he was crazy. For three days, the military had him in an office near El Morro, in one of the buildings they had in the fortress grounds in Old San Juan. The army was trying to figure out if this boy with a lame leg and a bad ear could be shipped off to Vietnam. What's Vietnam? Amaury asked the officer across the desk, feigning, ducking. He was playing roulette with his life, scared to death. What's that, Vietnam? Where? You want to send me there? Fine with me, I don't care, I'll go. Sure I've done drugs, LSD, uppers, downers, you name it. Later, recalling the interrogation, he mimicked himself, his eyes rolling, his body jerking, his words slurring. Three days of these questions, his mind was pummeled. They finally let him go, and he left the windowless room and walked into the ocean-smelling air of Old San Juan and went home and slept for a long time. He had escaped.

But to what?

Sally went back to New York. He didn't. He got into the Inter-American University in Puerto Rico, and thought he might become a veterinarian (I liked dogs, I liked animals, was his explanation). Another girl took Sally's place, but Amaury had no drums to play, no band. My father paid for his school and set him up in an oceanfront condo in El Condado, with a balcony where birds nested and left their droppings.

The new girl became Amaury's wife, a nice girl, mother wrote me. Dot was her name, from New Hampshire. They moved there. New Hampshire? Amaury in Concord? I could not imagine it. The marriage lasted four years. Amaury got work loading and unloading trucks, making a living, but the marriage didn't survive. The surprise to me was that it had lasted that long. And afterward he went back to San Juan.

He couldn't sit still. Just as his leg jerked back and forth and his hands pointed and circled when he spoke, his mind couldn't settle down. He found only the dead past in San Juan. His friends were scattered, married, playing in clubs here and there.

He was a man out of places to run to.

For him there was only one road—San Juan to New York.

[illegible]

[illegible] and began [illegible] ideas into [illegible]

[illegible] any way [illegible]

What [illegible]

Still [illegible] Nature [illegible]

[illegible] hard [illegible] animals [illegible] this [illegible]

[illegible] ground.

[illegible] New Mexico [illegible]

[illegible] Chicago [illegible]

[illegible]

[illegible] was found [illegible] in San Juan [illegible]

[illegible]

[illegible]

Chapter Ten

The Visionary

Watching Angeles pluck flowers in Sara's garden, trimming their stems, filling a glass bowl with water and placing the cuttings in it, arranging them with a gentle move of her fingers, I had the strange sensation that I was watching my mother. I thought of a picture I had seen on my mother's piano, in her house in Edgewood, mother and Angeles posing at a fashion show. Angeles was only fifteen then, but there was nothing of the child left in her face. She had her hair pulled up in a French twist. Her eyes were outlined in black, her eyelashes curled, longer than mother's. They looked like sisters.

When my mother looked at Angeles, she saw herself. When she looked at me, she saw my father. I had his small face, small eyes, small mouth, and when I was a child that made me an adorable figurine, my light hair falling in curls around a doll-like face. I was cute, mother liked to say, pinching my nose. Angeles has my eyes, my mouth, mother then would add, and I believed this brought them closer, gave them a secret bond, a deeper connection, and as we grew older, they became like mirror images in my mind. Angeles interpreted mother for me, as if she had absorbed her, deciphering her, explaining her, telling me things mother had told her that I had not known.

Now, so many years later, Angeles was graying, grayer than mother had ever been, and her hair, which once fell down her shoulders, was cut short, cut by herself, and she had gained some weight, soft flesh showing under her T-shirt and around the waist of her jeans.

But she was still beautiful, I thought.

She placed the vase in the middle of the kitchen table, two hands under the base, careful to spill no water. The roses, grown along a wall on the side of the garden in the backyard, their petals a pinkish white, imperfect, with tiny brown spots, were just beginning to open.

It was early, the house was still quiet. Sara, in her nightshirt and shorts, was making coffee. Her hair was uncombed, straggling to her collarbones. It was darker than I remembered, had grown darker with age, and she did nothing to it, let it fall down to her shoulders. She had a thin face, not oval or round, but narrow along the cheeks, coming to a period in the chin. She looked neither like mother nor father, but had the light appearance and the spriglike posture of Tití Angela Luisa when she was younger. It was a look that gave her more height. Her voice, too, was different from ours, higher, like the cheeping of birds. She was so Texan, had been born four years before our parents' divorce, and had moved with mother to Texas when she was just nine years old. She had inhaled Texas, married a high school boyfriend from Abilene, had given birth to two daughters who inherited Rick's all-Texan bones and frame. Sara even spoke the language, with that extended Texas drawl, as if she had heard it in the womb. She was the only one of us who had no trace of a Spanish accent.

Pushing her hair behind her ears, a habit she had, she wiped the immaculate kitchen counter for the third time, pulled off the plastic top on the Maxwell House can, and spooned the coffee into the filter. She moved automatically, the steps memorized, done day after day.

Her face had pillow lines this morning, her cheeks seemed more hollow.

She's exhausted, I thought, all these people disrupting her orderly life. This death!

Why don't you stay a few more days? Angeles said, looking at me. She was already smoking, her index finger tapping the cigarette. Her mouth is a bit crooked, I thought, like mother's. I turned to her. Her glasses reflected the sunlight. I couldn't see her eyes, the severity in them, but I knew the lids were swollen from sleep and from the beer of the night before.

She wasn't asking me, really, she was making a statement.

I picked up my coffee, lit a cigarette I didn't want. This was not going to be easy.

Oh, I don't know. I've got to get back. Have things to do.

Sara piped in: You can stay as long as you want. Olga is staying, but Carmen and Amaury are leaving tomorrow. There's plenty of room. She had only three bedrooms, hers and Rick's, and each of her girls had her own, but they were doubling up to make room for me, Angeles, and Amaury, while Olga and Carmen stayed with their husbands and children in a hotel nearby.

Sara would never say, Why doesn't everyone go so I can have my house back? Even if she wanted to say that.

No, I said. I think I should get back. . . . The landlady thinks I'm coming back tomorrow . . . the plants need watering. . . . I've got to meet an editor. . . .

Angeles shrugged. But I don't see you but every few years, she said. Think about it. . . . It'd give us time to talk.

She put out her cigarette and shuffled back to her room.

Sara said, How do you find her?

Better than the last time I saw her, I said, recalling the time, two years before, when she and mother had come to see me in New York. It was September 1992, and mother had come from Texas alone, just to see me, and Angeles had decided at the last minute to fly in from

Honduras. We were in the living room, mother and I, waiting for her. I jumped up when I heard the doorbell. I opened the door slowly, as if unwrapping a gift, and Angeles was right there—unbelievable!—wearing her thick glasses, her T-shirt and loose pants. We looked at each other for a second or two, unable to move, the years running through my mind, the five years I hadn't seen her.

The September before that, in 1991, I had received one of her rare letters. "So much has happened since the last time we really, really saw each other," she wrote, "something like fifteen years, that it would be like a novel when we catch up again." They were building a house on a hill in Tegucigalpa, she said, "our magnum opus, after Jose, of course."

It did seem like fifteen years had passed since we'd seen each other. The last time I had seen her was at Christmas in Abilene in 1987, when the six of us were last all together. Our paths had hardly crossed since 1979, when she had gone to Nicaragua. While she lived in Managua for eight years, I had moved from Charlotte to Philadelphia, and from Philadelphia I had moved, in 1986, halfway around the world, to Manila. My mother hadn't thought it senseless for Angeles to move to Nicaragua. Mother was thrilled, in fact; Angeles was joining a revolution she understood and supported.

But my decision to quit my job in Philadelphia to go to a country in Southeast Asia did startle her. She knew about Marcos and Cory Aquino and had been intrigued like much of the world with that story, but what would I do there, without a job? I will write, I told her, my usual answer.

A year later, Christmas 1987, for mother, for the holidays, I flew in from Manila and Angeles came from Central America.

That Christmas, the house held all of us, all six of us, and Leon and Leon Jr. And father. He had flown in from San Juan. It was odd to have both my parents in the same room, in the same house, and more awkward to see father and Leon together. Leon had never been a father to me or to Angeles and Amaury. He was a man my mother married, a good man, someone she loved, but he had no connection to us other than the piece of paper she signed when she married him. He had tried to make us his family, but we were too old when he came into mother's life. We were father's children, not his. Even to the younger girls, to Carmen, Sara, and Olga, who grew up in his presence, he was a stand-in, a substitute, not their father. But one gets used to nearly everything in a family, the strained arrangements, the silent compromises, and the fights. By now, father and Leon had their routine down pat, the roles they played, always polite to each another, keeping to light conversation, respectful, even friendly, roles that only men can play.

On Christmas Day, mother was in the kitchen all morning, setting up the platters of food and the table. She had a place for each of us. But Angeles, Amaury, and I took our plates to the living room, and opened one bottle of beer after another. It was then, after gifts were handed out and the family pictures were taken, when Angeles, who had too much to drink, said something, did something, I don't know what, and mother and father, together, came to me. We're worried about Angeles, one of them said, probably mother. She looks so frail, she smokes too much, she drinks too much. I crossed my arms, nodding, I didn't know if I was angry or sad looking at the two of them, mother in her nice dress, father in his suit, helpless.

What do you expect, you did this to her, I said. I blurted it, not knowing what I was saying. But I knew that her drinking, her bouts with depression, her stubborn will to defy convention and do what she wished even when it hurt her, all of that had something to do with them. Their divorce? My father's beatings? Had they not seen from the beginning, from the day she was born, that she was more vulnerable than the rest of us. The light that was her intelligence saw too clearly and too much.

Did you really say that? Sara muttered, her eyes popping. That was unfair.

Yes, it was, but I had been furious at them for years. It just came out.

What did mother say? Sara asked. Cried, no? She always blamed herself.

I said, Mother dissolved in tears and father got up from the sofa, pushing himself up like an old man and left the room, that's what happened. He was leaving the next morning, I remembered. You know, Sara, I never saw him again.

Between that Christmas in 1987 and the time of our meeting in New York in 1992, Angeles had left Nicaragua and returned to Honduras, and I had lived nearly three years in Manila, briefly in Tokyo, and had returned to New York.

The years had left marks. How could they not, but I still had no trouble remembering her as she looked at fifteen, at twenty-five. Now her hair had swaths of gray in it. Her face, the skin of her face, had acquired the softness, the looseness that comes with age, and she felt smaller and bonier, almost fragile, when I threw my arms around her, holding her head to my shoulder.

Hadn't she just flown in from Honduras? Sara asked.

Yes, she was tired, a lengthy trip, a long stop in Miami, immigration, customs, and you know how nervous she gets when she travels. But no sooner was she in the door than she was reaching for a beer and going through her handbag for her cigarettes. Mother embraced her once, twice, those crushing, frenetic embraces she had for us, tears on the border of her eyelashes. It had been a long time for her, too, since she had last seen Angeles.

Rummaging through her bag, Angeles found her cigarettes, her lighter.

You look the same, she said to me, lying. I touched my hair. We laughed. Well, you don't have gray hair, she said, patting her own head. I look ancient, don't I?

I was so riveted by her I had barely noticed Amaury standing at the door, dragging her suitcase. He had picked her up at the airport, but I'd nearly forgotten he was coming and, turning to him, gave him a quick kiss. He looks happy, I thought, always happy when he's with her. Bottles of Corona came out, glasses were set on the table, ashtrays, smoke soon hovered in wisps and then in clouds over the room, and mother sat on the sofa, taking polite sips of her beer, sitting straight up in her dress and her heels, filling the air with her exclamations, her eyes like gaslights, flickering, lightened by the sight of her three oldest children there, together.

But Angeles, Sara interrupted my story, Angeles, how was she really?

Nervous, I said, but joking with Amaury, you know how they are, until we had drunk all the beer, and Amaury left with mother—she was going to stay with him and his wife in their house in Queens. After they left, Angeles and I took a walk down the street, got something to eat—of course she doesn't eat, just picks at her food—and we got a six-pack for her, some wine for me, and some flowers at the corner grocer.

Did she talk then about her years in Nicaragua? Sara asked.

I knew little about her years in Managua, mostly secondhand stories. I had not gone to see her there, not once in eight years, never saw where she lived and how she lived. Angeles had gone to Managua when the Sandinistas took power, in 1979. She became a senior government official, director of housing—finding and building homes for hundreds of thousands of displaced people, dirt-poor families, orphans, widows, bomb victims—in a devastated country, in a country at war, where there was no food in the stores, no toilet paper, no lightbulbs, or streets with names, nothing but disaster . . . and Flor de Caña. Never out of rum, never out of Flor de Caña.

She threw herself at her work with alacrity and a fervor she had shown for little else in her life. As an architect with a mind for mathematics and strategy, she had the qualifications for a job that, in a poor country at war, required more zeal than talent, more patience and political savvy than diplomas on a wall. And for eight years, without a break, she fought without funds, without materials, and, increasingly, without much hope. She worked night and day, hungover and sober, sick to her stomach, she lived off coffee and Flor de Caña and the idea—the idea!—that the people, el pueblo, could rise against history, against centuries of exploitation and colonialism. For a time, she was one of them, down to the uniform, going through hours of training to fire an AK-47—"They kept telling us, 'Annihilate the enemy, annihilate the enemy,' and I kept telling them, 'But I don't want to kill anyone.'" She worked around the politics, the intrigues going on in the junta, the backstabbing and casual betrayals, and the corruption that inevitably came to touch almost everything and everyone in power. She had such will, such an obsession. What she couldn't do in Puerto Rico to help bring about independence—she had talked about this since she was young, since the days when she read the works of the independence leader Albizu Campo, since her miserable days in Pennsylvania and then in Florida, since then, she had dreamed of a free Puerto Rico, not this island that had been, in her view, bought and sold, its people fed false dreams, its identity truncated, a United States passport in one hand and Latin blood in its veins. She couldn't fight for Puerto Rico; she would then fight for Nicaragua. She made it her country.

And it almost broke her. She left when she saw the end coming, when the end came for her. The war and the American embargo had left Nicaragua broke, its coffee and banana fields ravaged, the countryside charred, its people in tatters, whole towns in ruins, Managua a crater for a revolution. In an atmosphere of desperation, rulers turn on one another, and everyone is suspect. Foreigners were no longer welcome, and Angeles, not only a foreigner but an American citizen no less, was no longer of any use. In late 1987, she left Nicaragua. Two years later, the Sandinistas lost the presidential election. By then, there was little left of the revolution.

When she came to New York in 1992, I hadn't seen her in five years, I repeated to Sara, not since that Christmas in Abilene in 1987.

But in 1992, in New York, Angeles wasn't as frail as she had seemed that Christmas; she didn't have that sick pallor. She stayed with me a few days, and we talked and talked, with her spilling ashes all over the sofa bed. One night she was talking about father and mother, and she started crying, and she doesn't cry easily but she was crying that time, and she said there was something inside her she couldn't get out, but she didn't know what it was.

I know, I said, but I didn't know. I put my hand on her shoulder, barely touching her. I didn't want her to shrink back as she usually did, as if her skin hurt. She seemed so young then, at that moment, but just as soon as she started crying she started laughing—Such drama, she said.

We analyze everything to death, she said, and we can twist anything anyway we want. She reached for her beer.

So how was Managua? I asked her. I remember her lifting her shoulders and making a face, her mouth turned down. I could see the ridges around her mouth.

I said to Sara, She never talks about it, not much, about her years in Managua. Instead she asked me about Manila, about Imelda and the article I had just written for a big magazine. So, no, she didn't tell me what happened to her in Managua.

I heard footsteps behind me and I stopped talking.

Were you talking about me? Angeles had come back from her room and was standing at my side in Sara's kitchen, pulling at my hair, joking.

Her hair was fluffy, blow-dried, brushed back, and her face had some powder on it, smoothed, bright. She was wearing a clean top, those loose cotton jerseys she had in every color, each the same, just so she wouldn't have to think about what to wear. Her feet were in sandals, black rubber-soled sandals. She was locking the clasp on her Rolex.

So, she said to me, pulling her top down over her hips, are you staying another day or going tomorrow?

No, I said, grabbing her hand, I know you want me to stay, but I can't. I really need to go.

Well, she said, shaking her head. She had expected that answer.

I always left first, last one to arrive, first to go. My family visits were bracketed, as if staying longer would in some way pull me down into the endless mire of their drama, but I knew there was something else. My life had been separate for so long that I had become an artifact to them, more an idea than a person. I lived a life they didn't really understand, with no husband, no children, in cities they didn't choose. I felt set apart, had set myself apart. For a long time, I believed that seeing me hurry away freed them, freed them from me, just as it freed me from questions not asked, from answers not given, from their embrace.

It was so much more complicated than that, I knew, but I settled for the easy explanation—I was different, I didn't fit in. I didn't want to admit that I left quickly only because I couldn't bear to part from them. Leaving them would bring on an emptiness I couldn't stand to feel—like the solitude I felt when my mother first left me, when I was fourteen, at my new school in Pennsylvania—and so I had become accustomed to quick good-byes, turning my eyes immediately on the road ahead while knowing they were standing together waving, watching me go.

What time do you leave? Angeles asked. Around noon, I said.

Good, she said, late enough for me. We'll all pile into the cars and go like a caravan to see you off, she said teasing. I could see that, the interminable ride to the airport.

Uh, Carmen offered to take me, I said. You know how I hate these things with everybody going. Better just Carmen, no?

I didn't want Angeles to go to the airport—I would not have been able to leave then.

~

Angeles was born exactly two days after my first birthday, in the same month, in the same hospital, our stars set on a similar course from that day. For all our childhood we celebrated our birthdays together, dressed almost identically. We attended the same schools, found the same presents under the Christmas tree, always a roomful of packages, toys and clothes, dolls, tricycles, roller skates, and, when we were a little older, Schwinn bicycles, hers dark blue, mine deep green. We shared a bedroom and playmates. We played the piano side by side, we danced together, staged singing skits for our parents and poetry readings. We brought them perfect report cards.

Mother called us las nenas, even when we were grown-ups. We were always indistinguishable in her love, but from the day of her birth Angeles was a child quite different from me. She chafed at the world, this child, crying to go back, wailing at night as if she had been pulled away, torn, from the only place she would ever find safe.

There was no peace in her.

She grew up so fast. Everything she did seemed ahead of her years (except getting married—for that she waited). At thirteen, she confronted our father with his infidelity; at fifteen, she made a movie; at sixteen, she was expelled from the University of Florida; at seventeen, she fell in love with a middle-aged artist whose radical politics made him irresistible in her eyes, but it was an impossible affair, and, escaping from him, she left Puerto Rico to study architecture in Monterrey, Mexico. She came to see me in New York on her way there, and she brought me a small painting he had done of her that I later lost in one of my many moves from city to city.

I was living in Brooklyn then, after finishing college, in a second-story walk-up across from Prospect Park, where I opened the windows in winter and dangled on the sill, playing Grieg and Rachmaninoff at full volume, the snow hitting my face, and the ambitions I had then rolling in my head like the dense clouds across the sky.

Are you writing? she asked me that night she stayed with me.

I had no job, had floated from one fifty-dollar-a-week job to another, desk jobs, licking envelopes, filing magazine-subscription renewal cards. I had been fired once, twice. I was lying to my mother, never telling her in my letters that I was broke, that I had walked up and down the avenues knocking on the doors of every publishing house I had ever heard of, looking for a job, any job, receptionist, secretary, anything to get me close to books, and that every time I had been turned away at the door. Applications filled and filed away forever. I couldn't even get to the junior assistants. I didn't have the right credentials—I had gone to a college in South Carolina nobody ever heard of. Did you go to Radcliffe, Vassar, Columbia (the names tolling in my head like the bells of a cathedral), the receptionists asked, barely looking up at me, giving me a pen so I could fill out the application forms. And my accent and my unpronounceable name!

Where are you from? they asked.

I didn't tell mother that my phone had been cut off, that I was sleeping on a mattress on the floor, that I spent evenings aimlessly walking in the Village, that once, on Fourteenth Street, a street like any other in the barrios of San Juan, with the blaring mambos and the garish clothes and the tacky shops, and the oily Puerto Rican men shifting their legs in the come-on of the streets, places I would have never walked into in Puerto Rico, I didn't tell her that once, walking by a store, someone yelled out, Paisana! Are you from the island? And I kept walking, shaking my head.

In a few months in New York, I had learned shame, had learned that being a Puerto Rican meant the back kitchen, the bottom, something I had not felt in the Deep South or in Pennsylvania. But in New York City, where I had not expected it, it came at me from all sides. There was the day when my boss at the Long Island University library, a refined academic who adored Adlai Stevenson and John F. Kennedy, told me, while in a tantrum over her withering potted plants, which I was expected to water, that I was like the Puerto Ricans who hung out laundry on their balconies in the projects. I was so stunned, I could only glare at her, but vomited every morning before getting to the job.

Taxi drivers, shop clerks, people at work felt it necessary to remark time and again that I didn't "look" Puerto Rican. What does a Puerto Rican look like? I would invariably ask, but I knew what they meant. It was unmistakable.

How could I tell my mother? How could I tell Angeles? For them, and for myself, I kept silent. I pretended my life was great.

So, are you writing? Angeles repeated that night in the apartment on Prospect Park. She looked around the bare floors, bare walls, two chairs and a foldout table in the kitchen, the bedroom window that let in no light but looked out on a brick building and the garbage dump in the alley.

I was writing some poetry, I said, but I tore it all up.

You're not writing, she guessed, an accusation that went right through me. She was right, I was not writing. I had tried, but I had no idea what to do with it. I couldn't figure out who could help me, where to take it, and I didn't have the courage to show it all. There were thousands of writers in New York, I told myself. I was just another one.

Who's this girl you liked so much? Angeles said. I knew she would ask.

Hmm. I knew her in school. She paints . . . she was in my dorm, a year older than me.

Those are her paintings? Angeles asked, looking at a stack of canvases leaning against a wall.

Yes, I said, glancing over at them, dark, crazed portraits of women.

Not very good, Angeles said casually, an offhand statement I didn't bother to argue with, and she turned back to me.

Where is she? she said.

She's gone, she was here for a month or so, then she went home. She cracked up. It's what happened, her personality began to change until she believed she was three different people, and I didn't know from one day to the next who was living with me. I would spend afternoons at a Brooklyn library reading about multiple personalities, trying to understand, trying to hold on to her. But I couldn't tell Angeles that. Who would believe it?

So that's the problem, she said, that's why you stopped writing. What happened?

Her parents, I said. They came to get her, threatened to write mother. So I wrote mother . . .

Yes, I heard, Angeles said, waiting to hear the rest, her eyes fixed on my face.

I didn't want to talk about it, but Angeles kept staring at me.

She was great, mother was, I said. Wrote me a beautiful letter, said she would come to New York if necessary to stand by me. She believed I had done nothing wrong. Angeles nodded. I'm not surprised, she said, mother understands in her way, she may not like it because she doesn't want you to be unhappy, and she believes, you know, that without a man and children, a woman can't be happy.

Then, rising from the chair, planting her drink on the table like a fist, she said, You have to get out of this place. You're doing nothing here.

But where am I going to go? I thought.

A day later, she left for Monterrey.

I left New York shortly after, in January 1964, to stay with mother in Texas. I was broke and she gave me a home. She was pregnant with Leon Jr. and had no job to keep her mind occupied. My company was the closest she could come to her previous life in Puerto Rico. Days became weeks, and I got a job at Texas A&M University, editing pamphlets on drought and corn and cotton growing, boring work that paid me well enough to buy a car and a stereo. Abuelita died that spring, and mother went to Puerto Rico for the funeral, and when she returned she said, Mita would have liked the funeral. Everyone came, even Muñoz Marín.

Mother gave birth to Leon Jr., and the time came for me to leave. I couldn't stay in Bryan, Texas, one moment longer. I was dying in that town, just as Amaury had been dying, and my mother knew it.

She didn't try to stop me when a newspaper in South Carolina offered me a job. She had Leon Jr. in her arms as I packed my car, the stereo, books, one suitcase, my pillow. I knew she stood on the carport a long time watching me drive away.

All this time, Angeles was planning to leave Monterrey and go to Italy to study. Father was paying her way. He was making up for what he hadn't given me, I thought, the money to go to college. She had a way with him I didn't have. She tolerated him, even liked him, and she flew often to Puerto Rico to see him, staying with him and his wife in the house he had built on his farm. She enjoyed his jokes, repeating them years later, and she liked his family stories—she understood him, and had long ago forgiven him. But with me there was no forgiving.

I could hardly imagine her in Milan. I could barely imagine Milan. Milan, I had to say it aloud. Angeles walking the avenues of Milan, the most beautiful girl in any cafe, drinking vino in little glasses, chain-smoking, the ashes of those skinny, filterless cigarettes piling on a saucer, her body exhaling as if her soul were being expunged, smoke rings twirling, breaking off around her hair. Angeles, bella.

Milan bored her, and she took the train to Paris, and from Paris I got a postcard, a copy of a painting by Klee; on the other side, in black ink, in her handwriting—blocky, with a designer's angles, an architect's cubism, it said, "What can I say? Paris is Paris."

I knew she felt lost, and horribly alone.

Next I heard, through mother, who was our hub, where all the family news was deposited and circulated in every direction to us, that Angeles had returned to Monterrey, had gone back to the Tecnológico, and was living with an architecture student, Guillermo, a nephew of one of the former presidents of Honduras—prominent family, mother would add unnecessarily. This news came in bits and pieces. Details were left out or unknown. But I knew Angeles and Guillermo lived in an old colonial apartment in Monterrey—I had a picture of the two of them, handsome in wire-rimmed dark glasses, as if they had just signed a film contract, her chin turned up, her eyebrow raised, posing in front of door No. 4, a picture I so loved I had it blown up poster size and framed. Their marriage came eventually. She was in no hurry, and the piece of paper meant nothing, a formality.

You can only think about her as if she were broken-up lines of poetry, I told myself.

She was dressed in a white silk suit Guillermo had designed. A thigh-length, embroidered formfitting jacket, flowing sleeves, flowing pants, her hair, long, dark, and straight, fell along the contours of her face, framing it. Her eyes, lined in soft black, had a far depth in them in which you could read anything—sorrow, longing, serenity, only she could know—and in her hands, between her palms, between her bare fingers, she held a long red rose.

She was getting married. My father held her elbow as they walked into the room. He walked an inch or two behind her, very straight, almost trim in a tuxedo he had bought for the occasion, his face set in a stare, neither smiling nor frowning, but commanding, as if he were walking down the nave of a great church. But this was mother's house in Abilene, Texas, not a church, and we were gathered in a small group, family mostly. Even Amaury came, left whatever he was doing (in California? in San Juan?), his mustache plucked, his long hair trimmed, his rock 'n' roll days already fading, his leg yet to be crushed in his car wreck.

Angeles was twenty-six years old, the first of us to marry. Mother, who would have liked a big wedding, organ music, and ushers and flower girls, stood on the other side of Angeles, as it seemed only right, puckered up in her heels, exquisite in her short beige sheath. Was she not always exquisite? She was fifty-two but no one would have guessed that, her face too young to be the face of the mother of the bride. Her hem came just above the knees, revealing legs more shapely—firm calves, trim ankles—than any of ours. But she had worried about it for hours, that a small bandage on her right knee, where she had hit the corner of a chair, spoiled the picture. I watched her to catch her the minute the tears started flowing. But she was smiling, no dabbing at the eyes. She was giving flashbulb smiles, moving her body to best advantage, coquettishly whispering to Guillermo's older brother, the one with the self-satisfied look on his face that said he thought he was lord of the manor. And he was in Guillermo's family.

When Guillermo took her hand in front of the judge, in mother's living room that last day of January 1970, he seemed every inch the prince, rolling waves of thick dark hair barely brushing the back of his gray coat, a face so Roman, so aristocratic (ah, the aristocracy of Latin America, the power that is built into bones and flesh, that survives, even thrives, in the squalor around it). I could only think of portraits in dim galleries, somber portraits by Velázquez. He had that sculpted face, that baronial posture, but he glanced at her like any man, adoring her.

They looked like movie stars.

We got drunk that night, and I remember nothing else about Angeles's wedding.

After their wedding, they got into their new MG and flew up the icy roads from Texas to New York. They lived in Chelsea, and spent hours in museums and galleries, and visiting the offices of the great architects. Philip Johnson! Paul Rudolph! They lasted less than a year in New York. Nine months.

They had been offered work, presumably good jobs, drafting and copying drawings, working in large offices filled with other architects bent over drawing tables, doing nothing that was their own, living in tiny apartments, spending every cent to keep afloat in Manhattan. They wanted none of it, and Angeles hated the cold (she was cold even in June). We can't live like this, she said to him one day in Central Park. He agreed. He wanted to go home, to Honduras, and she didn't care. She just wanted to leave New York; she wanted to leave the United States. They packed up, and on their way to Tegucigalpa, they came to see me in North Carolina. I was working at the newspaper in Charlotte, and had just bought a house, a small Tudor-style cottage that needed some work but had a fireplace, a yard of trees, and a lot of light.

How do you stand it here, she said, it's so quiet. She didn't say it to offend me. She had a way of asking a question that left you no choice but to answer it. She didn't push, she didn't dare. She simply intoned it, gently, like plucking a petal. It wasn't the first thing she said. The first thing she said was, It's so pretty, putting the cushion first, letting me relax before wondering, ever so slightly, how I could stand the quiet, the fact that nothing really happened in Charlotte, North Carolina.

It's a good job, I have this house, I tried to explain, sounding hollow even to myself. But I don't plan to stay here . . . I didn't wonder why she was moving to Tegucigalpa. To me it was clear. She was Latin American, she had to be in Latin America. And she was married to a Honduran.

So you are writing, she said, going directly to the point. You were going to write, she said, you were going to write books.

What happened? I wondered myself. She believed that writing was what I had to do, one reason I was here on earth. I said, The job keeps me busy, there's not much of a market for bad poetry, for books, you know. Can't make money that way, and I like it here, I'm doing fine, have friends.

She gave me a look, that look of hers, like mother's, the way she arched that eyebrow. Why I had stopped writing? Fear, I thought, but I didn't say that. She knew. She didn't pry, she knew when to stop, but I saw the doubt, and worse, her disappointment. She had expected me someday to be on the cover of *Time* magazine. So she said once, in Mexico, when I went to see her in Monterrey. She said it during one of our late-night incantations—lighting candles for each other—when I told her she was the brightest of us all, I had such faith in her, and she threw that back at me—No, it's you, you will do it, not me.

But now I was working in North Carolina of all places (they were not looking for Radcliffe graduates). I was laying out pages and making marks on other people's stories, telling myself that this was important, that it mattered if the headline was 24 points or 36 points.

I had gone as far from writing as I could go, had not lifted the cover of my typewriter at home for a long time, not since the day I had torn up the pages of poetry that I, melodramatic to the end, had titled "The Hours of Glass."

Angeles and Guillermo stayed several days, fixing dinner, insisting on doing everything, rearranging the furniture, hanging up my *New Yorker* posters, patiently putting coat after coat of varnish on bookshelves, redesigning the kitchen. We spent hours on the back porch—Needs new screens, Angeles said. The house was too hot in August. Nothing seemed to bore them, and they would even sit through evenings with my friends, people whom they invariably described as "nice."

One day, when we were alone, just she and I, Angeles said, Louise is very kind, very nice. Louise had just arrived from a trip out of town, and now Angeles had met her. It was a meeting I dreaded. But Louise, who could make anyone feel at home—coffee, wine, coq au vin, a shoulder to cry on—had taken Angeles in, my flesh and blood. Almost me. Angeles saw that.

She's good for you, she said, a question. I said nothing. She's a better artist than that girl in New York, Angeles said. She's serious.

We could hear Louise in the basement, rolling the ink-soaked squeegee over the silk screen she had stretched over wooden frames she had sawed and nailed. She was doing a poster of Virginia Woolf for me. She disappeared into the basement for days, with her inks and tubes of paint, pots and silk screens, her long hair musky from the basement's stale air and turpentine fumes, her face colorless and dry, aging quickly, lines deepening around the palest blue eyes, a face that reminded me of Edna St. Vincent Millay.

Yes, she's good for me, peaceful, you know, I finally said. But I thought, I no longer love her. I said, blurted out, I'm having an affair with a man at the office. He's married, now he wants to leave his wife. I told him, no, can't see breaking up his marriage, he's got kids. Angeles looked stunned. A man? Married? You keep going back and forth, she said, shaking her head. She wasn't making one of her definitive judgments, I knew, but she was puzzled. Like me, puzzled, perplexed, how could I love men and women?

What am I going to do about Louise? I wondered, asking not her but myself. She won't leave no matter what I do.

Be kind to her, Angeles said, turning off the conversation. She didn't indulge me in my affairs; she really didn't want to know the details. Like mother, who didn't bring up the subject though she had finally stopped asking me when was I going to get married.

Their visit was over too quickly, as usual. Just as suddenly as they had arrived in Charlotte, they were off, on the long trip to Honduras. They were driving all the way.

Mountains shield the valley where Tegucigalpa lies, the capital a crumble of old buildings and narrow streets, and new buildings rising oddly over terra-cotta roofs here and there, glass and steel coming out of the earth like huge exclamation points. Airplanes fly in over the mountains and then, suddenly, without the ease of the landing slide, drop down into the valley in one stomach-turning jolt. Tegucigalpa, at the end of the world.

They lived on La Alhambra, on a hillside, a steep climb from the city, in a large apartment with views all around, the city appearing like a beautiful painting below, red-tile roofs, church towers, the mountain range lavender in the distance, the air crisp and clear. From their hillside, you saw only the colors of the city, the shades, the shadows, mansions scattered in other hills, and all around, flowers, ravines, trees. You couldn't see, you couldn't smell, the belly of the town, the dirt encrusted on buildings, the skeletal dogs with oozing wounds, and the hovels, the children, always the children, shy, big-eyed, hands in mouths, and the laundrywomen with their elbows in tubs of water, washing Madame's clothes, and the stink, that stink that doesn't lift in rain or sun.

Poverty in the countries at the end of the world has a specific smell, like burning rubber and burning trash, of sewage floating in rivers, of things left to rot.

Angeles thought of little else, up there on her hill, on her picturesque hill. But she had a good life, anyone would agree. She had finally talked me into taking the long flight from North Carolina and

I was there for my first visit. They were starting their architecture firm, they had clients, acquaintances, relatives, connections. Nothing happens here without connections, she said, rolling her eyes. It's like San Juan, very small. But you know me, she went on, I hate the parties and the showers and the weddings. Guillermo has to do some of that, it's his family, his city, he has to show up.

Look around this town, she went on, there's nothing here, but the rich live very well, they travel, they shop in Miami, they buy condos in Coconut Grove. She poured beer into her glass. It was night, my first night in Tegucigalpa, and the lights of the city below didn't illuminate the city as much as disguise it, dress it up. It looked splendid. At least it's not as bad as Nicaragua or Salvador, she said. It's not Vietnam, I countered.

We had arrived finally in Tegucigalpa, but I had already been in Honduras for days. I had landed in San Pedro Sula, on the Caribbean coast, a town lying prone in the heat, a commercial port town, miserably charmless.

I rushed down the line of passengers to the immigration counter, the clerk taking what seemed an eternity to look at my passport, study my picture, my face, glasses, shaggy long hair. At last, he stamped the page, the first stamp on my new passport. What a wonderful sound, the rubber stamp coming down on the thick leaf, the fading ink, barely readable: Aeropuerto La Mesa, Migración, Honduras, C.A., 1 Agosto 1972.

I was not traveling alone. Olga was with me. She had stayed with me in Charlotte that summer and was now moving to Honduras to live with Angeles. Mother had no choice but to let her go. Once Olga made up her mind about anything, she had to do it. She was seventeen but had the tenacity of two of us, and she wanted to leave Texas, to leave life with mother and Leon, not a bad life but one that was boring. Nothing seemed as exciting to her as life with Angeles in Central America.

Angeles came toward us slowly—she never hurried—carrying her son in her arms, six months old. I held them for a long time, and then she put him in my arms, a gift. Here's Jose, she said. She didn't say José; she said Jose. I looked at him, his eyes, his mouth, trying to see her in him.

Isn't he beautiful? she said, grinning at him, touching his head.

Of course, I said, he is yours.

We were not going directly to Tegucigalpa, a four-hour drive away. We were on the way to Tela, to the ocean. Angeles wanted to give me the grand tour, from the Caribbean to the ruins of Copán, and days later, to Tegucigalpa. The beach house in Tela, down a dirt road in a field of banana plants, rose in a grove of coconut palms, set back from the high, voluptuous sand dunes that bordered the shore. The sun was fierce, an angry sun, pitiless. But we sat in the breezes, on the veranda, drinking lukewarm beer and milk from the coconuts that the house guard cut down for us. Angeles hovered over Jose, as if he would vanish if she didn't keep him close to her. The maids from the village came every day and rinsed the clothes and made arroz con pollo and fried fish caught that day. At night we talked endlessly, the same conversations, circles that we made, and the cockroaches came out, overrunning the kitchen and the shower stall.

In the mornings, I walked down to the dunes and sank in the sand, bareheaded, letting the sun toast my face, looking at the Caribbean, the flat sea reaching out, if you looked north and west, to Puerto Rico. I hadn't seen the Caribbean in years, hadn't been in Puerto Rico since the mid-sixties, the family now dispersed, mother and the girls in Texas, Amaury here and there, in California or New York, or maybe at that minute in San Juan. Only father remained in the island, father and Tití. I didn't want to see father, and I knew that if I went to see Tití, word would reach him, and I would have to see him. So why go back? I hardly ever thought of it, hadn't even visited since mother had moved to Texas. Father came to see me in Charlotte once, brought his wife, in her spandex pants and tight tops, her hair bleached. She hardly said a word but put up with him, cooked all his meals. That was the visit (I could see him so vividly in his brown suit, always wore a suit when he came to the States), when he offered me money, ten thousand dollars, if I got married. I sat in my porch in Charlotte listening to this, hurt, furious, and glowered at him as if he were someone I didn't know at all. I would never again have anything much to say to him.

Sitting on the empty beach in Tela, I was remembering that scene, when Angeles's maid interrupted me. Your sister wants to know if you want a beer. I looked up into the sun and shook the sand off my shorts and went in.

A few days later, after Tela, Guillermo drove us to Copán, high in mountains that border Guatemala, Mayan country. The telegram reached us there, in Santa Rosa de Copán, at a hotel of Spanish vintage, a relic from the nineteenth century. Mother had known where we were staying and sent the telegram. Sara was getting married. We were shocked, but she's only eighteen! She's not finished high school. We knew mother was beside herself, but her telegram put the best face on it—Rick is a good boy, good family, they are so in love. The usual mother things.

That was the excitement of Santa Rosa de Copán. I can't even remember the ruins.

So on our first night in Tegucigalpa, after Tela, after Copán, we had to discuss Sara's decision. Nothing happened in the family without hours of inspection, introspection, and analysis. Sara has always wanted a husband and children, even when she was a little girl, I said. Remember how she was with dolls? Angeles had put on her disapproving look, so familiar, pressed lips and raised eyebrow, but she shook her head and wondered, I can't see it, can't see how they'll last.

A few people, university students mostly, came to Angeles's apartment, usually in the evenings, and they sat on the floor, on cushions, on the Mexican rug, rolling cigarettes, passing them around, talking about the situation. "The situation," in quotes. Somoza came up, but I didn't catch on. I didn't know then that Angeles's apartment was a safe house. She was secretly keeping up a collaboration with anti-Somoza forces in Nicaragua, a collaboration that lasted for seven years, until the Sandinistas took over and she moved to Managua.

She was, in those evenings, the quietest of all. Drinking and joking and humming to the Beatles, and swaying to the music (she danced in her sleep) but she said little, moving forward to listen closely to something that pricked her interest, then moving back, offering no comment, when she had heard it.

When I was with her, that August 1972, she seemed indestructible, I thought, watching her with her friends, with Guillermo, seeing the circles that formed around her, as if she were the center of gravity. She had such command in her voice, in her face. And she was radiant, holding Jose in her arms, lifting him above her head. Her attention, if it had ever been fixed on Guillermo, had now shifted. Now it was on Jose.

One day she said to me, I told Guillermo when Jose was being born and the doctors were so worried that I wouldn't make it, that if anything happened to me, he had to give the baby to you.

Maybe she didn't tell me that right there, in Tegucigalpa, maybe it was later, another time, another moment, but when she said that, she was giving me everything she could give me.

Seven years later, in August 1979, a month after the fall of Somoza, when the Sandinistas came to power, hailed as heroes around the world, received with a standing ovation at the United

Nations and celebrated in the most exclusive salons of New York City, adulated like rock stars in a frenzy not unlike that for Castro in 1959 (Daniel Ortega's fatigues, aviator glasses, and guerrilla mustache treated as sex symbols), Angeles was arriving in Managua—Angeles, Guillermo, and Jose.

Managua lay flat, flattened, impossibly hot, in ruins on top of ruins, the debris of war, broken buildings, bombed-out homes, streets that ran out of pavement. Nearly destroyed by the earthquake of 1972, Managua was now a vast hellhole, too dry or too wet, its life sucked by dictatorship and bullets, and what was left, well, nature took care of that.

Angeles fell in love with it—the way one falls in love with a place, not for its beauty but for its very ugliness, its roughness, its desperation. And there was hope then—that idea—that this country, this cave within the greater cave of Central America, corroded by corruption and pain and futility, that such a country could be saved, resurrected (had it ever truly lived?), its greatness or its insignificance, either, lying just below the surface.

She would never talk like this. But she did think like this.

They found a small house near a park, a school for Jose (he was seven years old), and Angeles went to work. She had laid the ground for this work in Honduras during all the years of collaboration; she was an architect, she was an organizer, she was zealous, and in her way, in her defiant way, she was a masterful politician. Now she was in charge of housing for tens of thousands. She had a title, a private office, a car; Jose was enrolled in the French lycée; Guillermo worked in the agency for planning, supervising construction. She was la Señora Directora. She tried to build and rebuild homes for the homeless and looked for money where there was none. At times, she had to leave the country on official duties, as a delegate to Vienna, to the United Nations, to Cuba, one of the representatives of the revolutionary government of

Nicaragua, traveling without passport, neither a Nicaraguan nor an American—an interloper, a foreigner, a woman about whom little was really known.

By the early 1980s, she was entrenched, something of a figure, I suppose. People crowded in her small house, cars parked all around it, queues of people waiting for her at her office. There was no end to the paperwork, to the demands, to the expectations she had for herself, but try to imagine rebuilding a whole country, she told me, in the middle of a trade and economic embargo, without international aid, without resources, and, at the same time, fighting a civil war.

She had to borrow clothes to wear in Vienna, she remembered laughing. You should have seen that hotel, she said years later. Here we were, a few of us from one of the poorest countries in the world, just as bad off, worse off, than Cuba . . . here we were in Vienna, like we were somebody, in this imperial hotel, incredible. My room was twice the size of my house in Managua. In Managua, I couldn't find a lightbulb for my kitchen, there was no food in the stores, no flour, no rice, no beans, no milk, but here we were in Vienna, dining on fancy tablecloths, eating off gilded plates, drinking Austrian wine, wasting money we didn't have. . . . That's what happens when you become a government.

She's doing everything, mother wrote me after she saw Angeles in Managua in July 1984, the anniversary of the revolution. Mother flew down there from Texas just for that, to see Angeles standing with the comandantes at the parade. She works night and day, mother said, she's a little too thin, doesn't eat enough, but she's happy—Jose is so smart, a brilliant boy, he takes care of her, makes sure she eats. He is the only one she listens to. And Managua, you should see it, mother exclaimed (I was reading this but I could hear her voice, so excited, in boldface, in italics). Managua es una maravilla!

What about the war, the contras? I wrote back. Those things mother didn't mention, the war was far off, in the mountains.

But I knew, we all knew. The war was destroying the countryside, displacing more and more people, and Managua was being strangled. I was living then in Philadelphia, working at *The Inquirer,* editing foreign news and sending reporters off to Managua, giving them my sister's name, their conduit to Ortega, I hoped, but one by one they would return to Philadelphia with a similar story. Your sister was very nice, she gave me some names, people to talk to, and she talked about the work she was doing, but she really said nothing about the war, or the problems, the corruption and the fights among them in the junta.

That was Angeles, I thought, she wasn't about to play up to the press, she wasn't going to give a thing away.

She told me years later, I used to go to work so hungover the floor was weaving. There was no end to the work, day and night, late into the night, all those people waiting for me, waiting for some miracle, and I knew I could do nothing. Of course I drank too much and I lost weight and I got sick.

I could've gone to Managua. She asked me, not in letters because she never wrote, she never had the time to sit down and put her life down on paper, and she really didn't want to do so. She had sent me books when she was in Mexico (a book of poems by César Vallejo, I remember, "Yo nací un dia que Dios estaba enfermo" / I was born on a day when God was sick . . .). And she had sent me books from Honduras, but none from Nicaragua. Mail was a problem; the outside world was a problem. She did leave Managua occasionally, went to Texas once a year or once every two years, to visit mother, and she stayed a week, ten days, hardly leaving mother's house, talking, drinking, talking. She would call me, Why don't you come to Managua, why? I found an excuse—work, money, the long flight. Excuses, it's all they were.

Managua was her dream. It wasn't mine. I was afraid that her dream was better, grander, and that the life I had chosen was smaller, mundane and petty, and I felt small next to her. I didn't want to go see her because I didn't know how to explain myself, the easiness of my life in the face of hers.

One time she called, Christmas 1985, a horrible winter in Philadelphia. I had just broken off a long relationship, another one that had died long before it actually ended. We do carry dead loves around with us, the comfort of the familiar, the habits of mornings and nights, the routine, and then we feign surprise, shock, when we notice the carcass, the bones. I had put my house in the suburbs up for sale and moved downtown to a row house on a street of boarded-up buildings and junkies on the corner. I was leaving the nice furniture, the big house, the half acre of yard. One of those nights in the row house, when I was by myself, watching the news from Manila—Manila had eclipsed Managua, and now the attention of the world media, the beam, had turned to Marcos, on his last days, and I was editing those stories, living the story from such a vast distance, watching it every night, memorizing the names, the places, so familiar it all seemed to me, like Latin America.

At the newspaper, we were preparing to send reporters to the Philippines, and the list of reporters competing to go was long—everyone wanted the latest hot spot, the assignment that transforms an obscure city hall reporter laboring day after day under fluorescent lights into a celebrated foreign correspondent.

The phone rang that night. Angeles. Her voice a jolt, always a jolt, and I sat up straight on the edge of my chair. I lit a cigarette, I took a sip of wine. Suddenly, I was alive, excited. It seemed so close, as if she were there, and her voice, very soft, with a touch of laughter, would take me to other parts of my life, to childhood and the island, to all those dreams we had once had.

She was recovering from a fall, she said, had twisted her arm, nothing major.

What fall? I said, startled.

We were at a party, up on a terrace, but there was no railing. I leaned back and fell to the ground. . . .

Oh, God, I muttered.

Guillermo was leaving Nicaragua, she said, going back to Tegucigalpa to get his architecture business going. He couldn't stand it anymore. So he was leaving.

I'll be fine, she said, I have Jose, that's all I need.

But I knew she was falling apart. Olga had been there, had seen her. She's down to eighty-five pounds, Olga said, she works late every day and then goes off to the bar. Sometimes she doesn't know when to stop. You know how she gets—she gets angry, she throws words around, she insults Guillermo (She's like father, I thought, when he drank). The only one she never hurts is Jose. Jose never.

Olga exaggerates, Angeles said. You know she gets very upset with me when she sees me drink. I'm perfectly fine . . . maybe I'm a little too thin.

So why don't you come to Managua? she prodded, never giving up.

That would've been the moment, the right moment to be with her.

But I was going somewhere else. I was going to Manila.

Two years later, in 1987, while I was in Manila, she left Nicaragua. For a time she stayed in Puerto Rico, sorting out her life, her marriage, her future, though by now she hardly believed in the future. She would've stayed in San Juan, perhaps, but she couldn't take Jose away from Guillermo, and she couldn't quite leave a marriage of nearly twenty years.

My life ended in Nicaragua, she once said to me, my world ended there.

She went back to Tegucigalpa and to Guillermo, and they lived in a modest apartment building for a while and built their business—Guillermo built it, she would say—starting with nothing, two thousand lempiras, which is to say, nothing. Slowly, they recovered, and then began to build their "magnum opus," a house at the very top of their old hill on Calle la Alhambra. She turned the dry, rocky grounds into a garden and from that hard soil she brought forth jacarandas and bougainvillea, lime and avocado trees, guavas and mangoes, a flamboyán tree from seeds she had gathered in Puerto Rico, and dozens of flowers only she could name. They call their hill La Giraldilla.

Chapter Eleven

A Raw Passion

The evening was closing in, the sun had finally slipped beyond the farthest tree you could see out of Sara's kitchen window. Sara suggested we all go out to dinner; it was our last night together. She was looking at the leftovers, bowls and plastic bags, plates wrapped in foil—tuna salad, egg salad, a few slices of country ham, grilled chicken, macaroni and cheese, garlic mashed potatoes. She opened each bag, lifted each lid, everything looked stale, with that gelled surface that food gets in the refrigerator. We had been in and out of the kitchen all afternoon, making sandwiches, emptying the last carton of orange juice, drinking the last six-pack of beer, picking up dirty dishes and scraps of conversation.

After four days together, we were pacing in and out of rooms, leafing through the same magazines, recycling the same stories. There was just so much we could say to one another. By now I had heard about mother's last years, her years in Edgewood. She had a good life, Sara said, painting those last years in watercolors. She had seen mother often, more frequently than the rest of us had seen her. They lived only some fifty miles apart, a straight shoot from Edgewood to Dallas. Mother liked knowing everyone in Edgewood and was happy that everyone knew her, even if it was a town that didn't rate a mention in maps, a town of churches and men who tilted their heads slightly when greeting the ladies, a folksy town. Leon and

Maria, that's how they were known. Leon had grown up in Edgewood, and sixty years later people still remembered him; that's how long people stayed in Edgewood. Mother was making plans for the beautification committee and, in her way, she took up gardening (she hosed the yard, I imagined, I could hardly see her digging into the ground). That last year, the one that turned out to be her last, 1994, she spent her afternoons organizing her scrapbooks and trying to trace her family tree back to Spain. She kept busy.

That was one picture. I had another one, the other side, the inverted mirror. In those last six months, even in her letters, where she usually tried to put a gloss on things, I noticed a weariness. She seemed resigned, as if she had reached the last stop. How did she end up there? Her answer, when I asked, was always the same. Leon wanted to be there, she wanted to be with Leon. It was that simple. Sometimes, when she and Angeles were alone, when Angeles went to see her on her annual visits and they gossiped and reminisced like old friends, she talked about Puerto Rico, her trips there—how she was when she went back. She thought everyone would remember her, but how could they? She'd been gone so long, and then she was so hurt. She realized it was too late for her to return there, that she'd been left behind.

Let's go out to dinner, Sara repeated. I had been lost in thought—of mother, the scrapbooks, the prayer pamphlet she had by her bedside. (How odd, I thought, when I saw it, I had no idea mother had become religious.) I had been thinking about her letters to me, the most recent ones pleading with me to come see her—We are not so backward here, she had said sadly, almost apologizing. She had to have known, she was getting ready.

Looking at Sara, I said, That's a good idea. Let's go to dinner. Where?

It took an hour to round up everybody. We went back to the Mexican place, ordered up margaritas and Corona for Angeles. Platters of tacos and enchiladas, bowls of guacamole, and we toasted ourselves, our last evening together. The jukebox drowned out our conversation, though we were hardly conversing, we were exclaiming, joking, moving our shoulders to the Tejana songs. After a while, Amaury and Angeles started to sing, clapping their hands on the table, jerking their heads this way and that to the beat of the music. I ran my tongue around the rim of my glass, tasting the salt, instantly remembering the margaritas in Manila, but it didn't take much for me to realize that that's not where I was. I was in Dallas, with my sisters and brother, on the third night after our mother's burial.

We never knew how to end a night, Angeles and I. Somehow we didn't know how or didn't want to put a period to it. A simple good night didn't come easily to us when we were together. There was always one last drink, cognac, brandy, Courvoisier, Grand Marnier. But that night, our last together, even Carmen, Olga, and Sara stayed up, as if this, staying together, would keep mother alive.

When we got back to Sara's house, I asked her, Where's mother's last scrapbook? She went to her bookshelves and brought it to the sofa. We crunched up together around the coffee table. Some of the black stickers at the corners of the pictures had fallen off. We turned each page very slowly, remarking at each picture. There you are. How old were you then? What an awful picture, let me tear it up. Children, we were children even that night.

The pictures were arranged chronologically, dated. The more recent photos were in the back, pictures of me I didn't even know existed and others I had sent her from Manila, from Philadelphia, from New York.

I held up one page, stopped cold—a large black-and-white picture of me in Manila. I studied it for a long time.

Who's that with you? Carmen said.

A friend. We were at the Cowrie Grill at the Manila Hotel. She was wearing a scarf around her neck, her pen in her shirt pocket. I was dark brown, tanned, my arms were very thin. I was smoking, we were obviously talking, not aware of the camera. I had a glass of white wine, she had red. It was 1987.

I want that picture, I said, carefully lifting it off the stickers. I don't have a copy of it.

Who is she? Carmen asked.

Elizabeth.

Carmen looked at me, a question on her face, as if she had found the last piece of a puzzle but was still not quite sure what it was.

Angeles interrupted before I could answer.

Mother liked her a lot, when she met her in New York two years ago. It's too bad, she said, looking at me, touching my shoulder.

Oh! Carmen said, looking at the picture more closely. That's Elizabeth. I'm always the last to know, Carmen complained. It was her usual complaint that because she lived in Sweetwater, a four-hour drive west of Dallas, out of the way of the family circuit, and because she lived such a tidy, conservative life, she was often left out of family business. This time, she was right.

What happened with Elizabeth? she asked again.

She's gone, I said. The last thing I wanted was to talk about that. Happened months ago, I said casually, as if it had been the most ordinary thing in the world. We had come to that point . . . took a long time, but we had drifted apart, you know how it is.

I smiled, reassuring them and myself, took the picture, and put it aside on the table.

Let's see what else is here, I said, turning to the next page.

Angeles and Amaury didn't go to bed that night, or maybe they did after I had finally pulled myself away. My flight was leaving the next morning. Carmen was taking me to the airport. I could count on her to get me there on time.

Seven o'clock in the morning and I was already showered, dressed, packed, and ready to go. I went to the kitchen to make coffee, thinking I was the first one up, but Sara was already there, the coffeemaker percolating.

She loved you so much, mother did, Sara said suddenly. She didn't talk about your life, I mean she talked about your work, your writing, but didn't go on about your relationships—your friendships, she called them. She was happy if you were happy, like she was with all of us.

What did she say? I insisted.

She didn't understand, not really, Sara said. Wished you'd get married, have children, and she wished you had been closer to her, that you hadn't gone so far from her. It made her very sad. But she was so proud of you.

I could say nothing. I thought, I never talked to mother about it, about my love for women, and she never asked me. That silence ran deep, and it was perhaps more than any other thing what kept me away—I was afraid she would ask, and at the same time, I resented that she didn't want to know, that a whole part of my life was unacknowledged and not talked about with the ease she talked about my sisters' husbands and children. The tacit understanding was not enough; the silence set me apart from the others.

Sara was looking away from me. She was thinking about mother, about all the Septembers she would drive to Edgewood to leave red carnations at my mother's graveside. She was about to cry.

Here, don't, I said, rushing to her.

I could hear the shower, doors closing and opening, Amaury folding the sofa bed, Angeles in her slippers, dragging behind me.

These hours were so long, waiting for the ride to the airport. I dreaded going, I dreaded the good-byes, the tears, the parting of flesh.

Later that morning they gathered on the sidewalk by the carport. It was time for me to go. One by one, they reached out, Amaury, Sara, and Olga. Carmen, who still had to take me to the airport, was already in tears, packing her car. We were all leaving pieces of ourselves, I thought, more alone now that mother, our center, was no longer there to hold us together, or perhaps closer than we had ever been when she was alive.

I turned to Angeles, who was standing back, waiting. I wanted to take her with me. I turned to her and held her desperately, touched her hair, her face. Then, I let go and got into the car.

~

In the tropics, in late summer, the wet season, there are no gray colors and no pale colors and murmur of voices. The heat makes the colors brighter, the voices louder. The smells explode in the air. There is a way the sky looks after a rain shower, the way a rainbow suddenly appears while you sit on a porch and watch the rain dry up in a matter of minutes. The sky turns a blue so pure you think you can see through it.

The bamboo raft swayed gently with the waves, held in place by ropes the beach boys had tied to poles in the water. It had rained earlier that morning but now the sky was cloudless, the sunlight spread out, the sun climbing directly above my head. The beach was crowded, as it was on weekends, the wood boats swaying with the weight of families, children jumping off the boats' rails into the sea, girls dancing to the music from boom boxes playing at top volume. My legs dangled in the water, water so clear I could see to the bottom. Elizabeth dived in and out, splashing water all over me. I rarely went swimming. I only wanted to smell the sea, to feel it near me, to feel it like air.

In the distance, beyond the shore, the mountains seemed painted, a sweeping, dark green backdrop. Small clouds scuttled over their peaks. Whitish smoke rose in wisps from hillside huts and the scent of burning wood wafted back to the sea, even from that far.

It was my birthday, and I was floating on a raft in the South China Sea.

Elizabeth came out of the water and leaned on her elbows on the edge of the raft. Our food had arrived. The beach boys had waded in the water and brought it in boxes they carried on their heads—fried fish, bones and all, and lumpy white rice. We spread the food on a dry palm leaf and ate it with our fingers, drinking lukewarm San Miguel beer.

Nothing I had eaten since I had left Puerto Rico tasted like that fish, crispy and salty. No sea had looked like that sea. No sun had burned quite like that.

I had arrived in the Philippines that week, on an early spring day. Marcos had already fallen and fled to Hawaii. Corazon Aquino was president, and the yellow banners of her campaign, what came to symbolize the end of the dictatorship, still flew off telephone polls and the roofs of shanties. I had expected the heat of the tropics, but this heat had a meanness to it, like a swamp. Waiting for a taxi at the airport, jostled by vendors and girls throwing sampanguita garlands around my neck, I felt no sweet breezes off the bay, only a suffocating, damp heat and the bitter smell of too many bodies packed too tightly in too little a space. The cab had air-conditioning, the driver said, but it was useless. All I got in the backseat were puffs of lukewarm air. I rolled down the window. I wanted to breathe real air, even dirty air, and smell the city.

The road that ran from the airport to downtown Manila followed the contours of the bay. It was lined with dry palm trees, squatter camps, condos, discos, fleabag motels, cocktail lounges, fish markets, churches, massage parlors, and food stands—all of Manila seemed jammed along one road. At one time, Roxas Boulevard had been a prime address for the rich, with mansions facing the harbor. Roxas was hardly grand now, but there was still a touch of that lost beauty in the sweep of the road, in the panorama of the bay, even in the frayed royal palm trees along the way.

Elizabeth was at the Manila Hotel waiting for me. When she left Philadelphia for her job in Asia, I had told her I would see her there, in Manila. Two months later I arrived on holiday. I had wanted to see Manila for myself after all those months that winter, in January, February, and March 1986, when Manila was all I thought about, the stories I edited, the images on television, the fall of Marcos, and Elizabeth's voice on the phone. I booked a flight, Philadelphia to Los Angeles to Manila, thirty hours, ten thousand miles, thirteen time zones, because I simply had to be there, because I had to be with her.

As the taxi approached the Manila Hotel, my blood was racing. First, I saw the tower wing of the hotel, a white rectangle that looked like all the Holiday Inns in the world. But as we got closer, driving past the American embassy, I saw the hotel of the postcards, the original facade. It was set back near Rizal Park, with a curving driveway and an overhang to keep rain off the guests.

Bellboys and doormen in white uniforms and white pillbox hats rushed to greet me, saying my name. I was startled; how could they know? The lobby was enormous, furnished with dark burgundy sofas and armchairs under a carved-wood ceiling hung with palatial chandeliers.

It was a hotel for grand entrances and passionate intrigues, drunken reveries and moonlit dinners by the water. I could see myself growing old in those rooms, having coffee by the pool every morning, an eccentric character in a straw hat and sunglasses, wandering absentmindedly through the garden.

She was not in the lobby. A manager greeted me and took me up to my room. It was two floors above hers, but I knew she was in her room, waiting.

A vase with freshly cut flowers and a bowl of fruit with a note from the hotel management were arranged on my room's coffee table. A bottle of wine rested in a bucket of ice. On the bed, wrapped in plain brown paper, was a thick book, a journal. On the front, she had written me a note, welcoming me to the Philippines. "Mabuhay! You will soon fill all these pages," she wrote. Along with the journal, she had left me a Philippine flag and a T-shirt. I rubbed my fingers on the journal, feeling the leather covers, and tried on the T-shirt. I looked around the room, the jolt of arrival, the idea that she was just an elevator ride away, making my hands shake. You travel thirty hours and suddenly you're sitting in a hotel room in a place you could only imagine just the day before, a place so far from everything you know and yet strangely familiar.

I yanked open the drapes and unlocked the sliding glass door to the balcony overlooking the swimming pool and the bay. A blast of sunlight hit my face. Freighters in the harbor lay motionless in the lull of the afternoon. A few children played in the pool. I fell in love with Manila right there, just as I had fallen in love with New York at first sight when I was fourteen years old.

Leaving the sun of the balcony, I unpacked slowly, hung every shirt, every pair of pants, and washed my face. I walked down the corridor to the elevators. Moments later I was on her floor. I knocked on her door. Time stood still, and then I heard the doorknob, the crack of the lock. She was standing before me.

Without touching her, I walked in and stood by a sofa, paralyzed, looking at her.

You look great, she said.

I thought, I've been flying for almost two days, I cannot possibly look great. She was blonder than I remembered, and thinner, her hair sun-bleached, her light skin deeply tanned. She'd been staying at the hotel for more than a month, had had no time to find an apartment. But her room had her life in Manila all over it. Flags and maps hung on the walls, and telephone messages, telegrams, and faxes were pinned to a bulletin board. She looked totally at home.

She walked to the bar and offered me a beer, and when she brought the bottle to me, she put a hand on my shoulder, a second only, and sat on the sofa across from me, her legs stretching down the length of the sofa, making it seem casual, this meeting. But we were both scared, as if meeting for the first time after an endless wait. No, as if meeting new parts of ourselves. She asked about my flight, work, acquaintances, and I asked about her latest story, the wreck of her Jeep near Davao in Zamboanga province, and all the while my eyes roamed around her room. I couldn't quite fix my eyes on her. I got up and examined up close the things on her bulletin board, opening another beer, sitting down again. Funny, I thought, the way this setting makes her seem different, looser, as if, in this foreign country, she had found some freedom. Happens sometimes when you travel, gives you a sense of being new, unburdened by familiarity, even your own familiarity with yourself. You can be anybody, for a time.

It fits you, I said, this place, this room, all of this.

She smiled, dimples deepening around her mouth. Slants of sunlight fell on the sofa, on her hair, making it brighter. She had cut it, and it fell, thick and shaggy, just below her ears. She opened a pack of cigarettes and tapped it on the table and lit a match with a nail of a finger, a habit of hers.

Yes, she said, taking a long drag, I would have to say, you were right.

I had told her, months earlier when she got the assignment to cover Asia and she didn't know if she could change her life so radically, I had told her then, Do it or you'll regret it all your life. I hardly knew her then, but that much I knew.

You know, she said, people know you're here. Reporters, photographers, freelancers—people I had met at one newspaper or another. The hotel was occupied by journalists. Yes, I nodded, I know, I have messages in my room.

Do you want to go down to the lobby to see anybody? she asked, making it clear without saying it that she would not be going with me. She had an aversion to groups, and she defined more than two people as a group. But more than that, she wanted me to navigate alone. She didn't want to stir up the gossip that she knew would go around about my presence in Manila.

No, I said, I don't want to call anybody or see anybody until tomorrow.

That evening we went to a cafe in Ermita, the nightclub district nearby. We sat at a wobbly table on the sidewalk, under a Cinzano umbrella, drank wine, and picked at gambas al ajillo. Children played hopscotch and jumped rope on Remedios Circle across the street, and vendors meandered around the tables, selling cellophane-wrapped, long-stemmed red roses for a dollar a bunch. The table candles flickered, and the night was bright with the headlights of passing taxis and the neon signs of other restaurants and clubs around the circle.

Es un carnaval, Elizabeth said, throwing her head back, laughing, trying out her Spanish. She had learned it in Europe, the year she spent in Spain, and she spoke it like a Madrileña, with the sybillant *s*'s and *z*'s, something I never did.

Reminds me of home, I said, when I was growing up. San Juan

was like this, loud music, noise, lights, people everywhere. I couldn't take my eyes off the children playing hopscotch, just as I had played when I was young. The buildings around the circle seemed like replicas of 1930s buildings in San Juan, especially a two-story house with rounded corners and casement windows that resembled the apartment building across Pérez Galdós where my childhood friend Julia lived.

I felt instantly at home, as if I had known this place all my life.

Late into the evening, half drunk on wine and carefree as young girls, we hopped on a street taxi, the sort where the windows don't work and the seats have springs breaking through the worn upholstery, and rode back to the hotel, the breeze in our faces, and lights flashing by. I went up to her room for one last drink, and she put Brahms on her tape deck, and we saw the night pass and the sun come up.

I spent mornings by the pool, my skin getting darker, my face losing the winter pallor (I imagined I was getting younger); I sipped calamansi juice and read for hours under the canopy of the banyan trees, making up stories in my head, scribbling in my notebook. On weekdays, the hotel seemed empty. Tourism was down and the press was out working. But by late afternoon, just around the time when the pianist started playing in the Lobby Lounge, the tables began to fill with reporters and photographers filing back from a day out in the muck of Manila. We jammed tables together, ordered up beer and margaritas, and soon the tables piled up with bottles, bowls of peanuts, overflowing ashtrays. Every rumor was passed around and traded, rumor for rumor—gossip was the lifeblood of Manila—and before you knew it, a rumor of a coup or of a love affair was stated as fact. Diplomats and visiting congressmen dropped by, and freelancers came in flocks, looking for strings with the major newspapers and the networks, while shady types, treasure hunters, and old war veterans lazed around in the Tap Room and in the Lobby Lounge, drinking Johnnie Walker in those wood-paneled rooms fragrant with orchids.

I'm coming back, I said to her one day. Want to live here.

She looked shocked. You can't, she said, you can't quit your job. She wanted me there, and she didn't want me there. Mostly, I knew, she was afraid, afraid of the gossip, afraid of a relationship that she knew would completely change her life, devastate her family, and perhaps destroy her. Passion was something she dreaded. She knew the force it had, and the dangers that came with it, and the pain. It was the story of her life, as it had been the story of mine. But hers had been tampered, tamped down, buried, while mine came in bursts, in explosions, taking me with it.

I refused to listen to her. I'm coming back; I'll get a leave of absence, I said finally.

I returned to Philadelphia, and on my first day back, I resigned. You have a bright future here, an editor said, why are you doing this? People are going to think you're wacko. Well, maybe they will, I said, but I've got to do it. Okay, he said, so take a year and go and then come back.

Are you kidding? my friends at the paper were saying. I laughed, No, I'm not. I really am leaving.

But one night Tim, who was my closest friend, who had seen me through one breakup and the misery afterward, who owned the place that had become my refuge when I put my house in the suburbs up for sale, he said to me, You are crazy. Coming from Tim, I had to listen. We had sat up too many nights in his row house, those nights when his girlfriends weren't calling him and he and I were alone, drinking Maker's Mark and smoking cigarettes until the blood vessels in his eyes were like spidery roads. There was nothing about me he didn't know or couldn't guess.

It's Liz, isn't it? he said.

Liz? It's Elizabeth. She hates being called "Liz," I said.

All right, he said, sighing, Elizabeth, it's Elizabeth.

No, I said, well, not entirely, it's writing. I was spinning this story. I've got to write and I can't do it here, can't do it with this job. I've got to get away from here. I've never felt about any place like I feel about Manila, I went on. I knew that nothing I said made sense to him, or to anyone else. Lying, I said, I don't really know what it is.

Tim had been to Manila, covering the fall of Marcos. He had smelled the tear gas and the garbage in Manila Bay. He had fallen in love with it, too. It was all he could talk about—the stabbing of a protester in front of his eyes, the blood that splattered his black boots, the first killing he had ever witnessed; and there was Marcos on his last day, singing with Imelda on a balcony at Malacañang; and the hundreds of thousands of people who massed in Rizal Park to celebrate people power, a spectacle televised around the world, but Tim was there himself, in the middle of it, with his backpack and his notebook. And he had to be thinking of the nights at the Manila Hotel, the dinners with a girlfriend there, and the street kids who surrounded him, pulling at his shirttails, following him, an American cowboy in black boots and white jeans.

He had wanted to stay, but once Cory Aquino was installed as president, once the story dropped off, the paper called him back.

You can't do this, he said again. He was pacing the living room, going to and from the kitchen, shaking ice in his glass, putting an old Coltrane album on his turntable, emptying ashtrays, stirring a gumbo stew he was making. You're ruining your career, he said, handing me a glass of wine. I thought of the evenings at my typewriter, the cold pizza from the corner diner, and the evenings at restaurants with friends, the endless chatter about real estate, the drab routine at the office.

Elizabeth's letters and her phone calls came day after day, her voice the only voice in my head. I waited for her letters, read and reread them, and bundled them in rubber bands. The weeks passed very slowly. I went to work in the mornings, my mind halfway around the world, and I came home every evening, picking up take-out on the way, hurrying to get to the mail, to sit in Tim's old armchair by the phone. There was no other life left for me in Philadelphia.

After I sold my house and my car and gave away stacks of books, my bookshelves, the dresser, and the bed, the posters and the sofa, I left for Manila. It was August 1986. The rainy season had begun.

This time, on the day of my arrival, Elizabeth was waiting for me at the airport, not in a hotel room. She was scanning the crowd. But I saw her first. She caught my eye, gave me a palms-up wave, and moved toward me without any apparent rush. But she had a smile of wonder and a slight swing to her stride, a tilt of her head, neither looking directly at me nor away but focused all the same. She reached toward me and stroked my hair, light and casual, as if anything could be casual about this, and picking up a piece of luggage, she led the way out of the terminal.

Watching her walk ahead of me—she always moved so much faster—I studied her back, her neck, her hair, streaks of white in it. She was wearing what she always wore, jeans, long sleeves rolled up to the elbows, and running shoes. In the taxi, I sat far from her, looking out the window, not so much at Manila because Manila was no longer new to me, but to avoid her eyes, to find a proper distance, to avoid being drawn in too quickly. But then, for one second, I glanced over at her, the fine cheekbones, the wide mouth, the eyes that in sunlight turned a pearl-gray blue, the arc of her long neck, her hair brushing the top of her upturned collar. I was startled—she was so distinct, so oddly beautiful—that she was there. I had not invented this.

We had a year, or perhaps only weeks, months, maybe an eternity. We did not know how much time we had because nothing about us had come arranged, nothing had been easy, nothing had been like anything else in our lives.

The maids washed the laundry out back, on the roof over the garage of our apartment building, hunched over tin tubs, sinking their arms up to their elbows in soapy water, pounding the clothes on washboards. They were girls from the provinces, brought to the city by uncles and brothers, and passed around, offered up for a few dollars a week.

The building's manager, a rotund little man named Alex who lived in a room by the garage, procured the maids—nieces, cousins, he called them—and made the arrangements with the tenants. The building was a landmark where, according to Alex, the Japanese had fought room to room with American troops, where MacArthur had lived (MacArthur had lived everywhere), where diplomats had once occupied its stately rooms. But the building had fallen on hard times, like just about everything in Manila.

Alex came to our apartment periodically, checking up on us, I supposed. He never sat down. He stood by the doorway, rubbing his fleshy fingers on the stucco walls of the apartment, telling this story about the Japanese and MacArthur, saying these walls—his palm planted on the wall—had been covered in blood. Now the walls were light gray, like the facade of the building, like all white buildings in Manila, which turned dirty gray in a season.

We had an apartment on the second floor and every day noticed the spider webs that hung off lightbulbs and in the far corners of the ceiling. A statue of Jesus gathered dust in the hallway, the wood stairs creaked, the lights went on and off, geckos appeared at night, and cockroaches crawled over our bathtub. I loved it.

In the mornings, soon after Elizabeth was out the door, her heavy canvas bag strapped to her shoulder, notebook in hand, ready for her interviews, I walked around the corner for cigarettes and the papers. Garbage was piled up five feet high on the sidewalks and vendors scurried about like ants, clacking their wood boxes, boxes stacked with Marlboro reds and Marlboro Lights, Winstons, Carltons. They got American cigarettes on the black market, stolen from the PX at Clark Air Base, sold by the carton at the Cash-and-Carry and in the mercados. Just about everything could be found here, on the streets of Ermita and Malate, the tourist district (the word *tourist* was a euphemism for the red-light district). Vendors of all ages, wearing the uniform of the streets—cutoffs, ragged T-shirts, and flip-flops—hawked flowers, sticky sweet pastries, grilled pork slices, fish heads, chicken parts, and whores. The air stank of humanity, fumes, trash, and food. Filth stuck to the city, but the street sweepers in orange aprons and bandannas were out there in the mornings with their short brooms, sweeping the sidewalks, moving trash from one place to another, from the sidewalk to the gutter, and then the rains would come.

The rain came in gulps, torrents, slashing across the city, drowning it. The sky, a crisscross of flashes, the lightning snapping, exploding, became a vast black cloud. The palm trees lashed by high winds bowed to the ground, and people caught in the storms were washed away, like the cardboard homes in the squatter camps. An afternoon could suddenly become night, and the city, a city of eleven million people, would become a phantom, ghostly.

We would watch the storm come, our candles burning and the wind hissing through the cracks in the windows, the lightning close enough to touch, but we had no fear, no sense of disaster. We felt pure, and the rain, the fury in the sky, seemed a miracle, an omen.

The rain didn't stop, it rained day after day, month after month, from August until late November, and the backstreets became rivers, people traveled by boat from one part of the city to another, the roofs of buses served as rafts, and the floorboards of taxicabs flooded.

Days and nights fused for us, and everything around us took on a meaning, the places we made our own, the cafés, the streets, and the moments when, sinking into this city so foreign and so intimate, we lost ourselves. Mornings came after nights when the geckos crawled up the walls and Albinoni was left playing over and over on the tape deck. I would wake up to the splash of her shower, the sun already above the horizon, the ceiling fan turning, buses and jeepneys rattling on the street below.

She was up and gone early in the morning, giving me her quick wave, sauntering down the stairs two steps at a time. I wanted to go with her. I wanted to run as she did from interview to interview, from coup rumor to coup rumor. I wanted to meet the generals, the senators, the coup plotters. I wanted to write those stories.

You didn't come here to do that, she would say, you came to write a book. So, here, write. She gave me a lamp for my desk, she got me copy paper, pens, pencils, books, and a wastebasket for all the pages I crumpled. She read every word I wrote and patiently marked up the pages with her fountain pen.

I stayed behind in the apartment, hunched over the typewriter, staring at the walls, at the flags and maps. I made lists, I played tapes she had mixed—Aretha, Van Morrison, the Rolling Stones—and I wrote page after page, tore up half of them, began a sentence and crossed it before I got to the end, my back stiffening as the hours passed. I wandered around the apartment, a cage at times, flipping through magazines, reading Graham Greene, Naipaul, Didion, thinking up titles for my book and discarding them instantly. Late in the afternoon, I would sit in the long-armed wood chair, a relic from provincial times that she had picked up at a market along with all our other furniture. I would open a book from the stack on the side table, and settle myself for the end of the day, a beer glass leaving wet circles on the chair's arm. That's when Gina would come out of the maid's room in the back, long after she had waxed the wood floors in the bedrooms and the living room with a husk of dry coconut she held with her bare foot. From the back room, she carried the laundry folded in perfect squares, the shirts on hangers, the clothes still warm from the iron. She made no noise and she hardly spoke. She was eighteen, from Tarlac province, that much she told us. She left the apartment as quietly as she had come in, around the time Elizabeth arrived, sweaty and harried, ready for a drink.

We ate out nearly every night, usually at Café Adriatico, sometimes with a crowd of reporters. Adriatico was a Parisian scene, with the Cinzano and Pernod umbrellas and the alfresco tables with checkered tablecloths and the old waiters in long black aprons. We lingered hours over garlic shrimp and cheese fondue, the house wine and cigarettes, running home bareheaded in a thunderstorm.

Twice a month my mother's letters came, already outdated by the time I read them. Amaury had gotten married to the woman he had met when he was going to school in New York to get his teacher's certification. He was teaching math and science to fourth-graders in a public school in the Bronx. Mother assured me that he liked it. He had gone to see her in Texas, had taken his new wife, a very nice woman, very serious and mature, mother said. They lived in the Bronx, in the projects. I winced reading that, in the projects? His wife's family lived there, in the barrio, humble people. Mother hadn't met them, hadn't gone to the wedding, a quick ceremony, apparently.

I tried to understand, but all of it seemed so far from me. Angeles never wrote, so I couldn't have known that the revolution was fading for her, that it had worn her out. Things had gone terribly wrong. She was anemic, sick. Finally she was beginning to consider what she had once thought unthinkable. She would leave Managua.

But I didn't know any of that. Mother's letters couched bad news, glided over these things. I believed, sitting in my own little revolution in Manila, that now Angeles and I had found places of our own, that I was living a life like hers, in a foreign country in the middle of historic change. She had her stories; I had mine.

So I wrote long letters to my mother, the way she liked them, making her feel that she was there with me. But she wasn't with me. I hadn't ever felt as far from my family as I did then, not far in miles, but far, their lives so remote, so unlike mine. Even Angeles's life seemed distant, but hers was the only life I could really understand. All of the United States seemed unreal, the clean streets, the malls, the dead quiet of the towns where my mother lived, and those grainy images of Ronald Reagan I saw on TV in Manila. Nothing seemed to happen in the United States, and everything seemed to happen in Manila. I told mother those stories.

Christmas in Manila came early. The stores put up the twinkling lights in early November and set up their mangers and their imported fir trees, draping them in angel hair. Santas glowed red and white, night and day, in display windows. The temperature was ninety degrees, but shopping malls played their scratchy tapes of "White Christmas," and grocery stores stocked eggnog and fruitcakes, canned cranberry jellies, glazed hams and turkeys. That's what Manila has in common with San Juan, I told friends in Manila, those four hundred years of Spanish rule followed by years of American colonization. As the Filipinos never tired of saying, they had lived four hundred years in a convent and fifty years in Hollywood. Weeks before Christmas, offices in Manila began to close at midday to give employees time to shop and party, and the government ceased to function—not that it really functioned the rest of the year. Rumors of coups disappeared because no one was going to have a coup at Christmastime. Churches tolled their bells, barrios had days of fiestas, processions filled the streets. There was a run on fireworks, and the hotels advertised evenings of choral music.

The city, like the towns of my childhood, became a festival, one very long festival. Parties every night, gifts spread out under trees, eggnog cocktails to make your head explode. Then, on Christmas Day, Boracay. Half the foreign press, it seemed, left town for Boracay, a spit of an island two hours south of Manila. Only bucket planes flew to Boracay—to be exact, to Panay, a short boat ride to Boracay. We wanted to go, not with a caravan of reporters, but alone, the two of us. We left on Christmas Day, after opening the gifts under a tree in our living room, a potted ficus tree Elizabeth had decorated one night with white lights and handmade trinkets from the local market.

Our six-seat plane sputtered to a landing on a grass field surrounded by coconut groves just a mile from the South China Sea. It jerked to a stop near a thatched hut, what passed for a terminal, where tourists waited with the chickens for the motor tricycles that took passengers to the docks to catch the next banca to Boracay. There was a long crossing of water, the banca roiling over slapping waves, and then, the sight of chalk-white sand and palm trees, a Gauguin painting.

Our days in Boracay began at sunrise, a walk to the village half a mile away, a cluster of taverns, cheap motels, and vendor stalls. I bought waist-string shorts made of flour sacks, a beach towel, a straw hat, and walked on burning sand, slapping at sand flies. I lay on the beach, my skin turning brown, dark brown, black. Before sundown, the houseboys at Casa del Pilar lit the garden torches and brought around our gin and tonics. We put our bare feet up on the balcony's rail and watched the sun sink into the water. Night fell quickly, and the sky sparkled, stars like diamonds set against black velvet, a darkness that was not like the dark of night anywhere else.

Six months later I had a third of a book written and was filing articles for a West Coast newspaper, earning some money, and traveling all over Southeast Asia, from Manila to Hong Kong, to Bangkok, to Seoul. Seoul was, in the summer of 1987, the hot spot of Asia, millions of demonstrators on the streets, another dictator under siege. But these were no peaceful protests with statues of the Virgin Mary guarding the crowds, as they had done in Manila in 1986. These were bloody street fights, and the first thing you did was go get a gas mask. Nasty mustard gas spewed out of cannons, and policemen in helmets and shields, armed with batons, marched against students armed with stones and bricks.

The crowd of reporters and photographers from Manila was there, and correspondents from Japan, from New York, from the Middle East. On the day that Chun Doo Hwan fell, when he resigned, the Seoul press office was mobbed. Hundreds of reporters were clamoring for the text of the president's statement of resignation, front-page news all over the world. I stood on a stool, scribbling, watching a scene similar to ones I had often seen on TV, during big press conferences, during crises, but I had never been part of one. Finally, after hours of waiting, copies of the text were handed out, thrown out like confetti. Reporters, photographers, the network cameramen stepped on one another, elbowing their way out, scrambling for their rented cars back to their hotel rooms. I had no idea where Elizabeth was, or our friends from Manila, it was such mayhem. I found a way to our hotel and wrote the story and phoned it in to my editor in San Francisco. It led the front page, which was not a surprise—it was the lead story on the front page of just about every newspaper in the world. The surprise to me was that I had written it.

You're good at this, Elizabeth said later. I raised a glass. Few things made me happier.

Junctures, there are junctures that you see only when you are looking back, when things change, when decisions are made that are immutable, irreversible. My life had been a life of junctures. I made decisions without weighing consequences. I assembled and disassembled my life in one moment. I didn't even know in Seoul, or later, back in Manila, that my life had changed entirely. I knew it only later, when that life no longer existed, when I had passed through it, had lived it, and it was gone.

In one year I had transformed my life, had willfully destroyed the career of editor I had carefully made step-by-step, from one newspaper to another, from one job to the next, rung by rung. I had left the hemisphere I knew, the people closest to me, and had traveled far from all of it because of a mere notion that I had to break free and find a way down to the bottom where the words I wanted to write had long drowned. I had to go away from the origin of the words, my birthplace, my island, my family, to find them again, to recapture them, and to write them. And I had to go that distance to understand passion. Words and passion came at the same time. It was no coincidence that Elizabeth and writing became one and the same. One could not have lived without the other.

I was working in my bedroom when the letter came. We had moved from the apartment building into an old big house in a compound of foreigners, a provincial-style house with large rooms, plank floors, bleached cedar walls, shuttered windows, and a yard of frangipani vines, tamarind trees, marigolds, and bougainvillea. From the moment we saw it, when we swerved into the dirt driveway and ran up the steps to the porch, we wanted it. There was a rough beauty about it, and a sense that it would soon come to ruin. Winds had blown too hard against it, and time, too, but it was still beautiful and unspoiled.

All day long doors banged, and cars pulled in and out of the driveway beneath the porch. Dogs barked, the whippets that guarded the compound and preyed on cats. Maids shuffled in and out, washing clothes in their tubs in the backyard, whistling, humming, singing. Everyone was a singer in the Philippines. From my bedroom, where I had my desk, I could hear Gina waxing the floors with her coconut husk, and her sister Edna dusting the window screens with a broom, and the cluck of the rooster the guard kept in the yard. Only the gardener made no noise. He walked on bare feet, spoke only when he came up to be paid, sticking out a scarred hand and mumbling apologetically, but the rest of the day he kept his head down, literally almost on the ground, hunched over the bushes and plants, clipping the grass with his scissors.

Edna brought me the letter that morning and closed the door behind her when she left the bedroom. I had been dreading this letter.

The paper was asking if I was returning to Philadelphia—I had agreed to a year's leave, and now it had ended. I knew my answer before I folded the letter and slid it back into the envelope. I put it in my top drawer, like things I needed to keep around but didn't especially want to see in front of me. I waited days, weeks, to answer it. I talked to Elizabeth night and day about it, but she left it entirely up to me and refused to be dragged into the decision.

You have to decide, she kept saying. I can't be responsible.

She had a strong, one might say forbidding, sense of division between us. We were together, true, but we were not one and the same. We were not a two-headed monster, she liked to say. I had to set out my own course just as she had to set out hers.

How well she played that hand, born poker player that she was.

My decision was clear. I couldn't leave Manila. I couldn't leave her.

Something happens when a story dies, like a passion oozing out slowly, unnoticeably, until nothing is left. Manila was falling off the front pages, and many of the foreign correspondents had left for other parts. I hardly saw Elizabeth in 1988. She was in Sri Lanka for two months, in Vietnam for a month, in Bangkok. I had her telegrams from Hanoi, from Saigon, and letters and postcards. But I was now living alone most of the time in our house in Manila, and when we were together, reality was unavoidable. Her assignment was ending, and I had a job offer in New York. We had three months left in Manila, plenty of time, it seemed, but once you know you have to leave a place where your life has changed, each day becomes a departure, peeling away your skin, tearing pieces away until the waiting to leave becomes almost as painful as the leaving itself.

We didn't know what the months would bring, what our new life in some other place would do to us, but we knew it would never again be the same.

The last months rushed at us. Horrid things happened in the Philippines. Typhoons battered the country, ferries sank, coup rumors swirled again. Edna and Gina left us.

December came, the Christmas lights went up in stores, on the buildings on Roxas Boulevard, on the tree in the lobby of the Manila Hotel. And I bought my one-way ticket home, to the United States.

The rain was still falling in December, and our house was damp to its seams. My clothes had the smell of rain, of something old; the pages of my books were curling in the humidity; and the yard was deep in mud. At night, the rain seemed harder, louder on the tin roof. The tree branches slapped the shutters on the screen windows, like the storms in Puerto Rico when I was a child, when I hid under the sheets on my grandmother's bed.

For so many years I hadn't remembered much about the place, but the color blue, all the shades you see all over Latin America, and the noise that fills the spaces in those towns, the noise of people who explain their lives on the street, in bar corners, at the drugstore, the noise of infinite longing.

I had moved farther and farther from it, until this night in an archipelago in the Asian tropics, in this house of bleached cedar walls and wood floors, a house shaded by tamarind trees and coconut palms, where rain fell in torrents on the tin roof, slashing down to a ground planted in marigolds, the island of my childhood, the island I had abandoned, came back to me in fragments, fleeting, brilliant, elusive, raw like the rain, like passion.

But just as swiftly, it left me again. Someday, Manila, too, would come back to me the same way, in fragments, in flashes of overlapping moments, like photographs taken too quickly, one frame lying on top of the next, out of focus, cut off.

Two months later, in February, we were living in Manhattan, in a five-story walk-up near Central Park. I had a job editing copy and writing headlines, deskbound from four in the afternoon to midnight. After life in Manila, this was extreme tedium, a routine bound by the clock, by deadlines, by the coffee cart that came by the desks every afternoon at five. Watching the wall clock tick ever so slowly, waiting for the nightly "good night" from the desk chief that meant I could finally go home, I wondered, what am I doing here? My Manila tan faded quickly, my face seemed aged, furrowed, and sour. I wrote in the mornings, lashing myself to my desk in the small room in the apartment I used as a study. But my mind began to close again. I was putting up walls all around me.

The first one to notice was Elizabeth. She waited for me at night, bringing me a beer, listening to the stories of my day, trying to lift the depression and anger I didn't bother to hide. She would finally go to bed wounded, a bird shot down from the trees. Once, when we were in Manila, she warned me that someday I would destroy us. I thought of that now, in New York. These nights when she waited for me became nightmares for her. I can't listen anymore to this, you're bent on destroying yourself, she screamed one night, and picking up her trench coat, she ran out of the apartment. It was one in the morning. She didn't come back for hours. When she returned, I was still on the sofa, drinking.

Her face was a fury, and a sorrow. She had cried for hours on the steps of a church nearby. You get over these things easily, she said when she came in, but they take everything out of me—they kill me.

The passion was leaving me, the days when touching her was all I had ever wanted. I didn't see it then. I saw nothing but my own misery. I was beginning to leave her. I was pushing her away. But we could not let go. Life without each other was not imaginable.

We decided to leave New York.

Over the next three years, we crossed the Pacific again several times. For a while we lived in Tokyo. She worked for a magazine, and once again I was writing, flying to Manila for long periods, leaving her to her steamed rice and beans, to nights where she didn't sleep at all. Tokyo was a prison for her, no place for a woman like her, no place for someone who, like so many wanderers the world over, came alive in the heat and murk of the tropics, in those backwater places of the third world. All that time she spent alone in our apartment in Tokyo was far more difficult and lonely than she ever let me know. She didn't complain. She didn't demand anything. She had wanted it all for me, wanted the book, the magazine assignments, the smile that had returned to my face, my tanned face.

After nine months in Tokyo, we moved back to New York. She had a new job, and I was traveling all over the world for a magazine. I didn't see her for months. I didn't see the changes, the end that was coming.

On the day I returned from South America after two months away, she sat me down and said, I can't live like this anymore. Were those her words? I don't know. That's one of those photo negatives that overlaps another and another and another.

What is there, what is the picture?

Only this.

Chapter Twelve

San Juan, 2001, "This Sea, These Long Waves"

The light falls faintly on the rocks rising along the shore, right where the waves roll up in an unbroken rhythm and come crashing down, swallowed by the black sea. All other sound is drowned, only the incantation of sea against rock, of water heaving and rising and falling, again and again.

How dark the night is in this place where I was born.

My journey back to this island has been unimaginably long, thirty-five years, a span impossible to measure that stretches over a life, mine, my family's, the island's, and my mother's death. I left when I was sixteen years old, but at this moment, sitting on a balcony high above this point of earth and sand carved out of the Atlantic, in the silence of two in the morning, the years fall away, and there's no sense of time having passed, of the distances I have traveled away from the island.

I have finally come home, to this stillness, this insistent sea.

Strange, my own banishment from the island. How could I have been gone for so long? We grow up and too often drift away from family and birthplace, from the towns of our childhoods, but few of us leave behind everything as I had. I used to tell myself there was nothing for me in Puerto Rico. My mother had moved to Texas. My sisters and brother had scattered far from the island. My father was still there, but what could the two of us talk about, what did we have in common but blood and flesh? He was not a stranger to me, but worse, he was someone I knew too well and didn't want to know at all. Those were the things I told myself, but I knew that was never the whole truth.

We had emigrated like so many others. We had separate lives in separate places and the island was no longer our address. But I had gone farther away than Angeles or Amaury and certainly farther in her heart than mother. Something of them, something unchangeable, remained in Puerto Rico. But I had wrenched away and had transplanted myself entirely. I had grown new roots—frail roots that I could pick up and move at a moment's notice—reinventing myself as if there had never been that old soil beneath me, and in me. What a liar I was, pretending that these threads could be cut off if only I didn't go back to the place of my birth, the home of my childhood.

Sitting on this balcony on this night, I finally see that for thirty-five years I had been a wanderer, restlessly moving, tossing and turning from place to place, from lover to lover, a citizen of the world, which, of course, means a citizen of nowhere. I had been seeking a home, yearning for something I could put no words to, something I had misplaced somewhere.

Now I am here, home, but perhaps it's too late. Perhaps the island won't take me back, perhaps my place in it was erased by the years, and I have no markers left.

Morning comes full-blown. The sun absorbs the world. The palms waft in the rising wind of spring, and the sea, soothed by the light, appears translucent where it touches the shoreline and vast, interminable, gray green toward the horizon. It is seven in the morning and on the beach the sweepers are raking the sand, picking up pebbles, and the pool boys are setting up the lounging chairs and the towels. The sand is already burning.

On the spot, just where the beach curves, where my mother would be sitting, shading her face from the sun with her hand, a chair lies unfolded, its chrome legs glinting orange in the heat. She would be reclining there, under that palm tree. I take the chair and imagine myself being her, seeing the water the way she saw it, her head tilted toward the distance, her eyes half closed.

On a hot, cloudless day in September 1994, ten days after her birthday, we had buried my mother in a country cemetery in the Texas town where she died, two thousand miles from her island, from this place in the sand that had been hers for so long. In the church, the pews were filled with people who had not really known the woman I had known, who had not heard her speak the lines of García Lorca, who had not seen her move on a dance floor, who had not seen her eyes reflected in the sea. And after the last prayers were said, they lowered the mahogany coffin into the ground, and we, her children, standing together, but apart, outsiders like her, did not look.

It is late March 2001. The six of us are together again. We have flown to the island from New York, New Orleans, Dallas, Honduras, to bury our father. We had expected his death because he had been ill for several years, during which I didn't see him once. But when the news came that he was dead, I shuddered, the distance that had been ours during so much of my life was suddenly gone, and I knew instantly that I had to come to his side in his death.

The island has become over the years in my memory a series of still lifes, which I recall in furious winds and hot rains, a place of trammeled beauty. Flying in, floating over the jagged coastline of San Juan, gliding over the five-hundred-year-old fortress of El Morro and over the peacock-colored colonial buildings of Old San Juan and the rows of beige-and-pink hotels along the shore, the plane had dropped slowly onto the runway of the Luis Muñoz Marín International Airport. Just as the brakes screeched and the wheels rolled to a stop, applause broke out, as it always did. People scrambled for their bags, the door opened, and a blast of hot tropical air hit my face. I had not forgotten that smell, that air; that was not a still life.

Along the road in San Juan, there is hardly room left for one more building. Hotels clutter the view of the ocean, expressways cut into old neighborhoods, and every other stop seems to have a Burger King. High-rise condominiums and gated communities rise along the beach, and the slums are mostly gone. San Juan spreads out before me in all directions, in pastels and undiluted colors, the sea speckled with sunlight. The Caribe Hilton, where I had learned to swim when I was a child, has been renovated once, twice, three times in the years since I had last seen it, and is painted a rich vanilla, its entrance a spray of yellow flowers.

Olga is already there, the first one to arrive. She is in her room, her eyeglasses on, her hair combed down in girlish bangs, and she's on the phone talking to her sons in New Orleans. She drops the phone and bursts into tears when she sees me. We had seen each other several times since mother's death. We had had our sisters' reunion in Miami and visits in Dallas, but this is the first time that all six of us would be together since mother died. What we don't say because it doesn't need to be said is that it had taken the deaths of our parents, nearly seven years apart, to bring all of us to the same place at the same time.

Arrangements, Olga, we have to make them all. You, Sara, and Carmen stay in this room, and Angeles and I will stay in my room. A memorial service has already been planned by father's family, his wife's family. We, his children, I think, are like guests of honor, making our brief appearance.

Sara and Carmen, looking as if they had just gone for a stroll instead of a four-hour flight from Dallas, come in, lugging their bags, just as Olga and I are talking. Sara looks very thin, though she isn't; it is only her face that looks thin, sucked-in cheeks, that sharp, birdlike face she has. Carmen looks perfect—how does she do it?—diamond earrings on, hair curled, fresh makeup, her ladies' jeans creased as if she had just ironed them.

No noise in the world is like the noise of sisters seeing one another after a long time. It's not only the words and exclamations, but the noise of memory and joy and awful sorrow, all at once. Everyone is talking at the same time, exchanging flight stories, and everyone but me is dialing up on cell phones to husbands and children back home.

Angeles is arriving later tonight, after a ten-hour flight. She had to go by way of Costa Rica and Caracas. We'll have to go and pick her up at the airport, I say, you know she can't stand not having someone waiting for her. And Amaury? someone asks. He's already here, staying at Jacobo's. He brought his wife. We're going over there to Jacobo's and then we can all go get Angeles tonight. Arrangements, always the arrangements.

Later that evening, Angeles comes out of the airport terminal, past the sliding doors, pulling her roller suitcase. She stops immediately to light a cigarette, and I'm at her side in a second. I can always spot her, no matter how crowded the airport. I can tell her apart from the crowd by the way she walks, slowly, as if she had all the time in the world. She is wearing her worn sandals, baggy pants, and has not a speck of makeup on her face. Her hair is hand-combed off her forehead, a cap of bright gray. She is embracing all of us and trying to smoke at the same time.

Seeing her, holding her, I think of some lines she had sent me, like so many she has sent me through the years, passages, stray lines from books, from poems, lines she can recite from memory.

"Eligió el fracaso, la negación de si mismo, de su arte, como venganza pasiva contra el mundo, sin perder por ello el humor, la elegancia, el aire de gran señora. . . ." She chose failure, denying herself, denying her art, as passive vengeance against the world, without ever losing the wit, the elegance, the air of a great woman. . . .

The night would go on forever, a family party. More than a dozen of us filed into Jacobo's penthouse; the bottles of wine were uncorked, the beer chilled. Family reunions being what they are, this one had its awkward silences, too much food, too much wine, everyone talking, the funeral plans discussed, father's death in the night, his body finally giving up. Amaury had glazed eyes. He had a picture of father in a frame, when father was in the army. Amaury said he carried it with him everywhere. He took one of mother with him, too. He was getting drunk, holding court, jumbling his jokes. Tamara, his wife now for almost fifteen years, sank into the sofa by his side, patting him on his leg, there, quiet down.

I want to go hear Carli, he was saying, asking us to go with him, to Carli's club in Old San Juan. Carli was one of the guys in the old band, in The Living End. It's too late, someone said, the funeral is tomorrow. He grabbed another drink, and began talking about father, half sentences, nothing coherent. Olga, Sara, and Carmen looked at one another as if saying, There he goes. Jacobo tried to interrupt, to change the subject, but Amaury was not stopping for anyone. He was crying, wiping his nose with the back of his hand. You didn't love father, he cried out, no one but me cared about him. I can't stand this, I thought. Time to go, I whispered to Angeles, yanking her shirt. No, she shook her head. She wanted to comfort him, to shut him up. She could always outlast him, could outlast just about everybody, but I insisted. I wasn't going to sit there and let him wreck all of us. Sara, Carmen, and Olga were already out the door, and I dragged Angeles with me.

The funeral service was in Gurabo, the last place on earth I wanted to see, but this was father's final moment, what he had wanted, and we had no choice. Gurabo had sprawled like every other town in the island, but it was still ugly. The plaza seemed smaller, and the houses around it had been replastered and cut up and built up and converted into five-and-dimes, travel agencies, lawyers' offices. My father's old dairy farm on the outskirts was now a subdivision named after him. He had sold it lot by lot, but kept the house on the hill, which was no longer a simple blue cinder-block home. It wasn't blue anymore, and it had been expanded to two floors, and iron grilles had been put on the windows to keep burglars out. He had lived there the last forty years of his life; it was his last home, where he had hung his hammock.

Our house, the house with the terraces, the house in front of the plaza, the last house where our parents and the six of us had lived together, had been turned into a funeral home, painted a gaudy pink, the tin roof replaced with a flat top, the words *Funeraria de Gurabo* chiseled above the second floor.

The memorial service for him was there, in that house. Incredible, I said to Angeles, father is having his memorial service in the house where we lived. We looked at it from the street, looked at it from all sides. The front porch had no French doors, and my bedroom had no balcony. Men in shirtsleeves and straw hats sat on chairs on the porch, passing the time of day.

Like being drawn by an invisible rope, we walked up to it and went in. I was the last to enter, Angeles the first. The living room, where my mother had had her piano, where she had her glass-topped coffee table, had been opened up, the arched wall that had separated the living room from the dining room torn down, the stairway shortened, or so it seemed to me. Sara, Carmen, and Olga stayed at my side, sitting on a sofa, the only one in the reception area. Amaury and Angeles went about greeting the townspeople who filed in, old people mostly, people none of us knew or could remember. I looked for familiar faces, my father's nieces and nephews. His brother, the only one still alive, was ill; his sisters lived in Florida. None came. I didn't move off the sofa, sitting close to Tití, who was now frail, her memory fading, but who was still the most elegant of all of us in a silk gray suit.

This is awful, having this in this house, she murmured in my ear while smiling at everyone. Who are these people? They were ambling in, lining up on a bench against a wall, peering at us, at the six of us. Who is the architect? one asked. Who is the journalist?

Angeles worked the room, occasionally glancing over at me and rolling her eyes, playing mother's role perfectly.

At last, we were called into a room near the reception area. The room had no windows. This used to be the carport, where father parked his Pontiac. A worn lavender shag carpet covered the floor and foldout chairs had been placed in rows. We walked up the aisle and took our places in the first row. My father's ashes had been placed in a plain white box set in the middle of a table covered with a white cloth. There were no flowers.

We stood looking at the table, Angeles, Amaury, and I in front; Sara, Carmen, and Olga behind us. I wondered, What's upstairs, where my bedroom and my balcony used to be? I imagined embalmed bodies. The service seemed interminable.

It was mid-afternoon when we gathered in the yard of father's house, the one on the hill. Amaury was carrying the box with the ashes. We fell into place in clusters. Carmen, Olga, and Sara waited close together, arms around one another. Angeles and I stood to the side, arms behind our backs. Amaury held the box in the crook of his arm, opened the lid, and took a handful of ashes and sprayed them on the ground. It took more time than I had expected to empty the box. The last fistful hung in the breeze and then scattered. Amaury held the box with both his hands, close to his chest.

We made the rounds in the next few days. The house on Pérez Galdós, my grandmother's house, had decayed with time and weather. Water marks ran down from the gutters and the coats of paint had faded, bleached by rain and sun. The garden had been paved over and the flower-bordered path to the front porch had been widened and turned into a carport. The living room windows, once wooden slats that you cranked open, had been replaced with ordinary glass windows protected by iron bars.

I had loved my life there, running across the street to see my girlfriend Julia, listening to my grandmother barter with the street vendors, keeping her company at the dining table in that room with the gaudy flowery window trims, dunking chunks of bread in her coffee. I could still see her in the kitchen, the door to the yard open, letting in the gusts that came after the afternoon showers.

Can you ever return to Puerto Rico? Angeles asked me that night. It was our last evening together, and we were drinking Medalla beer on the balcony of our room at the Hilton. The sun was fading, the sea turning dark.

I don't know, I said. You are lucky, you have La Giraldilla, a home you love, a place that is you, yours. I don't have that. You are leaving tomorrow morning, and you are dying to get home, it's something you miss. It's your cave, your refuge. I don't feel that, I don't know that I will ever feel that anywhere.

The next morning she was packed at dawn, and I walked her down to the hotel lobby. I promise I'll come see you in Tegucigalpa, I said, a promise I made every year. Everyone says La Giraldilla is like a dream, so beautiful, so peaceful, your garden, the birds, all those flowers you have around you.

She loved it there, I knew, but not because it was una maravilla. No, it was because it was more than she had ever expected in life.

I know that for some of us who left it, the island is a remote place, a long-lost home we will probably not see again. But for others of us who left it, this is a place of dreams still, where we return time and again. We are caught somehow in whatever it is to be Latin American and puertorriqueña, the quickening of the pulse at the sight of the Caribbean, the exhilaration that comes for no reason at all, maybe it's just the taste of the heat, the way it feels on your skin. And the longing that comes by surprise, one evening in a country halfway around the world, or one day standing on a street in New York and hearing a sound out of nowhere, words in Spanish, lines of a song long forgotten. It's that, the sudden longing.

Each of us sees our past differently. How could we not? Each of us has her own story, her own chronicle of those days. Each of us composes pictures of what it was and pretties them up or makes them wretched. Each of us moves in the circles that we create to sustain us and re-create over again, but for all of us, the six of us, my sisters and brother and myself, life began here, on this island, and that defines us, that completes us.

The last time my mother was here on the island, she sent me a postcard of an old plaza, El Parterre in Aguadilla, where she remembered playing as a little girl. She looked for the house where she had lived as a child, not far from the plaza on the postcard, and found it. It looked no different to her than it had looked when she was growing up, as if the seventy years that had passed had barely touched it. And she found her grandparents' house, this one nearly in ruins, and she remembered the laughter that had been in it so many years ago. She drove through the island, reliving her life, collecting memories, trying to recapture what had been lost under the surface of change and years.

For a long time, for most of the thirty years she lived in Texas, she dreamed of going back to Puerto Rico to live. She had the islanders' blood, she felt the pull of the sea that haunts the people of the tropics, the nostalgia on certain days, in specific moments, for the salt smell of rain on warm earth. She wanted a simple house on a hill near the town of her youth, and she talked about the flashing sparkle of the fireflies that light the fields at night and the singsong of the coquís at dusk. But mostly she saw the colors, the scarlet of the blooms of flamboyán trees, the canary yellow of the hibiscus, the transparent turquoise of the Caribbean.

She had kept returning nearly every year, but the plans to go back to stay, to live out her last years on the island, becoming what she had been when she was young and living the life she had lived then, began to lose their radiance, and the pictures in her mind began to lose their color, like the old photographs she annotated and pasted in her albums. The dream was leaving her, but even in those last years her eyes would light up when she remembered Puerto Rico, and her illusions. Her voice would break with longing, as if she were living her life there all over again.

Her death came just six months after her last trip.

I can only believe, because she didn't say, that she had imagined herself where the air was light and the sky sheer, looking out to the sea, this same sea I'm looking at now, from this spot in the sand where, when I was a child, she watched me run into the waves.

Acknowledgments

Books are born slowly, the date of birth really unknowable. This book has been with me in different forms, and in no form at all, for more years than I can possibly remember. But I do know that it would not be here at all without the vision and guidance of my editor, Henry Ferris, who understood what I was trying to do even before I did. He and his colleagues at William Morrow and at Rayo have given this book a wonderful home.

A writer labors in obscurity or fame, whichever luck brings, for all her life. I have been fortunate in many ways, but no gift has been more important to me than Kathy Robbins, my literary agent and great friend. Through more than a decade as my rock—adviser, confidante, but more than anything, as my most loyal champion—Kathy has never faltered. She pulls me back when I get too close to the brink; she pushes forward when I am afraid. Everything I write in some way has her imprint. I owe this book to her. The crew at the Robbins Office, taking its lead from her, has been unfailingly gracious, efficient, and comforting. Each of them—John, Sarah, Sandy, David, and many others—has over the years jumped to my rescue in matters large and small.

Friends come and go. But all have offered support when I needed it. Most especially I want to thank Tim Weiner and Catherine Manegold.

Finally, my family. Their trust in me to tell this story sustained me. They answered my questions and generously shared their experiences without ever questioning my right to write this book my own way, through my particular prism. Without them I could not go on. They are everything to me.